# Praise for
## *The Learning Power Approach*
## by Guy Claxton

In person, Guy Claxton balances the precision of academia with the warmth and wit of our most beloved teachers. He challenges, engages, and inspires in equal measure. It is the same when he writes; he transforms complexities of learning into recommendations that are both inviting and inspirational, and he does so without ever losing the subtlety of nuance or culture. He is the perfect "critical friend," and *The Learning Power Approach* is the exemplary handbook.

**James Nottingham,** Author
*The Learning Challenge: How to Guide Your*
*Students Through the Learning Pit*
Northumberland, United Kingdom

We have to radically reimagine education if we're going to fulfill the potential of today's students as leaders who will address our increasingly global challenges. *The Learning Power Approach* is a valuable map not just to student success but also to a more peaceful, prosperous, and sustainable planet.

**Steven Farr,** Executive Director
Global Learning Lab at Teach For All
Washington, DC

*The Learning Power Approach* helps to validate a belief that the subjective goal of education should be about the liberation of the self, freeing us to choose our own essence in life. This book helps to emphasize optimal learning for all students.

**Ken Austin,** Associate Professor
Stephen F. Austin State University
Nacogdoches, TX

Guy Claxton challenges the traditional approaches to learning that exist in so many of our schools and presents a compelling and practical strategy to foster authentic thinking and learning for all. *The Learning Power Approach* is rooted in the belief that we must move beyond systems that categorize and judge people merely on their ability to do well in exams and tests, or learning that promotes the myth of the "one right answer"—to cultures that focus on "the cultivation of the confidence and capacity to be a good learner." Claxton identifies and describes the diverse variety of strengths essential to successful learning and presents practical approaches to make these a priority.

This is a great book. It is a must-read for those who understand the uniqueness of abilities in all of their students and would like to set in play a culture of learning that makes this flourish—a culture of learning that is inclusive and personal.

**Peter Gamwell,** Author
*The Wonder Wall*
Ottawa, Ontario

Reading this book was a joy. As a writer, Claxton is beautifully able to express the whats, whys, and *hows* of the learning power approach. His argument is urgent, but it is expressed with great warmth, making it a compelling read. Claxton's work has just the right mix of accessibility and challenge.

Central to the Learning Power Approach is the belief that it is every teacher's responsibility to nurture the student as learner and to grow learners who are "mind fit." Learning itself is learnable! I challenge any teacher to read this and not come away questioning their practice and inspired to tweak their classroom spaces, language, and the way they design lessons. Reading this book will help teachers understand more clearly the way "every lesson, every day" gradually shapes the way students see themselves as learners and their understanding of the process of learning itself. This is the beauty of the Learning Power Approach. It is not a program, not a subject, not an add-on—it is something all teachers can integrate into their practice on a daily basis. Claxton's work helps us notice what lies beneath the surface of our teaching and to attend much more closely to the way we shape dispositions and attitudes to learning. As an ardent inquirer, I found the "Wondering" section at the end of each chapter particularly stimulating. These wonderings would be a great way to prompt conversation and action among teachers, making it a marvelous text for rich, collaborative conversations across an entire school community.

Claxton often uses the metaphor of a coach to describe the work of teachers using the Learning Power Approach, and there are some fascinating and helpful case studies of such coaches in action throughout the text. After reading this book, I feel as if I have spent time with one of the very best learning coaches there is. I can already envisage *The Learning Power Approach,* dog-eared and lovingly littered with sticky notes, on my shelf. This book deserves a place in every teacher's collection.

**Kath Murdoch,** Education Consultant
University of Melbourne
Melbourne, Australia

We are always trying to see through the eyes of learners and guide them on their way to become their own teachers. This is that guide.

**Michael McDowell**, EdD, Superintendent
Author, *Rigorous PBL by Design*
Ross School District
Ross, CA

*To David Perkins, unassuming giant of our field*

# The Learning Power Approach

## Teaching Learners to Teach Themselves

**Guy Claxton**

Foreword by Carol S. Dweck

**CORWIN**
A SAGE Publishing Company

FOR INFORMATION:

Corwin

A SAGE Company

2455 Teller Road

Thousand Oaks, California 91320

(800) 233-9936

www.corwin.com

SAGE Publications Ltd.

1 Oliver's Yard

55 City Road

London EC1Y 1SP

United Kingdom

SAGE Publications India Pvt. Ltd.

B 1/I 1 Mohan Cooperative Industrial Area

Mathura Road, New Delhi 110 044

India

SAGE Publications Asia-Pacific Pte. Ltd.

3 Church Street

#10-04 Samsung Hub

Singapore 049483

Acquisitions Editor:   Ariel Bartlett

Development Editor:   Desirée A. Bartlett

Editorial Assistants:   Kaitlyn Irwin and
                                     Jessica Vidal

Production Editor:   Melanie Birdsall

Copy Editor:   Cate Huisman

Typesetter:   C&M Digitals (P) Ltd.

Proofreader:   Tricia Currie-Knight

Indexer:   Sheila Bodell

Cover Designer:   Alexa Turner

Marketing Manager:   Margaret O'Connor

**Note From the Publisher:** The author has provided video and web content throughout the book that is available to you through QR (quick response) codes. To read a QR code, you must have a smartphone or tablet with a camera. We recommend that you download a QR code reader app that is made specifically for your phone or tablet brand.

Printed in the United States of America

ISBN 978-1-5063-8870-0

This book is printed on acid-free paper.

Certified Chain of Custody
SUSTAINABLE   Promoting Sustainable Forestry
FORESTRY
INITIATIVE   www.sfiprogram.org
SFI-01268

SFI label applies to text stock

17 18 19 20 21 10 9 8 7 6 5 4 3 2 1

# Contents

Foreword   xi
   **Carol S. Dweck**
Acknowledgments   xv
About the Author   xix

**Chapter 1. The Origins of the
Learning Power Approach**   1

Nuclear Family   7
Godparents   9
Friends and Neighbors   9
Near Misses   10
A Socket Set   14

**Chapter 2. What Is Learning?**   17

Why Do We Learn?   18
When Do We Learn?   20
What Is the Launchpad for Learning?   21
What Do Learners Actually Do?   23
The Beginnings of Learning Power   30
So Can You Get Better at Learning?   32
What Kinds of Learning Are Going On in Classrooms?   34

**Chapter 3. What Exactly Is the Aim
of the Learning Power Approach?**   39

Diving In: The Aim of the Learning Power Approach   40
Some Flesh on the Bones   49

**Chapter 4. How Do I Get Started?
Some Quick Wins**   55

The LPA Menu du Jour   59
Curious, Adventurous, Determined, Collaborative:
   A Starter Kit of Learning Dispositions   67
A Reflective Exercise   71

## Chapter 5. Why Does Learning Power Matter? 10 Good Reasons for Pumping Those Learning Muscles 75

1. Because Life Is Complicated 79
2. Because Learning Power Makes the World a Safer Place 81
3. Because We Won't Always Be There 83
4. Because Good Learners Are More Successful in Life 84
5. Because Employers Want to Hire Powerful Learners 86
6. Because Powerful Learners Do Better in School 88
7. Because Powerful Learners Do Better in College 90
8. Because It Makes Teaching Easier and More Rewarding 93
9. Because People Are Happier When They Are Learning 95
10. Because Young People's Mental Health Depends Upon Their Learning Power 97

## Chapter 6. What Is Learning Power Made Of? 103

The Elements of Learning Power 107

## Chapter 7. Learning Power in Action: Some Classroom Illustrations 127

## Chapter 8. Design Principles of the LPA Classroom 147

1. Create a Feeling of Safety 151
2. Distinguish Between Learning Mode and Performance Mode 152
3. Organize Compelling Things to Learn 156
4. Make Ample Time for Collaboration and Conversation 157
5. Create Challenge 160
6. Make Difficulty Adjustable 163
7. Show the Innards of Learning 166
8. Make Use of Protocols, Templates, and Routines 168
9. Use the Environment 171
10. Develop Craftsmanship 175
11. Allow Increasing Amounts of Independence 177
12. Give Students More Responsibility 180

13. Focus on Improvement, Not Achievement   182

14. Lead by Example   186

Chapter 9. What Is the Evidence for the
Learning Power Approach?   191

Does Curiosity Affect Learning?   192

What About Concentration?   194

Can Learners' Resilience Be Deliberately Increased?   195

Does Resilience Contribute to Raising Achievement
in School?   196

Does Imagination Improve Learning and Creativity,
and Can People Get Better at Imagining?   196

Do Deliberate Attempts to Teach Students to
Think Clearly Work? And Do They Improve
School Performance?   198

What About Collaboration?   199

Does the Same Apply to Empathy?   201

Does Reflection Aid Learning?   201

Does Learning Power Developed in One Context
Transfer to Other Contexts?   202

Chapter 10. Distinctions and Misconceptions   213

Focus on Learning Power, Not Just Learning   214

Learning, Not Thinking   216

Learning Dispositions Are Malleable, Not Fixed   217

Is the LPA "Traditional" or "Progressive"?   219

Evidence, Not Measurement   221

Precision About Language   223

Learning Muscles and the Mind Gym   228

Pedagogy Rules   230

It's Not Just Classrooms; It's the Ethos of the
Whole School   233

Provisional and Growing, Not Set in Stone   235

Chapter 11. Joining the Culture Club   241

Bibliography and References   247
Resources and Further Reading   257
Index   259

# Foreword

Many people now recognize that the drill-and-test focus in our schools is not preparing students for the modern world. This increasingly unpredictable world requires a zest for challenging ill-defined problems, an ability to see things through, and the resilience to bounce back from setbacks. It requires the desire and the ability to do this over and over and over.

Although many agree that schools are not equipping either our low or high achievers well enough for the real world they will meet after they finish school or college, far fewer have suggested practical alternatives. Into this comparative void rides Guy Claxton and his colleagues with their Learning Power Approach. This approach combines research-tested learning techniques that can be implemented in any classroom, and it includes these all-important factors: provoking curiosity and imaginative thinking, promoting "metacognitive" skills (such as reflecting on one's strategies and planning new ones), encouraging determination and perseverance, and fostering collaboration in the learning process.

In other words, the Learning Power Approach places the student in the center of an exciting, purposeful, and social learning environment—not an environment in which students are required to memorize things they may not understand, for reasons they may not understand, and to do so in isolation from other students. You can just feel your heart sink as you go from the description of the Learning Power Approach to the Business as Usual approach.

There are many reasons to believe that what the Learning Power Approach offers is so important. Here are just two.

First, it teaches generalizable qualities of mind—not just facts and formulas that apply in specific cases, but learning "mindsets" and skills that apply to many tasks and problems that students will encounter both now and in the future in all parts of their lives. For example, students in these classrooms (such as those in the EL schools; see https://eleducation .org) may often do projects that require them to learn about meaningful issues (such as issues in their community), formulate the problem in a manageable way, do research into possible courses of action, and make recommendations, including ones that they and their peers can act on. They may also present oral reports on their work to the school and community. How could this not be more useful in the long run than memorizing decontextualized facts and formulas that bear little relation to what they will encounter in life?

Second, more and more of our students are experiencing mental health problems such as anxiety and depression. Too often I am hearing of first or second graders who experience such high levels of anxiety about schoolwork that they do not want to go to school. The testing culture is now reaching down into kindergarten, with many students, younger and older, believing that these tests measure something deep and permanent about their intelligence and their ability to succeed in the future. Rather than places of joyful learning, many of our schools become places of dread. In contrast, classrooms that embody the Learning Power Approach can become places of tremendous eagerness as students question, explore, delve deeply, and collaborate in the service of learning. Upon entering such a classroom, you may hear laughter or squeals of excitement, or you may hear nothing as students devote intense concentration to the compelling problems they're grappling with.

So, you might ask, what's the problem? Why isn't every classroom using the Learning Power Approach?

Well, I think there's one big reason: the current incentives for schools, teachers, and parents. In the United States, schools are often evaluated and rewarded (or punished) based on their students' standardized test scores. Teachers, too, are often evaluated and rewarded on the basis of their students' test scores. I recently learned of a teacher who created a joyful and effective learning environment for her summer school students, using many of the principles of the Learning Power Approach. However, during the actual school year, with the test hanging over her head, she used a more structured drill-and-test approach. She felt it was a risk for her and for her students to do otherwise. Observers reported that the difference in anxiety between the summer and school-year classes was palpable.

The irony here is that schools that adopt a version of the Learning Power Approach often have *higher* test scores. Good test scores are a natural byproduct of deeper and more effective learning. Furthermore, in Learning Power schools teachers are free to experience why they became teachers in the first place. They did not become teachers to force-feed facts and formulas to anxious and depressed students. They became teachers to see their children avidly learn and successfully grow their brains.

Parents, too, can play a role in perpetuating the drill-and-test approach. Many parents see high test scores as ways of ensuring their child's place in top schools in the future. They may not want to risk new teaching methods that may not pave the way to these schools. Yet the same parents are puzzled when their child moves back home after university rather than confidently taking on the world. In the end, shouldn't parents prefer a K–12 education that prepares their children for life?

You will cherish this book. It's full of engaging and informative classroom examples, and the recommendations rest on solid foundations, such as research on mindsets, interest, metacognition, grit, and collaborative learning. Guy Claxton, himself a noted cognitive scientist, is a knowledgeable and entertaining guide to the future of teaching. I urge you as teachers not to stand by as the world changes but our teaching does not. I urge you to be leaders in the crusade to transform education, so our students can thrive now and in the future—starting with your own classrooms. This book will help you begin your journey.

**Carol S. Dweck**
Lewis and Virginia Eaton Professor of Psychology
Stanford University

# Acknowledgments

I'd like to say a big thank you to the people who very kindly read the first draft and offered feedback and advice. First, there were my friends and colleagues Becky Carlzon, Nusrat Faizullah, Graham Powell, and Susie Taylor-Alston, whose experience, enthusiasm, and excellent ideas for improvement were invaluable. Then there were five reviewers organized by Corwin whose detailed comments were really useful. And finally there were my two splendid editors, David Bowman of Crown House and Ariel Bartlett of Corwin, whose experienced eyes have helped me to craft a book that is, I hope, both persuasive and accessible.

Carol Dweck has long been an inspiration for my work, and her offer of a foreword was extremely generous, given so many calls on her time. Other gurus of mine—giants on whose shoulders I have tried to stand—include David Perkins, to whom this book is dedicated, Art Costa, and the late Neil Postman. Over the years, many friends, colleagues, and authors have challenged and enriched my thinking about education. They include Ron Berger, Mark Brown, Margaret Carr, Maryl Chambers, Margot Foster, Michael Fullan, Paul Ginnis, John Hattie, Faye Hauwai, Bill Lucas, Deb Merrett, Karin Morrison, Kath Murdoch, James Nottingham, Graham Powell, Ron Ritchhart, Chris Watkins, Val Westwell, and Dylan Wiliam. Even some of those who temperamentally or ideologically disagree with me have helped me sharpen my thinking and deserve my thanks. They include Katharine Birbalsingh, Daisy Christodoulou, David Didau, Kathryn Ecclestone, Martin Robinson, and Chris Woodhead.

Many schoolteachers and principals have helped me to understand where my ideas work and where they don't, and have been a huge source of practical wisdom. Far too many to name exhaustively, they include Hugh Bellamy, Sue Bill, Matthew Burgess, Robert Cleary, Liz Coffey, Andrea Curtis, Reagan Delaney, Robyn Fergusson, Gemma Goldenberg, Bryan Harrison, David Kehler, John Keohane, Debbie Marchant, Sarah Martin, Karen McClintock, Andy Moor, Kellie Morgan, Judith Mortell, Bojana Obradovic, Leah O'Toole, Tom Sherrington, Annabel Southey, Nicole Styles, Adam Swain, Luke Swain, and Michael Whitworth. Becky Carlzon in particular has been a massive source of energy and ideas. She and her husband Juan were responsible for many of the elegant photographs and illustrations in the book.

Judith Nesbitt, as always, has been my most precious source of support and reassurance.

Many thanks to you all.

# Publisher's Acknowledgments

Corwin gratefully acknowledges the contributions of the following reviewers:

Ken Austin, Associate Professor
Stephen F. Austin State University
Nacogdoches, TX

Jessica Baldwin, English Language Arts Teacher,
    Grades 10 and 11
Toombs County High School
Claxton, GA

Debora Banner, Retired Teacher and Assistant Superintendent
Lantrip Elementary School
Houston, TX

Donna Eurich, English Teacher, Grades 6–8
St. Ann Catholic School
Palm Beach, FL

Erica Ward, Elementary School Teacher
Public School 190
Roosevelt, NY

# About the Author

**Guy Claxton** is a cognitive scientist specializing in the expandability of intelligence. He is the author of many books on education and learning, including *Wise Up: The Challenge of Lifelong Learning*, *What's the Point of School?* and *Building Learning Power*. He holds degrees from Cambridge and Oxford universities, and is visiting professor of education at King's College London.

The Learning Power Approach seems to be the answer to so many challenges we [teachers] face at the moment: the need to prepare young people for a world where many professional jobs will be automated, the need to get good academic results, the need to engage all students (boys being the most likely to be disillusioned) in education, the need to get a good inspection report (where inspectors are now looking to see the development of independent learning), the need to be distinctive . . . and the need to deal with the growing problem of mental health in the young.

Neil Tetley, Headmaster,
Woodbridge School, Suffolk, UK

I constantly see people rise in life who are not the smartest, sometimes not even the most diligent, but they are learning machines. They go to bed every night a little wiser than they were when they got up, and boy does that help—particularly when you have a long run ahead of you.

Charlie Munger, Vice Chairman of
the Berkshire Hathaway Conglomerate
(from his University of Southern California
Law Commencement Speech, May 2007)

# The Origins of the Learning Power Approach

Live as if you were to die tomorrow. Learn as if you
were to live forever.

Mahatma Gandhi

It wasn't till I was working on my doctorate in cognitive
psychology that I began to unlearn to be taught. DPhil or
doctorate supervision in the Oxford University Department
of Experimental Psychology was, in the early 1970s, a very
loose affair. I had three supervisors over the course of the
four years it took me to complete my thesis, all of whom
practiced a form of benign neglect. It was entirely down to
me to make an appointment to see them, and when I did,
the response was usually some form of "very interesting—
what do you plan to do next?" What guidance I got came
mostly from protracted coffee break conversations with

other graduate students, and especially from conversations with the three young bloods with whom I shared an office, Stephen, Nigel, and Roger.

We read and argued. We thought up and carried out many experiments that never saw the light of day. And in the process, we were rehabilitating our learning faculties. We were learning to be curious, and to develop and discipline that curiosity through critical thinking and wide reading. We were developing longer-term interests and stretching our willingness to persist in the face of difficulty and confusion. We were learning to collaborate and discuss, to disagree robustly while remaining friends, and to reflect critically and fruitfully. We were learning to be creative and imaginative, dreaming up possible theories to explain whatever we were interested in. We taught ourselves to design and critique experiments and pick holes in our own and everyone else's arguments. We made dozens of mistakes and learned to learn from them. Above all, we were learning to trust our own minds: to believe that what we wondered was worth wondering, what we thought was worth thinking. We were learning to develop and rely on our own (collective and individual) resources. We were regaining the confidence, which we had all had as small children, to dive in, have a go, follow our noses, engage in trial and error (lots of error), but honing those attitudes into sharp, sophisticated research skills. We were learning to be powerful learners. (And we all went on to become productive and successful academics.)

It was a challenging, uncomfortable, and exciting time. We had to break free of all the habits and expectations that our previous education had embedded in our minds. We had to give up expecting a teacher to design learning for us, rescue us when the going got tough, tell us the "right" answers, or train us in how to write an A-grade essay. In the absence of that benign, authoritative, guiding teacherly presence, we had to learn how to become our own teachers. And so I will always be grateful to my supervisors for their neglect.

When I left Oxford I imagined a career as a psychology academic, but, to pay the bills, I took a temporary job teaching psychology at the University of London Institute of Education. I soon discovered that the real-world challenges of helping people learn to become schoolteachers were more satisfying, and indeed more intellectually interesting, than designing finicky little laboratory experiments—so I have never left the world of education. And those earlier experiences of education—of learning, and then eventually unlearning, to be taught—have shaped my work ever since.

It quickly dawned on me that everyone—not just academics—needs those powers of confidence, curiosity, and imagination that I had been strengthening at Oxford. No artist, no engineer, no plumber, no care worker is going to be followed throughout their lives by a kindly teacher marking their work and showing them how to close the gap between their current performance and a more advanced form of expertise (like passing an exam). If I had become a chef instead of a prof, I think I would still have needed those abilities.

OK, in some workplaces there are line managers, annual appraisals, and learning and development departments offering some advice and training. But if we are going to take advantage of those offerings to grow our expertise, we will need a mindset that has the confidence and enthusiasm to learn on our own. Even more, if we are to craft "trajectories of excellence" through life—as a parent, a lawyer, an athlete, or a gardener—we will have to design and manage those learning journeys for ourselves. We will need to notice what it is we need to get better at, and to think about how best to acquire the knowledge and skill we currently lack.

When you look at traditional education, we don't seem to be doing very well at turning out those independent thinkers and learners. Of course, some people turn out to be powerful learners despite their schooling, but many more do not. Their minds are shaped for the worse by their time in classrooms.

No one, to my knowledge, has ever gone into teaching saying, "My passionate commitment is to do everything in my power to turn out young people who are apathetic, passive, extrinsically motivated, dependent, dogmatic, timid, fragile, and credulous." However, I have seen far too many schools that have unwittingly developed exactly these dysfunctional attitudes—in high as well as low achievers. Under pressure to raise grades, they have felt obliged to teach in a way that creates such closed and anxious minds. They may bemoan the lack of creativity, initiative, or entrepreneurship in today's young people, yet respond by trying to paste some special activities over the top of routine teaching methods that are the real culprits. Not surprisingly, such Band-Aids are largely ineffective.

> It is possible to teach in a way that hits both higher grades *and* positive, empowering attitudes toward learning itself.

Such schools are neither run nor staffed by bad people. As I say, no one in their right mind sets out to create these attitudes. Yet these attitudes are the very antitheses of the mindsets that today's young people are going to need.

| | |
|---|---|
| *Apathetic* means you are lacking in curiosity and wonder. | Instead of apathetic, you will need to be **curious.** |
| *Passive* means you are uninterested in learning unless required to engage in it by someone else. | Instead of passive, you will need to be **proactive.** |
| *Extrinsically motivated* means you are interested only in getting marks, grades, and praise for what you have learned, not in the glow of satisfaction from having mastered something tricky or produced something you are personally proud of. | Instead of extrinsically motivated, you will need to be **intrinsically motivated.** |
| *Dependent* means you are unable to engage in learning unless constantly instructed, reassured, and corrected by a teacher. | Instead of dependent, you will need to be **independent-minded.** |
| *Dogmatic* means you are addicted to right answers and unable to think about complicated or uncertain things that aren't black and white. | Instead of dogmatic, you will need to be **thoughtful** and **open**-**minded.** |
| *Timid* means being so frightened of making mistakes that you are unadventurous and conservative in your approach to learning, willing only to tackle things you already believe you can be successful at. | Instead of timid, you will need to be **adventurous.** |
| *Fragile* means you are likely to get upset or go to pieces if you get confused or don't get good grades. | Instead of fragile, you will need to be **robust and resilient.** |
| *Credulous* means you accept uncritically whatever authoritative-sounding statements come your way. | Instead of credulous, you will need to be **critical** and **skeptical** of what you hear and read. |

Until recently, there was a prevalent view that chasing grades and building mental capacities were somehow at odds with each other. Without really thinking about it, some educators thought they had to choose. Am I going to go for the grades, in which case I have to adopt a rather didactic, teacher-directed style, or am I going to try to build those elusive "21st century skills," in which case the grades might suffer? This either/or thinking is an example of what we might call *limiting assumptions*—beliefs that we may not even recognize as beliefs, but that limit our horizons and aspirations: our sense of what is possible. And what *is* possible, according to the research, is to teach in a way that hits both targets: higher grades *and* positive, empowering attitudes toward learning itself. The Learning Power Approach is about turning this possibility into a day-to-day reality—in every school in the world.

---

Gradually the idea of "learning power" was born, and I developed it through a number of books: *Live and Learn* in 1984, *Teaching to Learn* in 1990, and *Wise Up: The Challenge of Lifelong Learning* in 1999, in which I brought together all the research that underpins the idea of learning power. A friend of mine, Graham Powell, who was working as a professional development adviser to teachers at the time, read *Wise Up* and suggested I boil it down into a practical book for teachers, so in 2002 *Building Learning Power* (BLP) was published by a small British education provider, TLO Limited (TLO stands for The Learning Organisation). For the next 12 years, I worked closely with TLO to develop practical training and resources for teachers that would help them put the ideas into practice in their classrooms.

Though I am no longer closely associated with TLO, and my own thoughts have moved on, I think BLP remains an excellent example of what I am calling here the Learning

Power Approach (LPA). There are now thousands of schools around the world that have put BLP into action. Many hundreds of these are scattered around the United Kingdom, but there are also chains of English-speaking schools in South Africa and Argentina; a network of schools in Ireland; a cluster of rural primary schools in the forests of Silesia in Poland; early childhood education centers across New Zealand; groups of independent schools in Victoria and New South Wales, Australia; and international schools in Amsterdam, Budapest, Dubai, Jakarta, Ho Chi Minh City, Suzhou in China, and Santiago in Chile. (The work of some of these is described in a book that Bill Lucas, Ellen Spencer, and I published a few years ago called *Expansive Education*.)[1] My colleagues and I are now developing Learning Power International to coordinate and strengthen the spread of the LPA around the globe.

As we researched more, we naturally discovered earlier pioneers who had been thinking along the same lines, as well as a variety of other groups around the world, especially in the United States, who had been developing very similar—or apparently similar—approaches. I divide those approaches into four categories: nuclear family, godparents, friends and neighbors, and near misses.

## Nuclear Family

The nuclear family—those approaches that exemplify the LPA most clearly—includes several of the approaches that have come out of Harvard University's Project Zero, especially those originated by David Perkins and his colleagues. There are the *Intellectual Character/Visible Thinking* initiative, now led by Ron Ritchhart, and the work on *Studio Thinking*, focusing on learning habits of mind through arts education, led by Lois Hetland and colleagues. Also influenced by Perkins and his codirector of Project

Zero, Howard Gardner, there is what is now known as *EL Education*, originally *Expeditionary Learning*, led by Ron Berger, which focuses on the development of a craftsmanlike approach to learning in all learners. There is the pioneering *Habits of Mind* approach, originated by Art Costa and his long-time collaborator Bena Kallick. There is Chris Watkins's elegant work on the powerful effect of getting students to tell their own stories of learning, and the implications of narrative approaches for the development of the *Learner-Centered Classroom*. And there is the careful work of Philip Adey and Michael Shayer on their *Cognitive Acceleration* programs in science and math (CASE and CAME).

And I would include as family members some of the more venerable initiatives out of which our current understandings have grown. There is the seminal *Project for the Enhancement of Effective Learning* (PEEL), founded by Dick White, Jeff Northfield, John Baird, and others at Monash University in Australia in 1985, and continued to this day by Ian Mitchell. In early childhood education there is the *Hundred Languages of Childhood* approach developed at Reggio Emelia in Italy. There are the pioneering approaches of the highly influential *International Baccalaureate*, and the global chain of *Round Square* schools, inspired by the German educator Kurt Hahn, not to mention earlier roots in the work of Maria Montessori and Johann Pestalozzi.[2]

We are now able to articulate, more clearly than these pioneers were able to, the character traits that underpin powerful learning, and to provide a robust foundation in cognitive science rather than just philosophy. But all of the nuclear family members share a concern to articulate what the core learning dispositions might be, and to target teaching and school culture deliberately and explicitly to build those dispositions, while also raising more conventional indicators of achievement.

# Godparents

The "godparents" are those who have made seminal intellectual and academic contributions to the development of the LPA, but who have not themselves been associated with the promotion of particular practical strategies for teaching and learning. Among the godparents are, obviously, David Perkins himself—a constant fountain of thought-provoking ideas, arguments, and terminologies—who laid a cornerstone of the LPA with his work on *learnable intelligence*. There is Carol Dweck and her army of collaborators, whose monumental body of work on *growth mindset* has shown the extent to which certain unconscious belief systems restrict people's learning ability, and also the relative ease with which these beliefs can be surfaced, challenged, and changed. More recently there is Angela Duckworth's work on the important concept of *grit*. And perhaps I should include here such giants as the Americans John Dewey and Israel Scheffler, and the Scottish educationalist John Nisbet.

# Friends and Neighbors

Among "friends and neighbors" I would include a whole range of kindred spirit initiatives across the world. They include the *Expansive Education Network,* cofounded by Bill Lucas and me, and now led by Bill at the University of Winchester; Kevin Bartlett's *Common Ground Collaborative*; *P21, the Partnership for 21st Century Learning; Whole Education,* led by David Crossley and Douglas Archibald; John Abbott's *21st Century Learning Initiative*; the *Tools of the Mind* approach developed by Elena Bodrova and Deborah Leong; the *Effective Lifelong Learning Inventory (ELLI)*; Matthew Lipman's *Philosophy for Children*; Bob Burden's

*Thinking Schools International*; Paul Ginnis's *Teachers' Toolkit*; James Nottingham's *Challenging Learning*; Jane Simister's *Future Smart*; Mary Jane Drummond and colleagues' *Learning Without Limits*; David Price's *Engaged Learning*; The UK Royal Society of Arts' *Opening Minds* project; and Australian Kath Murdoch's approach to *Inquiry-Based Learning*. There are many more, and forgive me if I have not mentioned your favorite.

## Near Misses

Among the "near misses" are some currently very popular approaches to the improvement of teaching and learning that focus more single-mindedly on raising achievement—literacy and numeracy levels, examination scores and grades, and performance on international comparisons such as the PISA tests. Sometimes despite their rhetoric, these near misses neglect to promote teaching methods that actually, effectively, address the development of learning power. In practice, for example, many *Formative Assessment* and *Assessment for Learning* approaches focus predominantly on what teachers can do to help students close the gap between their current performance on the conventional curriculum, and the level of performance that high-stakes tests require. Though the original writings of Paul Black and Dylan Wiliam, the two originators of *Assessment for Learning*, envisaged something much closer to the ideals of the LPA, many practical versions have reverted to an obsession with raising grades.

John Hattie's *Visible Learning* techniques likewise derive from research that evaluated different teaching methods overwhelmingly in terms of test scores. Impressive though this research is, it still works on the assumption that conventional kinds of test scores are the most important outcomes of schooling. By failing to engage with the—admittedly tricky—issue of how to evidence the development of learning attitudes and dispositions, Hattie's work strongly steers teachers toward getting those grades. (Over the course of the series of books of which this volume is a part, we will introduce and discuss various approaches to assessing the development of such attitudes. It *is* tricky, but that does not mean it can't be done, and many promising starts have already been made.)[3]

Doug Lemov's *Teach Like a Champion* strategies too are targeted at academic achievement. It is clearly all about getting more kids, especially from low-income backgrounds, to college. The strategies are grouped under headings like "Setting High Academic Expectations" and "Planning That Ensures Academic Achievement." (There is a category for "Building Character and Trust," but it comes seventh in his list of nine and is quite undeveloped.) And *Mastery Learning*, deriving from the theories of eminent educator Benjamin Bloom, again emphasizes ensuring high levels of academic achievement for all students, and fondly hopes that, as a result, confidence and a love of learning will somehow automatically accrue, though there is no evidence to support that belief. Meanwhile, some approaches to *Character Education* take a more moralistic stance, focusing on sex, drugs, and health education. *Service Education* also talks of character development, but without a clear sense of what exactly the "desirable residues" of experiences of service are expected to be, nor of how success in their cultivation is to be evidenced.

Even some of the earlier work on *Thinking Skills* I now see as a near miss, because it tried to tackle thinking and learning as if they were mainly matters of consciously applied strategy or technique. All you needed to do was learn how to produce a neat "spider diagram" or how to make use of other types of visual diagrams for organizing ideas on paper (or screen), and that made you a better thinker. But by and large, research has shown that such techniques tend not to become embedded in the way people actually think. They become "tricks" that students *can* call to mind and use when prodded, but that do not, of themselves, change underlying beliefs and attitudes. We have to tackle the problem of how to help people think and learn better at a deeper level: their habits of mind.

———————————

Many of the LPAs, like my own Building Learning Power, have become widely known and successful "brands." But it seems to me that it is high time to distill the common messages out of these kindred initiatives, and to create a broader alliance between them. The LPA is therefore not another brand; rather, it is an attempt to synthesize and synergize a variety of approaches that are already well developed and increasingly well evidenced. It is an umbrella, a broad canopy under which teachers who are used to more specific versions feel they can camp comfortably, as well as an introduction and an invitation to the millions of teachers around the world who know that education ought to be a proper preparation for life in a tricky world, and not just a blind obsession with grades and college and university entrance.

Of course this is one person's synthesis, and I bring my own preferences and biases to the process. So it is quite possible that not everyone will agree with my placing them inside—or outside—the LPA family. Each approach has its own strengths, nuances, and terminologies, and we could have animated discussions about terminology and priorities. (For example, Art Costa and I have had friendly conversations about the meaning and prominence of what is widely called "metacognition.") But, in the face of so much current pressure to focus solely on the mastery of literacy, numeracy, and subject matter—and the widespread misconception that somehow the development of these vital character traits will look after itself—I think it is very important for us LPA-ites to join forces, share experience and research, and sing in unison as loudly as we can. I hope this book and its companion volumes will help to find and strengthen that single voice.

We will explore the distinguishing marks of the LPA in more detail later. At root, these approaches share a belief that examination success is not enough. It is not enough partly because millions of kids around the world are destined to be "losers" at the examination game: some because they are no good at sitting and listening for long periods, some because life has taught them to be highly distractible, some because they are just not intellectually inclined, some because they have needs and disabilities that cut across those required for school, some because of poverty. And some because performance on high-stakes tests would lose its value (for example, for college entrance) if everyone did well, so grades are statistically rigged to ensure the right proportion of "failures." The system, if it is to do the job of selection, requires there to be failures, and to tell kids otherwise, especially in "the land of opportunity," is fake news. So unless there is another way of "winning" at school, those who get low grades are failures, period. And therefore there has to be another "game" that will enable even the low achievers to look back and say they had a good education. This second game concerns the cultivation of the confidence and capacity to be a good learner. Actually, examination success is not enough even for the apparent "successes." As we will see in the next chapter, high achievers too often suffer from an inability to grapple calmly and intelligently with genuinely difficult challenges. They love to be successful and go to pieces when they cannot be.

The LPA offers an alternative to programs that continue to focus overwhelmingly, in practice if not in rhetoric, on academic attainment. It declares that *the learning powers are valuable ends of education in themselves*, and not just means to better grades and college entrance—though they are that too. The key point is this: The "near miss" approaches I mentioned above see character, if they see it at all, as either instrumental to the achievement of better grades—resilience helps you get better marks—or some kind of automatic by-product of conventional examination success. The mental habits of powerful learners are not seen—and this is the critical difference—as a set of learned, transferable strengths that are valuable in their own right, which, if they are to be developed successfully, need explicit attention and cultivation. As John Hattie himself has said,

> Dispositions to learning should be key performance indicators of the outcomes of schooling. Many teachers believe that, if achievement is enhanced, there is a ripple effect to these dispositions. However such a belief is not defensible. Such dispositions need planned interventions.[4]

Indeed they do—and the LPA spells out what those "planned interventions" are.

## A Socket Set

This book is the first in a series. It is rather like the handle in a socket set, and the following books are different

---

The learning powers are valuable ends of education in themselves.

---

"sockets" that can be fitted on to the handle. This first book sets out the rationale, the evidence, the principles, and the frameworks that underpin the whole LPA. It spells out clearly what is distinctive about the LPA, and provides plenty of illustrations of what it looks like in practice. To make a success of the LPA, it is very important, I have found, to understand clearly what it is and what it is not. So I hope you will enjoy getting your head around these ideas, and keep this book by you, to check your bearings, as you develop your own teaching and the ethos of the school in which you work.

To follow, there will be a number of different sockets that can be fitted on to the handle: a book for primary or elementary school teachers; another specifically for secondary or high school teachers; one for principals and head teachers who want to embed the LPA across a whole school or even networks of schools; and one, we hope, specifically for early childhood educators. There might be others for parents, or for college and university teachers and professors—but they are just pipe dreams at the moment. Each book in the series will be cowritten with experienced LPA practitioners, and will be full of practical advice and examples. If this first book seems, in places, rather too "conceptual" for your taste, and you are eager to get on to the practicalities, can I ask you to be patient? You may want to dip into this one slowly, assimilate its messages and invitations more gradually, and keep it by you as a reference book against which to check your own practice. Even if you are not a practicing teacher—perhaps you are an administrator, a college lecturer, or a parent— I hope you might enjoy this first book for its own sake, as an argument about what is desirable, and what is possible, in 21st century schools.

## Wondering

Can you remember what you were like as a learner—facing challenges and difficulties—when you were young?

What attitudes to learning did you develop at school?

Are there particular subjects—math, art, or languages, for example—where school left you feeling blocked or lacking in confidence as a learner?

Have those attitudes changed much since school, do you think? If so, what do you think caused those changes?

What kinds of experiences since you left school have given you the learning habits that you now have?

Are the young people that you know today more or less inquisitive and resilient than you were at their age? How much is down to personality, and how much to changes in society, do you think?

# Notes

1. Bill Lucas, Guy Claxton, and Ellen Spencer, *Expansive Education.*
2. You can find information on key works by all those named in these paragraphs in the references at the back of the book. For Kurt Hahn, see Nick Veevers and Pete Allison, *Kurt Hahn: Inspirational, Visionary, Outdoor and Experiential Educator.* For Reggio Emelia, see Carolyn Edwards and Lella Gandini, *The Hundred Languages of Children.* For Pestalozzi, see Joy Palmer, *Fifty Major Thinkers on Education.* A selection of practitioners' websites is noted at the end of the book as well.
3. See, for example, research in the references by myself and New Zealand academic Margaret Carr, as well as the review paper by Angela Duckworth and David Yeager. One of Art Costa and Bena Kallick's books, *Assessing and Reporting on Habits of Mind,* is full of practical examples.
4. John Hattie, *Visible Learning for Teachers,* p. 40.

# What Is Learning?

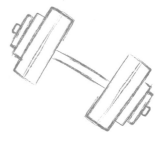

> A camel is stronger than a human being; an elephant is larger; a lion has greater valor; cattle eat more than a person; birds are more virile. People were made for the purpose of learning.
>
> Al-Ghazali, *The Book of Knowledge*

Learning power is the ability (and the inclination) to learn. As we grow up, we have lots of experiences that can either augment or diminish that capacity to learn. The Learning Power Approach (LPA) aims to ensure that, whatever we do in schools, we don't undermine our students' learning power. And then, we identify the different mental ingredients that go to make up learning power, and devise ways, in schools and especially in classrooms, that teachers can actively strengthen the learning power of their students. If we are aiming to prepare young people for a lifetime of confident, rewarding learning, the first thing we need to do is understand what it is that people do, out there in the real world, to increase their competence and understanding.

You can think of it like this. If you did calculus at school, you may have dim (or not so dim) memories of the relationship between distance, speed, and acceleration. Distance is how far you are from something. Speed is the rate at which your distance from something is changing. And acceleration is the rate at which your speed is changing. Speed and acceleration were called the first and second differentials of distance. There is a similar relationship between knowledge, learning, and learning power. Knowledge is what you know, or know how to do. Learning is a change in what you know, or can do. And learning power is a change in the way you go about learning. To understand acceleration, you have to know what speed is. Likewise, in order to understand what learning power is, you first have to understand what learning is (see Figure 2.1).

So what exactly is it that we want to help young people get better at when we talk about "learning to learn" or "building learning power"? The LPA takes a very broad view of learning. We are not just trying to make students more efficient consumers of the curriculum and passers of exams. We do want that, but we want more. We are trying to get them ready for the challenges and uncertainties of life, in all their messy glory. So we have to be clear from the start what that kind of learning involves: why we do it, when we do it, and how we go about it. That's what this chapter is about.

> Knowledge is what you know, or know how to do. Learning is a change in what you know, or can do. And learning power is a change in the way you go about learning.

## Why Do We Learn?

We learn because we are built to. As the 11th century Persian philosopher Al-Ghazali said, learning is our most

**FIGURE 2.1** Learning Power Is Like Acceleration

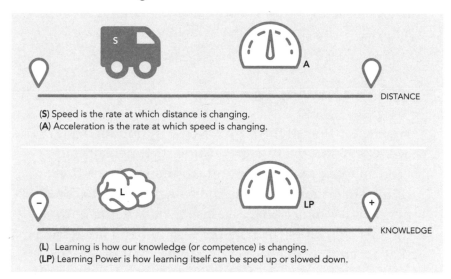

(**S**) Speed is the rate at which distance is changing.
(**A**) Acceleration is the rate at which speed is changing.

(**L**) Learning is how our knowledge (or competence) is changing.
(**LP**) Learning Power is how learning itself can be sped up or slowed down.

*Source:* By kind permission of Juan and Becky Carlzon

obvious characteristic as a species. We are born immature, unfinished, so that we can adapt ourselves to whatever cultural and biological niche we find ourselves in. Our brains are designed to pick up the patterns and nuances of the world so that we can mesh, when we need to, with a wide variety of conditions. The babies of Chinese parents brought up in England or America naturally learn to speak the local language, with all its dialects and idioms, flawlessly—and the babies of English or American parents brought up in China do the same. Through learning we are able to anticipate how the world will change, and the likely effect of our actions upon it. And in a fast-changing world, we are doomed if we cannot keep up. Learning is the one skill that you can be sure is never going to pass its use-by date. And without learning we not only struggle to live but

> Through learning we are able to anticipate how the world will change, and the likely effect of our actions upon it.

also fail to develop our interests, passions, and talents. So all in all, the ability to be a good learner is about as important an asset as you could possibly imagine.

## When Do We Learn?

We are learning all the time. Often without our being aware of it, our brains are adjusting their networks to keep up to date with the world around us. Babies don't think much about how they are going to learn to cope, but their learning-hungry brains are busy doing it by themselves. Out of the buzz of sensation and impressions that are continually impacting babies, their brains are striving to detect patterns: What goes with what; what precedes or follows what; and especially, how does what I do influence the flow of events? Infants love orderly rituals such as bath times, meal times, or going-to-bed times, because the patterns are clear. I sit in warm water and play with my toys. I get soap in my eyes if I don't learn the critical moments at which to keep them shut tight. I look forward to being wrapped in a warm towel and stroked and cuddled. All our lives, our brains are busy extracting and refining those patterns, because the patterns enable us to predict, and therefore exert increasingly sophisticated control over, the goings-on around us. When we move to a new town, when the train schedules change, when we start a new school or get a new job, our learning brains are hard at work altering their connections and making new ones.

> All our lives, our brains are busy extracting and refining patterns that enable us to predict, and therefore exert increasingly sophisticated control over, the goings-on around us.

When learning becomes more focused and conscious, it is because we can't immediately do or understand something we need or want to:

- I want to cook a nice meal, but the sauce goes lumpy.

- I want to build a tower of blocks, but they keep falling down.

- I want to get my academic paper published, but it got rejected.

- I want to help my team win, but I often lose the ball in a tackle.

- I want to be popular with my classmates, but my jokes just get a groan.

- I want to do well at school, but my math grades are poor and I often "don't get it."

- I want you to like me, but somehow I keep putting my foot in it.

When our first attempts fail to produce the result we want, we experience interest, surprise, frustration, confusion, or anxiety. These are the signals that—provided it seems possible and isn't too risky—learning is needed. These so-called cognitive emotions tell us when learning is required, and help to direct its course.

## What Is the Launchpad for Learning?

The stimulus for intentional learning is the desire to improve: to know more, to understand more deeply, to develop competence and expertise. The twin launchpads of learning are curiosity and necessity. We *want* to improve, in order to advance our interests; or we *need* to improve, in order to cope with the unavoidable, and sometimes unwelcome, demands that come our way.

Either way, learning won't happen unless we notice and admit the need for improvement. If we think we are doing fine as it is, we won't put in the effort that learning requires. We have to fess up—certainly to ourselves and oftentimes to other people—that what we currently know or do is imperfect or inadequate. We need to accept our current incompetence or ignorance in some regard, and not make excuses or blame it on someone else. We need to be able to acknowledge and tolerate feelings of uncertainty or confusion. We need to see mistakes not as a painful slur on our self-worth but as a prompt to engage what the LPA calls our "learning muscles." We need to be generally optimistic that our learning efforts are likely to pay off; hope of success needs to outweigh fear of failing or looking stupid.

Learning is like driving a car. To get going, you first have to engage the engine. That's what curiosity and necessity do. If nothing draws you in to learning, it won't happen. If you find yourself in a situation where your curiosity is unwelcome, it can wither away, and you become apathetic. Then you have to make sure the brakes are off. If we are defensive or imperceptive, unwilling to confront the need for improvement, the brakes will stay locked on, and no learning will occur. If you have learned to see mistakes or confusion as signs of weakness, for example, then you might be too busy trying to shore up your self-esteem to notice the learning opportunities that are right under your nose.

It will be obvious that learning isn't just a simple reflex, or even just a collection of skills; it is a highly complex activity that involves our personalities, desires, and beliefs as much as our intelligence. As we develop, learning becomes much more than forming simple associations between A and B, or committing "facts" to memory. Drill and rote memorization have their place. It is useful to be able to commit things to memory and retrieve them when needed. But they are just two of the tools in the powerful learner's toolbox. It is no use just being a parrot; you have to be able to think, talk, pay careful attention, and use your imagination as well, if you are going to be a good all-around learner.

## What Do Learners Actually Do?

So let us take a quick look at some of the other tools in the learner's toolbox. We will see that, like all tools, each of them has its pros and cons, and all have areas where they work well and others where they don't. Different kinds and different stages of learning draw on different tools in the box. Early on in a project, you might need to do a lot of reading and analysis. But then you may need to switch and make use of your imagination and fantasy. And then you may have to do some trial and error to find out which of your ideas actually work. And then you may have to be analytical and critical again as you review your progress.

Some subjects, like technology, involve close attention to the physical world; others, like mathematics, don't. Learning about other people may well involve a lot of conversation, but the kind of learning that happens in meditation needs a minimum of interaction. Some subjects (such as science) need a good deposit of knowledge on which to build, but many forms of valuable learning, such as the sophisticated practicing of a footballer or a violinist, are more embodied and intuitive. Some learning is deliberate, conscious, and effortful, but much of it happens incidentally and on the fly.

If school is a preparation for real-life learning, it ought to be sharpening all of the tools in the box, not just one or two.

Here is a quick overview of the common skills that the powerful learner needs to be good at.

## Observing

To learn, you have to be attentive and perceptive—using all the senses to gather information. Looking carefully, noticing small but critical details that might be easily missed, waiting patiently for perceptual patterns or trends to emerge: These are learning skills that can be easily overridden by impatience or the tendency to jump to conclusions. We can be amazed by children's perceptiveness—in finding a lost ball or helping a grandparent with a jigsaw puzzle, for example—yet remain unaware of how easily this invaluable kind of learning can be neglected or damaged in school. Studying a *Where's Waldo?* picture book can be as useful to a five-year-old's development as struggling to read text. The well-rounded mind needs perceptual as well as linguistic literacy!

## Reading

But, obviously, being a good reader is an essential component of being a good learner. To be a powerful learner, you need to be good at gathering and recording information, and a good deal of that comes through text. You need to be good at looking things up, whether in a library or on the Internet, and judging the validity of your sources. You need to know how to extract the gist of what you are reading, organize your notes, and follow references or hyperlinks from one place to another. You need to know how to extract the meaning from a difficult piece of writing (by highlighting, rereading, looking up definitions of critical terms, trying to summarize ideas in your own words, and so on). All these strategies need to be talked about and practiced, and we may need to help our young learners to explore their usefulness in a range of contexts—not just in school for school purposes.

## Critiquing

As well as the power to understand, good learners also need to develop the power to critique. As students mature, so we need to make sure that a respect for what others have written or said does not lead to generalized credulity. Of course there are people who are more knowledgeable and experienced than ourselves, and we do well to take seriously what they have to say. But as our students grow up, they are going to be bombarded with all kinds of dubious, if not downright spurious, knowledge claims (especially in this so-called post-truth, fake-news society), and it will not be in their best interests if we allow that attitude of respect to turn into a habit of uncritical acceptance of everything they hear. (They are going to need what Ernest Hemingway famously called a "built-in, shock-proof crap detector.") We will have to show them that their school textbooks are objects of inquiry as well as of authority.

## Experimenting

At the heart of learning is good, old-fashioned trial and error. In many areas of learning, including baseball, writing, and math, we tinker our way toward understanding and competence. Once we have the glimmerings of an idea about how to proceed, we give it a go, observe the effects and the success, adjust our action, and have another go. We can rarely figure everything out in advance so well that our first attempt is a surefire success. Watch an engineer sketching a bridge, an athlete adjusting her run-up, a teacher or an executive polishing their PowerPoint presentations, a child learning to dive, a cook tinkering with a recipe, and you will see the power of this kind of rehearsing, practicing, and drafting. Sometimes we know what we want to achieve, and our experiments are refined as we approach the goal. And sometimes we are just playing with material (as artists do), ideas (scientists), or bodily movements (choreographers) to see what happens.

Powerful learners often need to dive in and get things wrong on the way to getting them right. As Samuel Beckett famously said, of his own work as a playwright, "Ever tried. Ever failed. No matter. Try again. Fail again. Fail better." Yet some children, in some schools, learn to become afraid of making these kinds of productive mistakes, too timid to put pen to paper unless they already know the right answer.

## Imagining

Trial and error needs possibilities to work on. You have to have something to try—a hunch or a guess about what *might* work—and then you can set about testing, refining, or rejecting it. Imagination is one of the main ways of generating these ideas. These hunches are not foolproof, and are only as good as the bedrock of knowledge and experience from which they emerge, but they are often richer and more insightful than the careful deductions of the logician. To be able to make good use of our imaginations, we need to be able to slow down and listen for these intuitions. They aren't always right, but they often provide a fresh starting point for thinking and experimenting.

## Reasoning

Another important way in which we generate ideas is through careful thinking or reasoning. Sometimes, if the knowledge and experience from which we start is secure and accurate, and if our reasoning is rigorous and watertight, we are able to reach conclusions that don't need any experimentation to check them out. We know they must be valid because they follow logically. Mathematics exercises this kind of reasoning. In real life, things are rarely so cut and dried, but thinking as carefully as possible often enables us to come up with better guesses about what might work.

Often, we construct possible explanations for puzzling or inconvenient events, and these conjectures lead to plausible suggestions as to what a good next move might be. But we still have to go and check it out to see if it works in practice, as well as in theory. Science is a very sophisticated form of learning that combines observation, studying, experimentation, imagination, and reasoning into reliable ways of generating high-quality theories, which then enable us to know what we have to do to make aircraft stay up in the sky, drugs that will prevent malaria and smallpox, and phones that connect to the Internet.

## Imitating

Another source of good ideas on which to base learning experiments is imitation. To get a useful idea about what to try, you can find good role models—people who can do or talk about what you currently can't—watch how they do it, and try to copy them. Imitation is one of the most fundamental and effective learning tools we have, and we share it with many other species. Neuroscientists have found that our brains are deeply designed for imitation. Even very young children are predisposed to mimic the actions of those around them. Of course, as we grow up we become more discerning about who we imitate, and how much. We develop our own styles and interests, and your "solution" to a problem may very well not work for me. Nevertheless, borrowing ideas about how to proceed by watching what those around you are doing is a vital learning tool in all cultures.

## Discussing

We learn from others not just by watching what they do, but also by listening to what they say and sharing knowledge and opinions. Often two, or three, or fifteen, heads are better than one. But there is good and bad discussion, and students need help to develop these tools of interaction. They have to learn how to take turns, how to listen attentively, how to be good team players, how to disagree respectfully, and how to stay open and receptive to others' views and to the possibility that their own views could be improved. Many schools just put children into groups and assume that their conversations ought to be productive. But they aren't if one or two loudmouths hog the limelight, if shy people take a back seat, or if people just shout opinions at each other and become belligerent. In the LPA, we coach students in how to hold good discussions, how to monitor a group, and how to repair a group when it is not working well.

## Reflecting

After thinking up things to do, and trying them out, learners need to be perceptive and honest observers and critics of their own performance. How did it go? Did things work out as expected? Which bits worked well, and which need further thinking and tinkering? You may need to spend time reflecting on your performance more slowly, so that wider or deeper trawling of your own knowledge and experience can come up with more subtle adjustments. As a baseball pitcher, you watch the videos of the last game, intently looking for physical clues as to why your slider isn't breaking the way it used to. As a writer, you start the day by reading over yesterday's output with a fresher, more critical eye than you could muster the evening before.

Sometimes called *metacognition,* this self-evaluation can become quite sophisticated when it involves becoming conscious of and scrutinizing the assumptions behind your own thinking. Developing this kind of self-awareness is not easy, and it usually benefits from skillful coaching. As coach and athlete sit watching the video of last week's competition, the coach's gentle questioning—"What do you notice about your facial expression as you are winding up for the jump? Does that tell you anything about your mindset at that moment?"—can guide the learner's attention toward telling details that can deepen self-awareness, and thus open up more possibilities for learning. English teachers could be using the same kind of coaching to develop their students' ability to edit their own writing, for example.

## Practicing

As a last example of the learner's craft, we should mention the role of deliberate practice.[1] For a while, people thought that 10,000 hours of practice was what it took to become an expert at something. But now we know that this figure is a gross oversimplification, because the quality of practice matters even more than the quantity. Expert practicers get better faster. They have learned to pick out the difficult parts of what they are trying to do, and work especially hard on those. They make good use of recordings and videos of their own performance. They know what time of day works best for them, when to push on through tiredness or confusion, and when to take a break. A pianist knows that sometimes it helps to play a piece at half speed, to get the fingering exactly right, and sometimes it is worth trying to play it at double speed, mistakes and all, to get a better feel for the flow and cadence of the piece. A footballer is able to suggest to the coach a new way of practicing an attacking maneuver. Teaching and coaching so that your students become better at teaching and coaching themselves is not the same as teaching or coaching that is solely aimed at winning the match or wowing the audience.

## The Beginnings of Learning Power

From this brief survey, I think we can already see an image of an all-around powerful learner beginning to emerge. It involves a variety of strengths. The more you have and the stronger they are, the more all-around mind-fit for learning you will be. Powerful learners know how to make valid inferences and deductions, to critique their own arguments as well as other people's, to check knowledge claims, and to construct fruitful theories and explanations for puzzling situations. They are good at and enjoy using their imaginations: They can use visualization, mental rehearsal, fantasy, and reverie to create possibilities for further thought and action. They have attitudes of what we might call "interested sensitivity" and "respectful skepticism" toward their own intuitions, hunches, and gut feelings. They are meticulous and focused observers: able to look for both holistic patterns and telling details, as well as being on the lookout for productive role models. They enjoy reading things that feed their own interests. They like and are good at the process of tinkering and experimenting, trying things out in practice and revising them as they go along.

They know how to practice and develop new skills effectively, and in a way that preserves an element of playfulness and spontaneity. They happily put effort and thought into meeting worthwhile challenges to the best of their ability, and derive considerable pleasure and pride from their accomplishments. They are good at different kinds of conversation and discussion: unafraid to venture opinion and ideas, yet always open to reflection and revision, capable of listening intently and accurately and offering thoughtful and courteous responses. And, we might add, they are discerning in their selection of which learning challenges to respond to, being mindful of their own values and of potential benefits to their communities. They are also discerning in who they take advice and instruction from.

The key point is that these learning tools are all capable of further development. Learning power is something that is itself always subject to learning. The tools can be developed individually, but they also need to work well together as an ensemble, for all these strengths are to be used flexibly, appropriately, and in balance. To change the metaphor, they need to learn how to play together like the instruments in a jazz band of accomplished improvisers who know each other well. The powerful learning mind has to interweave its different strengths and habits according to the needs and rhythms of the moment.

Once we uncover all the things that learners do, the feelings they need to tolerate, and the attitudes that underpin their confidence, it starts to become clear what might get in the way of learning: what might make someone less rather than more powerful as a learner. Following are a few of them.

> Learning power is something that is itself always subject to learning.

- Being ashamed of making mistakes

- Being too proud to ask for help

- Being unwilling to look honestly at your own performance, or to take responsibility for it

- Being unwilling to wrestle or struggle with things that are difficult

- Being impatient for success, or unrealistic about the time and effort that learning is likely to take

- Being too scattered or agitated to focus on learning

- Being fatalistic or pessimistic about your own ability to grapple effectively with difficult things

- Being self-deluded about your own competence (Remember that 90% of car drivers rate themselves as better than average!)

- Or simply not having figured out that learning power is composed of all kinds of strategies and habits that are within your ability to master

Indeed, if the analogy holds, simply neglecting to make use of young people's learning muscles may lead the muscles to atrophy. "Use it or lose it" can apply to minds as well as bodies. All of these (and many more factors) can weaken people's learning power.

## So Can You Get Better at Learning?

Once you begin to think about learning not as something magical that you are either good at or not, but as a collection of skills, habits, and attitudes that can be influenced by experience, then the idea that learning itself is capable of being boosted begins to look like an interesting possibility. It may well be that your "general intelligence" or IQ sets some overall constraints on how far or how fast you can learn, but there are other factors, more under your control, that affect learning too. So it just seems good sense to focus on identifying what those factors might be. And what can be learned can also, potentially, be taught. So exploring the extent to which busy teachers, in regular classrooms, might be able to unfreeze some of the brakes and cultivate some of the accelerators of learning seems a worthwhile possibility. If it is really possible to fit a learning turbocharger to children's minds, so that all of them, whatever their path in life may be, can learn what they need and want to learn with greater confidence and success, then why on earth would we not?

Of course, it is perfectly possible to be a powerful learner in one context, and a timid one in another. I am pretty robust when it comes to reading difficult books that I think will expand my mind. (I've just finished one called *Surfing Uncertainty* by the Scottish philosopher Andy Clark that really made me struggle—but it was worth it.) Put me on the dance floor, however, and—though I would love to be able to dance well—I tend to go into my shell. Most people's learning power is a bit patchy. But that doesn't mean we can't stretch and strengthen our overall adventurousness or determination. We can. And it is the job of every teacher to help young people do so.

> Once you begin to think about learning not as something magical that you are either good at or not, but as a collection of skills, habits, and attitudes that can be influenced by experience, then the idea that learning itself is capable of being boosted begins to look like an interesting possibility.

# What Kinds of Learning Are Going On in Classrooms?

In every classroom, all the time, there are three different kinds of learning going on. Knowledge is being accumulated. Specific skills and techniques are being developed. And more general attitudes and habits of mind are being formed. I find it useful to think of these as if they were different levels or layers in a flowing river, as seen in Figure 2.2. On the surface, quite fast moving and most visible, are the subjects of the curriculum: the knowledge. As you sit on the bank, you can watch the different topics floating by. There go The Inert Gases. And close behind is Adding Fractions. . . . Ah, here come The Causes of World War II. . . .

Then just below the surface of the river come the forms of expertise that enable students to make sense of that content—linguistic, numerical, and digital literacies; the skills and disciplines of mathematical and historical thinking; the ability to read musical notation; and so on. Both of these layers are very familiar to teachers, and of great concern.

But lower down in the depths of the river, less visible and slower moving, the attitudes, dispositions, and habits of mind that shape students' engagement with learning more generally are being formed. Small details of the way classrooms and schools operate cumulatively impact the development of these critical attitudes and habits of mind. Every lesson, every day, affects the slow buildup of these attitudes—for good or ill. How we teach slowly shapes the way young people respond to the unknown—to change, challenge, complexity, and uncertainty. Our teaching can steer them toward becoming more positive, confident, and capable in the face of difficulty. Or it can steer them toward becoming more timid, dogmatic, and insecure. If we choose the former route, they will learn what they need to know

**FIGURE 2.2** The Layers of Learning in the Classroom

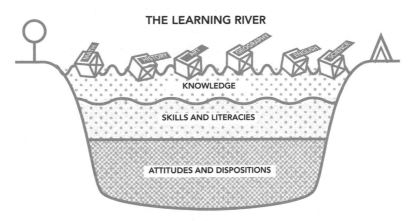

THE LEARNING RIVER

KNOWLEDGE

SKILLS AND LITERACIES

ATTITUDES AND DISPOSITIONS

*Source:* By kind permission of Juan and Becky Carlzon

more easily and effectively, and they will pursue their own dreams, interests, and ambitions more robustly throughout life. As my friend Art Costa puts it, we will have prepared them not just for a life of tests, but for the tests of life.[2]

As a teacher, you can't not be creating these currents—through your words, your reactions to students, the activities you design, your choice of what to display on your walls, the things you notice as you mark students' work, and dozens of other details that contribute to students' experience in school. This shaping is not inevitable—some students are "bent" more than others by these routines and expectations, and some resist being shaped at all. But the culture that a teacher creates acts like a magnetic field that attracts, stimulates, and rewards certain habits of mind and not others.

You can teach The Great Depression (for example) in a way that engages students' skepticism of historical accounts, their ability to research independently, their collaboration, and their empathy. You could get them to assess the reliability of different sources, to research new information for themselves, and to write about the same event through the eyes of three contrasting participants in the Wall Street Crash. But you can use exactly the same material as an "exercise machine" to develop their inclinations to accept what they are told without thinking, to depend on others to tell them "the truth," and to believe that there is always going to be One Right Answer or One True Story. All you have to do is get them, day after day, to copy down pages of notes mindlessly from the whiteboard, plow through prescribed pages of the textbook on their own, and take tests that focus only on the right/wrong recall of factual information.

Different lessons will, intentionally or not, contain different currents at the lowest depths of the river. You might be developing collaboration one lesson and reflection another. Learning to remember and recall things accurately is sometimes called for in life. Learning by rote is not a deep insult to the human spirit; it is sometimes an efficient way of nailing things you need to know. Developing a "good memory" is useful. But so is the readiness to question knowledge claims, or to put oneself into someone else's shoes. Over time, if your students receive a good mixture of lessons, they will get an all-around mental workout. They will become mind-fit for life.

> Over time, if your students receive a good mixture of lessons, they will get an all-around mental workout. They will become mind-fit for life.

However, if the regime of mental exercise your students get, day in, day out, is all of one kind, they will tend to be bent only in that direction. They will develop a lopsided mind, suited to one kind of learning but not others. If a student is going to go on from school to be a college professor, developing a heavily scholastic mindset at school will stand that student in good stead. But it won't if the student is going to become a nurse, a jockey, a farmer, or a drummer. For the majority of the population, the skill of being able to knock out a small essay is not one that they will have much use for after they have left formal education. It may have some use—especially for those who are going to be journalists or lawyers—but is it at the top of the list of the life skills and character strengths that *everyone* is going to need? Not for many people.

So the LPA invites you to think as carefully and imaginatively as you can about which learning muscles you consider to be the most important for the next generation to possess if they are to cope well with the mixture of pressures, demands, and opportunities that are likely to come their way. Then design learning in the classroom that stretches and strengthens those muscles, and not some other set that might have been good for the 1870s or the 1950s but that are less useful or relevant to the future we foresee. The world of the future is a moving target, so education, according to the LPA, has to keep adjusting its aim as best it can.

## Wondering

Think about your own experience of education and, if you are a teacher, your impressions of the schools you have worked in. To what extent do schools as you know them pay enough attention to developing these tools for real-world learning?

Where have you seen good or bad examples of students having enough time, opportunity, and encouragement to

- Practice just looking and listening carefully to things?
- Build up their ability and confidence to research independently?

*(Continued)*

(Continued)

- Try out their own ideas, regardless of whether they might make some mistakes?

- Discover when and how to make the best use of their imagination?

- See that science is a powerful way of knowing, and not just a big body of facts?

- Make several drafts, so they learn how to critique and improve their own work?

- Learn from each other and be generous with their own insights?

What have you seen that actively encourages students to be more independent, responsible, and thoughtful about their own learning?

What have you seen that seems to keep students dependent on their teachers?

Are there children/students in your class who spring to mind when you think of "strong" or "weak" learners? How could you bottle the traits of your strong learners and spread them among the class? How could you begin to encourage your weaker learners to become more resilient and take more risks in their learning?

## Notes

1. See Anders Ericsson and Robert Pool, *Peak*.
2. A very good treatment of these aspects of classroom climate is Ron Ritchhart's *Cultures of Thinking*.

# What Exactly Is the Aim of the Learning Power Approach?

Tomorrow's illiterate will not be the man who can't read; he will be the man who has not learned how to learn.

Herbert Gerjuoy[1]

I want to dive in and examine the aim of the Learning Power Approach (LPA) in more detail. In this chapter I will explain what its intentions and guiding principles are. We will look at some examples of the LPA in action, to put some detailed flesh on the bones and bring the skeleton to life. Then, in the following chapter, I'll get you to think about some smart tweaks that you might make, right away, to your own classroom. (If you are not a teacher, you can treat these suggestions as "thought experiments.")

## Diving In: The Aim of the Learning Power Approach

**The aim of the Learning Power Approach (LPA) is to develop all students as confident and capable learners—ready, willing, and able to choose, design, research, pursue, troubleshoot, and evaluate learning for themselves, alone and with others, in school and out.**

That's quite a mouthful! But I've thought hard about how to encapsulate the approach in as few words as possible, and that's about as short as I can get it.

### Wondering

To get into the spirit of things, you might like—alone or with someone else—to try to get inside my head and ask yourself, "Why does Guy think he can't do without each of those words?" Give yourself a few minutes, if you will, to think what would be lost, that shouldn't be lost, if a particular word was missing from that long sentence.

Here's my thinking. Let's take it in chunks.

**The aim of the Learning Power Approach is to develop all students as confident and capable learners**

I need the word ***develop*** to remind me that the cultivation of learning habits is a process that takes time. You do not become more imaginative, say, by committing a definition of imagination to memory or writing a short essay about it. Becoming a powerful learner involves much more than knowing how to knock out a mind map, or being able to parrot back to your teacher a list of multiple intelligences. It is a different kind of learning that is involved in cultivating mental habits, and this needs a different kind of teaching.

I need ***all*** to remind me that being a powerful learner is important for every child: both high and low achievers, academically as well as practically inclined, from well-off and poor families. Children from less well-favored backgrounds or complex and unstable families need all the learning power they can get, if they are to craft better lives for themselves. They simply have their difficulties compounded if they learn at school that they lack learning ability, and therefore that any efforts they make to learn are futile.

At the other end of the spectrum, thousands of 18-year-olds with impressive grades at top universities struggle with anxiety, depression, or self-criticism because they are not coping with their workload as well as they think they should, and are feeling stupid or fraudulent as a result. University counselors speak of a rapid rise in "imposter syndrome": the feeling among bright, successful students that they are being unmasked as unworthy of their place at Stanford or Bristol, and are there under false pretenses. In fact, they should be upset with their schoolteachers, not with themselves, because it was their teachers who, under pressure to squeeze out those top grades, forgot to include experiences that would build resilience and resourcefulness. And the same can happen to poor kids who have been helped to get the grades they need for college entrance, but drop out when they are there because they cannot cope without all the support they have gotten used to.

I need **confident** to remind me that powerful learners have a robust belief that their efforts to learn are, on balance, likely to bear fruit. It is that attitude of optimism about learning that enables them to commit their energies and their intelligence to a learning challenge when it comes along. It doesn't matter how high your IQ is, if a lack of confidence leads you to pull your learning punches and engage only half-heartedly. Learning power is not the same as "intelligence," conventionally understood. It's a matter of learned belief. As Henry Ford famously said, "Whether you think you can, or think you can't—you're right!"

I need **capable** to remind me that learning power is a matter of skill. In the phrase often attributed to Jean Piaget, powerful learners *know* what to do when they don't know what to do. Five-year-olds who are being successful at learning to read, for example, are more likely to have practical strategies to fall back on when they can't read a word than a child who is struggling. What we take for intelligence in a child is very often revealed, under closer inspection, to be more a matter of the child's having developed a useful toolbox of learning skills and techniques. Children for whom learning is more of a slow struggle frequently turn out not to be of limited intelligence but, for whatever reason, simply to have failed to figure out the craft of learning for themselves. It is untrue, and unjust, to infer that they "lack ability."

I need **learners** to remind me that it is what students themselves are doing that determines their success. Teaching is only successful to the extent that it successfully recruits learning. You can take a horse to water, but in the end it is the horse that has to do the drinking. Teachers design the learners' world so that they will want to learn what they need or want to learn, and be able to do so. When part of what we want students to learn is the craft of learning itself, then we have to think carefully about what kind of design will work best. The LPA teachers' role is twofold: They need to make sure that students *learn more* in their classrooms, by teaching clearly and marking accurately, but also that students become *better at learning,* by helping them strengthen their own learning muscles.

Now let's take the next chunk:

> **ready, willing, and able to choose, design, research, pursue, troubleshoot, and evaluate learning for themselves**

I've already explained why I need the words **capable** or **able**—but why do I need **ready** and **willing** as well? I need **ready** to remind me that learning is not just a matter of skill but of disposition. Skills are things you can do when the world prompts you clearly. If I have the skill of driving a car, say, I don't have to spend my whole life on the lookout for opportunities to use it. The right time to activate it is pretty clearly marked for me: I want to go somewhere, so I get the keys, get in the car—and it is pretty obvious what I need to do next.

But if the skill in question is "considering counter-arguments" or "putting myself in the shoes of someone I disagree with," the world does not automatically remind me when to make use of these abilities. If I am going to make use of them when it is appropriate, I have to be, as David Perkins puts it, "sensitive to the occasion" myself. Perkins has shown that a substantial part of what teachers often mistake for a lack of ability is actually learners' failure to notice that something they can do perfectly well is relevant here and now. In the LPA, we have to be thinking about how to cultivate not just skills but a sense of the situations in which those skills need to fire up spontaneously. Learners need to have practice in spotting such situations for themselves. In other words, learners need to be *in the habit* of drawing upon these ways of thinking so that they spontaneously come to mind when needed.

I need **willing** to remind me that learning is not just a matter of capability and belief, but it involves passion and feeling as well. Schools often treat learning as if it were—or at least ought to be—a purely cognitive affair, and emotions only become relevant when they are getting in the way. But learning is full of feeling. We have a whole vocabulary to describe the feelings of learning: *frustrated, surprised, determined, delighted, intrigued, blocked, fascinated, confused, puzzled, engrossed, disappointed, shocked, proud,* and so on. *Willing* reminds me that the key to learning is engagement—the inclination to lock on to learning, even when it gets hard, and not be derailed by these feelings.

I need the word **choose** to remind me that, in preparing students not just for further education but for life, I am preparing them to be proactive as well as reactive learners. They will need to be able to engage well with the many unbidden learning situations that will come their way: an end-of-year exam, a tax inspection, being made redundant from a job or posted to a strange country, recovering from a stroke, or the death of a loved one. But we are also preparing them to be enthusiastic constructors of their own learning agendas. Wholeheartedly pursuing your own learning projects is one of the most potent sources of happiness and fulfillment there can be. Indeed, we seem designed by evolution to push ourselves. Young people who seem entirely disaffected or apathetic in school magically transform themselves, like Clark Kent becoming Superman, into powerful learners when they dive back into their chosen learning worlds: their PlayStation, their guitar practice, their sports club, or their nighttime adventures. (Some of their learning exploits we might disapprove of—but that's another story.) We need to open up to them learning worlds that are not just exciting but wholesome and deeply fulfilling as well.

I need the word **design** to remind me that powerful learners need to be able to orchestrate their own learning. In traditional schools, all the learning design—the topics to be studied, the activities to be undertaken, the layout of the furniture, the displays on the walls—is done by the teacher. That is efficient, but if we do it completely, all the time, we are depriving our students of opportunities to learn how to design learning for themselves. After they have left formal education, they will have to be able to think for themselves: "What is it I need to learn here? What am I not very good at? What would be the best way of gaining the knowledge, understanding, or competence I need—can I find it online, is there a forum I could join, do I need to take a course, have I got a friend or a contact who can help, would it help to meditate?" . . . and so on. Can I just plug it in and fiddle about, or do I need to read the manual first? If we are getting young people ready to take charge of their own learning, we have to give them practice at it.

> Every minute was magical, every single thing it did was fascinating and everything it didn't do was equally wondrous, and to be sat there, with a Kestrel, a real live Kestrel, my own real live Kestrel on my wrist! I felt like I'd climbed through a hole in heaven's fence.
>
> Chris Packham, *Fingers in the Sparkle Jar: A Memoir*[2]

I need the word **research** for similar reasons. Powerful learners need to be good at tracking down and assembling the resources, the tools, and the information they are going to need. In schools, as I have just said, teachers used to do most of this work—too much of it—for their students. They neatened learning up into bite-size packages, where all the information and resources they needed were already determined, so students had neither the necessity nor the opportunity to go find things out for themselves. In the information age, all young people need to be able to do far more than simply "google it." Indian education professor Sugata Mitra has shown that even young children, fired up by a question that interests them, and with access to an online device that four or five of them can huddle around, are capable of generating an amazing amount of understanding for themselves. If they have this natural capacity, we ought to be protecting and strengthening it, not allowing it to atrophy through disuse.

I need the word **pursue** because that's what independent learners do—they have to carry out their learning plans for themselves. They have to find and protect the time for learning. They may need to ask for other people's help. ("Would you mind looking after the kids for a couple of hours while I work on my essay?") They may need to make a good guess as to the amount of time it is going to take. And they may need to revise their plans as they go along, in the light of experience. "This is taking a lot longer than I thought. . . . Let me check whether I really need to go into it in this much detail, or would a few shortcuts be OK?" Learners have to be able to manage their own learning and think on their feet.

In particular, I feel the need to emphasize the word **troubleshoot**, because learning always involves surprises, disappointments, and frustrations along the way, and powerful learners need to be resilient and resourceful enough to cope with them as they arise. I always remember Robert Pirsig, in his classic book *Zen and the Art of Motorcycle Maintenance*, writing about the inevitability of what he called "gumption traps": moments when unanticipated problems arise—like burring the head of an old screw so the screwdriver won't work anymore—and the importance, at such moments, of staying calm, maybe taking a break, and not allowing your frustration to make you do something stupid (like kicking the bike over) that would make the whole problem even worse.[3] Tolerance for the full gamut of these glitches and their attendant feelings is a vital part of being a powerful learner, and I have to remember that, as a teacher, I need to design experiences that build up that tolerance wherever and whenever I can.

I need the word *evaluate* because powerful learners need to be able to tell for themselves how well they are doing, and not wait for someone else to evaluate their progress for them—which is what traditional teachers tend to do. You do not learn how to self-evaluate by constantly being evaluated by someone else—just as you don't learn self-discipline by constantly being punished for your errors. But monitoring your progress, and checking it against where you want to get to, is not an ability we are born with. We all have to learn it, and that means developing greater expertise and sophistication over time, so that gradually our "nose for quality" gets sharper, and our unwillingness to settle for anything less gets stronger.

I've already explained why I need the phrase *for themselves*. Powerful learners need to be helped to become more and more independent of their teachers and coaches by learning to take on the skills and sensibilities of the teacher or coach for themselves. This requires a very particular kind of teaching or coaching—one that gradually, progressively seeks to hand over the skill and responsibility for learning design from the teacher to the students.

> Powerful learners need to be helped to become more and more independent of their teachers and coaches by learning to take on the skills and sensibilities of the teacher or coach for themselves.

And here's the last chunk:

**alone and with others, in school and out.**

The phrase ***alone and with others*** reminds me that powerful learners have to be good at learning on their own, and also in collaboration with partners, families, and teams. And they have to be good at being able to segue between the two when they have the choice. The phrase *independent learner* can often sound rather solitary and heroic—a Clint Eastwood kind of learner. But the ideal is obviously to have the freedom, the skill, and the perspicacity to know how and when to shut your office door or work from home, or to hang out in the coffee room shooting the breeze, or to call up an old and trusted friend for a heart to heart, or to convene a professional meeting. We need to help young people build up this kind of acumen and flexibility.

And finally the phrase ***in school and out*** reminds me again that the goal of education is not exclusively to pass more tests, get higher grades, go to a prestigious college, and graduate *cum laude* or with first class honors; it is to prepare all youngsters for the rigors and opportunities of life in the turbulent waters of the mid- to late 21st century. Not all young people can go to college or university. In many countries there is not enough capacity or funding in higher education for all to go, so many are bound not to—even if they wanted to and tried very hard. In such countries, somebody's daughter's top marks only have currency because someone else's son didn't get them. If—miraculously—every 18-year-old in the land suddenly became a straight-A student, there would be a Wall Street crash in the value of those A's, wouldn't there?

And anyway, not all young people want to go to college, nor should they. Many are impatient to become adults and assume the rights and responsibilities of employment. Many want to work with their hands and bodies as electricians, hairdressers, cooks, or musicians. For many, the kind of learning that universities specialize in does not suit either their interests or their temperament. They are not lacking in ability, nor undeserving of a flying start on life in a tricky world—so what of genuine value and utility are they going to take away from their 15,000 hours of schooling? That is the hard question that the family of learning power approaches—and many other schools besides—are trying to grapple with. It simply isn't true that schools are the way they have to be, and it is just bad luck that some substantial proportion of children are too unlucky or too unintelligent to benefit from it. That old idea is way past its use-by date. There has to be another "game" of education, alongside the "grades game," that every student can value and benefit from. Yet many schools have tended to obsess about academic grades and distinctions because they have not had a clear idea how to go about the other game. It is the aim of the LPA to show them how to do it.

## Some Flesh on the Bones

That's the design specification of the LPA. Before we go any further, a few examples might help to put some flesh on the bones. What might the LPA look like in practice?

> I've recently run several workshops for the youth coaches of the English Football Premier League Academies. These academies select and train the footballers of tomorrow, currently aged between about 8 and 20 years old. The coaches became very interested in the Learning Power Approach, because they could see its potential to accelerate these young players' learning. If the squad of 12-year-olds at Manchester City could, as it were, suck more learning juice out of every two-hour training session than the

equivalent squad down the road at Manchester United, they would progress faster. The coaches felt they couldn't afford not to pay attention to this simple fact, for fear of missing an important trick.

At one of these workshops, a squad of around 14 12-year-olds carried out a demonstration training session for us. Their coach, Elliot Dickman, had been trying something new. He set the boys up to do an exercise that involved members of an outer circle trying to pass the ball to a teammate across an inner ring of "defenders." The rule was, when you received the ball, you were allowed to touch it only twice before passing it back across the ring. "Just watch what they do," said Elliot, and we did.

After a few minutes of doing as instructed, the boys started to call to each other to say whether they were finding what they were doing too easy, too hard, or just right. As they told us afterward, "just right" meant that they were working at the edge of their competence, making a few mistakes, but making progress. As we watched, they quickly agreed that it was too easy, not stretching them enough. So, without any recourse to their coach, they changed the rules to make the activity harder. They agreed to allow themselves only one touch on the ball before passing, and to see how they got on with that. These were boys who did not always find communication or negotiation easy, but they made their decisions with impressive skill and efficiency—because Elliot and his team had gradually (but relentlessly) coached them to be able to think like coaches, and to be able to monitor their own learning efforts and adjust their activities accordingly.

The other coaches who were watching were visibly impressed by the boys' maturity, responsibility, self-awareness, collaboration, and ability to talk fluently about what they were doing. What we saw was just a small shift in coaching method. It didn't cost anything (except the coaching team's willingness to adjust their normal way of operating). The downside risks were minimal. The boys obviously enjoyed being involved in designing and controlling their own learning. The gains in their learning were plain for all to see. They were spending much more time in that just right spot of learning than a squad who were merely doing what they were told. And they were developing useful, transferable attitudes and habits toward learning itself. This is the Learning Power Approach in a nutshell. Later on we'll see how exactly this approach can be used, in regular lessons in school, to speed up the learning of mathematics, geography, and so on. We will also look much more, in later books in the series, at how to respond when you *don't* get instant success with these methods. As I've said before, none of them is foolproof, and the need for some troubleshooting is inevitable.

———————

A second example. A while ago I was visiting a primary school on the outskirts of a large town to the north of London, and went to observe a third-grade English lesson. The children were working on a poem—Alfred Noyes's *The Highwayman*, I think it was—but what struck me was the size of the groups they were working in, about six or seven children in each group. I asked their teacher, Haydon Ellis, why they were working in such large groups. He explained that two weeks previously the class had had a discussion about what their working lives might be like when they were grown up. Haydon had gently led them to think about the kinds of teams they might find themselves working in—groups of different sizes and compositions—and to see the value of learning to be the kind of person who could fit in with different groups quickly and even help them to function well. The children were quite interested by this possibility, so they decided, as a whole class, that, for the rest of that term, they would keep changing the nature of their working groups in order, as one child put it, to "stretch their collaborating muscles." As with the young footballers, I was impressed by their eagerness to be challenged in this way.

I was even more impressed as I eavesdropped on one of the groups at work. As I watched, one boy in the group held up his hand and said, "As the group monitor, I'm noticing that several of us don't seem to be joining in, and I'm wondering if it would be useful to stop for a minute and just talk about whether we are feeling OK." The group agreed, and indeed some of the children did say they were feeling a bit shy. After a quick discussion, the group decided that they might work better if they split in half for the next 10 minutes, and then came back together to share their progress. And off they went—without any need for Mr. Ellis (or me) to rescue them or intervene at all. I realized I had been in undergraduate seminars at Cambridge where students did not seem to possess that level of social and emotional intelligence. To be honest, I have been in staffrooms that didn't. These children were able to troubleshoot and redesign their learning with such apparent ease because they had been coached, over the preceding two years, to be able to do it, gradually building up to the level of sophistication that I witnessed that day. Goodness knows what they are capable of by now!

---

For my final example, let's take the case of the humble eraser. A few months ago, I was being interviewed by the education editor of a British national newspaper, and he said, "Guy, the theory is all very well, but give me a concrete example." I replied, off the top of my head, that I thought erasers were "instruments of the devil." This momentary bit of hyperbole got me a lot of publicity, most good, some troll-like. (Google it if you want to follow the action.) Within 24 hours I was on the front page of several national newspapers, had received an e-mail of support from a primary school in rural China, and had been invited onto national radio in Canada and Australia, where I had the opportunity to explain what I meant. Of course, it is not about those innocent little slabs of rubber. Lots of artists, architects, and designers make good use of them every day, and are not damaged in the process. It is about whether the way they are used in classrooms weakens children's learning power.

In some classrooms, teachers act as if being a "bright student" or a "good student" means getting all your answers right, quickly, the first time, and preferably without much effort. This is not a good idea to embed in young people's minds, for two reasons. First, because in what we might call the "real world," most learning worth its salt takes time, effort, and trial and error. Academic papers go through many drafts before they are published. Athletes spend thousands of hours being not very good at things on the way to becoming expert at them. Agile companies keep adjusting their practices in the light of ever-changing experience. So if this image of "brightness" gets installed in young learners' brains, it ill prepares them for the kind of learning they are going to meet.

And second, when this virus gets into your brain, it makes you feel stupid if you make mistakes, flounder, or need to take your time. And this makes you want to avoid effort and the risk of error, so your resilience and determination are undermined—you become a weaker learner. If you become addicted to your eraser because it enables you to quickly remove the shameful evidence of your own fallibility, then the eraser is doing you harm, and you need to be weaned off it. Many students (and some parents) object in the short term to not being able to rewrite their (or their children's) history to show them in a better light, but they will thank their teacher in the long term, because they will be better prepared for life. It is not rocket science, is it?

## Wondering

I hope those "trailers" have whetted your appetite for the Learning Power Approach. Take a moment to check (either on your own or with a partner) how you react to the examples, and to the approach in general.

- Based on what you have read so far, what do you see as the advantages and disadvantages of the Learning Power Approach?

- To what extent do you see signs of the learning powers in your students already? Where are they strong, and not so strong?

*(Continued)*

(Continued)

- What evidence, from the examples given, would indicate that the students are becoming more confident, competent, independent learners?

- How would this approach benefit your students? What are your hesitations in implementing this approach?

- What one thing could you do on Monday to implement this approach?

## Notes

1. This comment was made by Gerjuoy in conversation with Alvin Toffler, and is quoted in Toffler's bestselling *Future Shock*. It is often elaborated upon and misattributed to Toffler himself.
2. Chris Packham, *Fingers in the Sparkle Jar*.
3. Robert Pirsig, *Zen and the Art of Motorcycle Maintenance*.

# How Do I Get Started?

## *Some Quick Wins*

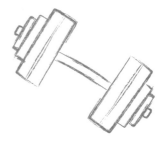

You should by now have a broad sense of what the Learning Power Approach (LPA) is up to. But after that orientation, the next step has to be to *do something different in the classroom*. This is critical—and it may feel risky. After all, you may have been teaching for some years, and many of your habits may have become so ingrained that you aren't even aware that they are habits. Unless you are right at the beginning of your teaching career, you will almost certainly have found a way that works—that keeps your learners interested, amiable, and on task—and now I'm asking you to put that sense of security and competence at risk. I'm asking you to be a learner, like the young people you teach, and try something that you can't yet confidently predict the outcome of.

To help people who are just setting out on this learning journey, this chapter presents suggestions that are pretty low risk, and fairly highly structured. At the beginning it can be useful to be given such clear directions. When you started to learn a musical instrument, you were probably pleased to be told what to do. But as you developed confidence, expertise, and a feel for what you were doing, you took more responsibility and became more creative. It's the same here. As soon as you feel ready, I would like you to start experimenting on your own. The suggestions in this chapter are just to get you going. Of course, if you are already fairly well down this track, you won't need the "training wheels" we have described in this chapter. I suggest you just skim through, but pause to check that you really have nailed the point of these suggestions, that they really are a core part of how you function as a teacher now. And then look to see if reading the suggestions sparks any thoughts about how you might deepen or enrich what you already do—how you can add the little bit more toward building powerful learners. (And remember, the little bit more is often a little bit less of something. Teachers often oversupport and overrescue their learners, for example, and you may have to learn to restrain that impulse.)

As I say, all the suggestions are pretty low risk. We have found that most teachers are willing to give them a try. However, one size does not fit all, and there are no guarantees. Every teacher is different. Every class is different. We often hear from teachers who think they have nailed it with one class, only to find that they have to go back to the drawing board and find new variations with the next year's class. For a dozen possible reasons, last year's surefire method turns out not to cut it with a different group. This inherent variability explains why, after we have explored a few simple possibilities in this chapter, we quickly have to extract and explain the design principles that underpin them, so teachers will have the knowledge, and the confidence, to make up their own variations. That's what we will do in Chapter 8.

Actually, you might have to do some adapting straight away—because each of the suggestions originates from a teacher working with a class of a certain age, and you might teach children who are significantly older or younger. I have chosen examples that are easy to adapt for quite wide age ranges, but still, you may want to change the language or the complexity of the suggestions to suit the classes you teach.

You will also need to judge whether the degree of challenge, for both you and your learners, is too low, too high, or about right. If what I'm suggesting feels too easy or familiar, then you might see if you can stretch it a bit, or try another suggestion. If, on the other hand, it feels way beyond what your students are ready for, adapt it down, or try another suggestion, though beware of underestimating what might be a tolerable stretch, either for you or them. Sometimes we have thought, "That'll be far too much for them to handle," and learners have surprised us by rising to the challenge.

It could work well like this. Find a partner in the school— maybe within the context of your professional learning communities, if you have them, or your local district—who is also going to try something. It doesn't have to be the same thing. Arrange three meetings with your partner. The meetings don't have to be long—around 15–20 minutes would do fine—but they do need to be focused, so try not to slip into talking about other agendas or unrelated issues. The first is a set-up meeting, where you clarify with each other exactly what you are going to try out, with whom, and what you are hoping the effect will be. This could be on the Friday before you plan to start on Monday. The second, at the end of the first week, is a "How's it going?" check-in meeting to share experience so far and, if necessary, adjust and refocus. The third, at the end of the second week, should be a roundup and sharing of any changes you have noticed in the learners' behavior and attitudes. If you want to continue with the same partner, this meeting could also be the set-up meeting for the second little tweak you are going to try out. And so on. If you like the effects that each tweak has had, don't drop it when you start a new one; keep going with the first one so that it becomes more and more embedded in the natural way you are with the learners. Research has found that formalizing meetings in this way really does help to make them meaningful and productive.

The LPA relies, certainly to begin with, on a gradual buildup of these small shifts. I call it the "mayonnaise model" of learning. Once or twice in my life I have made my own mayonnaise (rather than buying a jar of Hellmann's, which I normally do). I've learned what the trick is. You put egg yolks, mustard, and vinegar in a bowl and beat them together. Then you add just one or two drops of oil and keep beating until the oil is completely mixed in. Then add another few drops of oil and beat them in. Keep doing that till after a while you can add the oil faster. If you add too much too soon, the mixture curdles and separates. The same thing happens if you try to change your habits too quickly. You need to go little step by little step, giving yourself plenty of time and experience so that the new tweak becomes integrated into your natural way of being. Learn too fast, and the idea separates out from your behavior. You become knowledgeable or opinionated, but not altered in the way you spontaneously behave. When it comes to habit change, the tortoise beats the hare every time!

You don't have to play the game this way at all, but to structure your choices, I've created a simple menu with three "starters," three "main courses," and three "desserts." If it helps you to get going, choose one item from the starter menu as the thing you are going to try first, and give it a go. Then try one from the mains. And if you still have an appetite, finish up this introductory offer with one dessert. If you are already familiar with some of these strategies, choose different ones. And feel free to add variations to make them harder or more interesting. You know your students; I don't. So customize the activities to add an extra twist to what they already do. Here's the menu.

## The LPA Menu du Jour

### Starters

*The Wonder Wall*

Pin up a big display in the classroom (or use a whiteboard or an old-fashioned blackboard) headed "Our Wonder Wall." It is where your students will keep adding questions they are genuinely interested in. In high school they might relate to your specific subject, or to the current topic. In grade school, you could invite any of the children's own questions. Get them to use sticky notes or to write on the board. Regularly pick out some of the questions to wonder about. As a reward at the end of the day, get a child to pick their favorite question, and ask the rest of the class to make suggestions about how to investigate it. Ask the students if they can see different kinds of questions. Get them interested in the different kinds of "work" that different questions do. You absolutely do not need to know the answers—in fact you are forbidden from offering answers! One teacher commented, "This worked very well with my Year 2 class. It showed them that I valued their questions, and they responded enthusiastically."

A Wonder Wall: *How does the brain box work? How do eyes stay in my head? How does skin stay on my body?*

*Source:* Photo courtesy of Kelly Ellis and Amanda Valente

## The Chili Challenge

When you want your students to develop their expertise in writing or math, say, instead of getting them to plow through a worksheet, design three or four different challenges that are of differing levels of difficulty, and get them to decide which level of challenge they are going to attempt. In her class, Becky Carlzon uses cards with different numbers of chilies (like you might find on a Thai restaurant menu) that indicate how "hot" each challenge is. Learners can do this on their own, but it is probably better, at least to start with, if they work in pairs. As you walk around, you can ask them why they chose the "two-chili challenge" or went straight for the "four-chili challenge." When a pair of students think they have an answer to the challenge they chose, you could tell them whether it is right or wrong, but you could also ask them to work with another pair to see if they can check each other's answers. In high school there will be plenty of opportunities to offer students such choices of task difficulty.

## Try Three Before Me

Teach your students a little learning routine called Try Three Before Me. Explain to them that, from now on, they can put up their hands to ask for help when they are stuck, but that, when you come to them, you will expect them first to tell you three things they have tried to unstick themselves. If they can explain their three escape strategies and are still stuck, you could talk to them a little about the strategies they used, and give them the requisite nudge to get their thinking going again. If they haven't come up with three things to try, tell them you will give them another couple of minutes to think up three things. One teacher said, "Some of the children didn't like it at first, because they had gotten used to being rescued, and this forces them to think. But now it is just the way we do things around here; everyone plays the game—and I can see how much they have benefitted from it."

There are lots of variants of this routine that you may know—but do try this one, if it is different from the version you know. Some teachers call it Brain-Book-Buddy-Boss. When you are stuck, first consult your own brain; then reread the book or the instructions; then talk to your learning buddy; and only then, if all those have failed, can you consult the boss (the teacher). Your "learning buddy" is a fellow student who is your designated "phone a friend" when you hit difficulties. (Try not to allow students to choose their real friends for this—the role is different.)

## Mains

Now here is your next set of choices. Choose one again, and try to do your best with it for the next two weeks. (Remember, if you have success with your starter activity, keep it going as well. Just make sure it has become embedded in business as usual in your classroom.)

### No Hands Up

If you still use the traditional classroom routine of asking a question, getting students to put their hands up, and picking one of those to answer—try something different. (This example is often used in the context of "formative assessment" or "assessment for learning.") Ask your question—but try to ensure it is an open question—that is, one that invites opinions and ideas, rather than a closed, right-or-wrong response. ("What is the color of hydrated copper sulfate?" is closed. "Why do you think anhydrous copper sulfate turns blue when you add water?" is open.) Then give the students a minute or two to think and make notes if they like. They can do this either solo or in pairs or small groups. Then pick a student or a group at random to answer. Let the students know that this is what you are going to do. Some of them—especially the smug ones who know all the right answers ahead of time—will be furious about this change. Others, who usually try to be as invisible in the classroom as possible, may be a bit anxious. Carry on anyway.

### The Stuck Poster

The Stuck Poster is a display in the classroom that can build on Try Three Before Me (though you can introduce it directly). It is a list of suggestions, generated by the students, about what they could do when they are stuck.

These suggestions can be quite generic (possibly with younger learners) or can be tied to a specific discipline or topic. In grade school, it could be "Things to try when you can't read a word." In high school, it might be "Strategies to help with a Spanish translation." Resist students' attempts to get you to come up with the ideas; it is important that they do the thinking. Start with a few ideas, but keep returning to the poster, both as a resource to help your learners become more independent of you, and as something that they can keep adding to and developing. It needs to be something that is live in the classroom, not just a piece of wallpaper. If necessary, get students to brainstorm in small groups for a few minutes to get things going.

The Stuck Poster

**THINGS TO TRY IF YOU GET STUCK:**
- Ask a friend
- Read the question again
- Use a number line
- Split the question up
- Ask yourself – What do I know already that could help me?
- Use a reference book
- Use a dictionary
- Check the internet
- Share the problem
- Go for another question and come back to the bit you are stuck on later

*Source:* By kind permission of TLO Ltd

### The No-Put-Down Zone

This one could be slightly more demanding—and won't be applicable to all situations. It is not so much a tweak as a shift in your own standards for what is acceptable and unacceptable behavior in your classroom. It involves you instituting a zero-tolerance policy toward students disrespecting each other as learners. You want to create a classroom where all learners feel safe enough to venture ideas and answers that may be inadequate, incomplete, or just plain wrong. Some groups evolve a pecking order in which a bright, rather arrogant subgroup at the top feels entitled to poke fun at other students who participate in good faith but fail to come up with the desired answer. Using whatever sanctions you have, you make it clear that all such behavior is unacceptable in your classroom, and will be sanctioned. Unless the pack of top dogs is particularly vicious, they should get the idea within a couple of weeks. For many teachers this is basic good practice in any classroom, but check: Have you nailed it? Do you lapse when the put-down is particularly witty, and laugh along with the smart alecks? If so, practice upping your vigilance.

## Desserts

Now that you are beginning to get into the swing of the LPA, here is your third short menu from which to choose your last two-week intervention. (Desserts here are not especially sugary or bad for you; they are just a third band of options.)

### The Riskometer

The riskometer is a graphic display that looks rather like a thermometer, except instead of temperature, it registers the degree of risk or challenge.

## Riskometer Example

*Source:* By kind permission of TLO Ltd

The riskometer can be used in a variety of ways. In the version above, learners have used it to record how learning of differing degrees of risk or difficulty actually feels. Faced with something way beyond their capabilities, they have no choice but to flounder anxiously. Tasks that are well within their current sphere of competence, on the other hand, feel rather boring and uninteresting. Tasks that are in the "sweet spot" of learning—where learners are unsure of success, still making mistakes, but making progress—tend to be absorbing and enjoyable. Learners may also choose their own levels of difficulty (as in the chili challenges), and attach their own picture (on a Velcro strip) onto the riskometer to indicate the degree of "risk" they have chosen. With older students you can use the riskometer as a device for encouraging students to become more aware of and articulate about the nature of risk, and how they can regulate it for themselves.

### Circle-Ate

This is really an invitation to do something different, and possibly disconcerting, with the layout of the furniture in the classroom—especially if the default arrangement is individual desks in rows facing the teacher. With younger children, move all the desks or tables and chairs to the side, and have them work in pairs on the floor. Or, if they normally have their own desks in the classroom, change the rules so there is no assigned seating, and children just work with whoever they happen to find themselves next to. With older students, if the group is not too large, have discussions with all of them sitting in a circle. Develop ground rules for the discussions with the students, so they come to realize what makes for a profitable discussion. To begin with, these ground rules might be very simple things like "everyone gets a turn" or "speak respectfully," but you can build them up to suit the age and grade level of the students. You could get the students to brainstorm sentence frames as guidance and put them on a poster. "That makes me wonder . . ."; "What makes you say that?"; "At the moment I see it differently. . . ." Have them reflect on how successful a discussion was, and what they could have done to improve its quality.

### Ban Erasers

Finally on the menu, let's come back to the example of the use of erasers we discussed earlier. If you have learners in your class who are addicted to rubbing things out, and if you suspect that this is because they have come to see mistakes and "tries" as evidencing a lack of intelligence or ability, then ban erasers for a while, and notice the effect. Encourage them not to rub out mistakes but to highlight them, to treat mistakes as their friends "because they help us learn," to keep a scrapbook of their earlier drafts so they can look back and reflect on their improvement, and so on. It is best if you explain to the learners why you are doing this: to help them realize that trial and error is a vital and natural part of learning, and so aversion to mistake-making holds back their progress. Even so, you will probably get some resistance, especially from those students—predominantly girls, I have noticed—who have developed a deep commitment to making all their written work look neat and pretty, and an aversion to anything that looks scruffy or messy, like crossing out. (This seems to be a school-based version of the old adage about cleanliness being next to godliness: Neatness is next to intelligence!)

By the way, it's important to note that teachers of high school students sometimes think that the damage has been done in earlier years, and that there's no point in trying to change older students' learning habits. In fact there's every point (it's imperative), and small changes in teaching—applied consistently—can have a measurable impact at all ages.

## Curious, Adventurous, Determined, Collaborative: A Starter Kit of Learning Dispositions

So now, if you are being an obedient learner, you will have carried out three of these little experiments over the course of around six weeks, and noted the effects on your learners. Hopefully, some of those effects will have seemed beneficial to you—though the ride may have been a little bumpy. Students in school are often anxious about their performance, and this largely takes the form of resistance to any change that threatens their tenuous grasp on procedure. High-achieving students often show the most resistance, because they are the ones who have learned best how to negotiate the rather narrow boardwalk of "school learning," and consequently feel they have the most to lose from any unusual or innovative adjustments to teaching methodology. Nevertheless, if your tweaks are small, if you persevere undaunted with them for a few weeks, and if you do your best to explain why you are inflicting these small tortures on them, the benefits will soon come.

What exactly are these tweaks doing? They are attempting to strengthen a small set of vital attitudes toward learning. We call them by a variety of names: attitudes, qualities of mind, learning dispositions, learning habits, learning strengths, or informally "learning muscles." Most teachers we work with say they can see the value of these attitudes and habits in school and beyond, would like to see more of them in the classroom, and would like to know how to help their learners grow these attitudes more strongly. That's what I hope you will have discovered by doing these experiments. The specific muscles we have been illustrating in this chapter are *curiosity*, *adventurousness*, *determination*, and *collaboration*. Let's have a quick look at what each of these muscles is like in action. (We will explore the full range of learning powers in more detail in Chapter 6.)

*Curious* learners have lots of questions to ask. They like finding things out and are ready to be enthused and intrigued by new mysteries and challenges. So they are more enjoyable to teach. Teachers have more fun in a roomful of enthusiastic finder-outers. Yet, curiously, many schools and teachers have squandered this precious driver of learning and thus made it harder and slower than it need be. In the hurry to fill young minds with knowledge and expertise that others have deemed essential, we have sometimes turned off the fuel tap, and treated that as a necessary price to pay. Having a Wonder Wall in the classroom is a small indication—effective if you refer to it and make use of it—that your room is a place that values the learners' own curiosity, as well as a place where they are introduced to the cultural treasure chest of their society.

*Adventurous* learners are willing to take a risk, have a go, try something new, and rise to a challenge, without the fear of being thought stupid, ignorant, or babyish if they don't get it right the first time. As babies struggle inelegantly to learn how to crawl, they don't look anxiously over their shoulders to see if anyone is watching and criticizing their efforts. Yet put children in school, and many of them quickly develop that inhibitory self-consciousness. As Carol Dweck has so robustly shown, somewhere along the line, many of us, like our students, traded in our concern to Get Better for a concern to Look Good. We got fitted with a Learning Limiter, like the speed limiter on a truck, that caps our learning capacity. Yet simple teaching devices like the Chili Challenge or the Riskometer give us the tools to remove the limiter and regain our full learning power. By making difficulty and struggle things that are normal and inevitable, a proper topic for conversation in the classroom, we transmute them from being shameful into being interesting.

> By making difficulty and struggle things that are normal and inevitable, a proper topic for conversation in the classroom, we transmute them from being shameful into being interesting.

*Determined* learners are willing to persist intelligently with challenges in the face of confusion or frustration. They are not fazed by difficulty but take it as an opportunity to dig deep in their own resources to see if they can find a way to surmount the challenge. They have learned through experience that the feeling of pride and satisfaction that follows a successful struggle is a very good feeling indeed, and one that is worth working for. Yet young people who have learned to confuse effortless success with intelligence are deprived of this deep source of fulfillment, for they interpret the struggle that must precede it as a sign of stupidity. A simple classroom routine like Try Three Before Me aims to right this wrong and help learners rediscover the thrill of hard-won achievement. The Stuck Poster makes the process of struggle visible and aims to interest learners in the possibility of expanding their own ability to tolerate confusion and frustration, and to wrestle with challenges more effectively.

*Collaborative* learners know how to work well with others, and enjoy doing so. Two heads—or three or four—are often better than one, in the classroom as in life, so a school that grows powerful learners has to involve a good deal of teamwork and conversation. Sometimes you need to learn solo: there are kinds of learning that involve hours poring over a book or a screen on your own, or working quietly by yourself in your workshop or study. But just as often, as an adult, you are going to be problem solving in your project team at work or on the sports field, or sharing your learning journeys in prenatal class. So a school that only allows interactions between individual students and the teacher, and does not also invite discussion among students, is not a good training ground for real-life learning. When we train students to learn with and from each other by, for example, changing the layout of the furniture, we are helping to prepare them for real-life learning.

As I said, these learning muscles are drawn from a larger and more comprehensive framework that I will unpack in Chapter 6. But I thought it would help to start by illustrating the LPA with arguably the most basic subset, so you could see how it works in action. Learning in the real world of work, leisure, family, and friends relies crucially on curiosity, adventurousness, determination, and collaboration. These basic attitudes toward learning are often weak rather than strong in classrooms, and teachers constantly bemoan their lack. Incurious learners are hard to motivate. Unadventurous learners are reluctant to try new things. Brittle learners give up too quickly when the going gets tough. Solitary learners may be narrowly competitive with others, or cling to only one or two trusted partners. "They just want spoon-feeding," we often hear exasperated teachers say, not realizing that these attitudes of passivity, timidity, dependency, and conservatism might well have been a direct reflection of their students' previous history of education.

The LPA focuses on a particular kind of learning that goes on in classrooms: the encouragement, intentional or not, of certain attitudes toward learning. It does not ignore or undermine the acquisition of knowledge and skill; it just draws attention to a deeper layer of learning—a kind of mind training—that is there all the time. We try to identify what the unwitting teaching habits are that invite different attitudes toward learning, and we show teachers how they could adjust these attitudes so that narrow, negative, or defensive attitudes are progressively replaced by positive, robust, adventurous ones. If you have tried out the suggestions in this chapter, we hope you will now see that this is not such a difficult trick to work.

## A Reflective Exercise

Let me conclude this chapter with an exercise to surface your own ideas about learning power. Here is a short quiz you might like to try about how good a learner *you* are. (Again, this might work better if you do it with a partner.) Try to think about yourself generally, not in terms of any particular area of learning in your life. (I know this may be hard—if you are like me, you vary considerably as a learner depending on what domain we are talking about. I'm quite a different learner when I am concocting dinner out of various leftovers from the refrigerator than I am when trying to play foosball. But have a go.) For each of the nine statements, give yourself a mark from 1 to 5. 5 means "exactly like me, whatever I am learning." 4 means "often like me, in many areas of my life." 3 means "somewhat like me, in some areas, on a good day." 2 means "not often like me, only in a few areas." And 1 means "really unlike me/ hardly ever."

---

**The Learning Power Quiz**

_____ 1.  I know I can master new things if I try.

_____ 2.  I'm up for trying something new.

_____ 3.  I know what to do when I get stuck.

_____ 4.  I like working on what I've done to improve it.

_____ 5.  I get lots of creative ideas when I'm learning.

_____ 6.  I like working with others to figure things out.

_____ 7.  I don't mind if I make mistakes.

_____ 8.  I can tell you lots about how I help myself learn.

_____ 9.  I'm ready to take feedback and advice.

_____ 10. _____

---

Now, the point of this quiz is not to offer you some quasi-scientific insight into your learning soul. I'm afraid I am not going to give you a scoring rubric that tells you which box you belong in. The purpose is just to get you thinking about what some of the "instruments in the learning orchestra" might be, and also to raise some questions about how variable you are as a learner. What the quiz offers you is a rough sketch of what learning power might consist of—one that is slightly more elaborate than the four learning muscles we looked at above.

# Wondering

- How well were you able to look at yourself through this lens? Did it work for you? Did it feel natural to look at yourself this way?

- Think about your own view of the qualities of someone you could call a "powerful learner." As you reflect, can you identify one or two of the statements in the quiz you think you could improve upon, to make them clearer or better targeted toward what you think is important?

- You'll have noticed that there are only nine statements in this 10-item questionnaire. Can you think about an aspect of powerful learning that is missing from the quiz as it stands, and write a new statement for #10 that will make the quiz more comprehensive?

- Can you see any virtue in doing an exercise like this with (a) your colleagues in your school, and (b) your students (suitably adapted for age and reading ability if necessary)?

You'll see that I have done two things by framing the activity in this way. First, I have given you a strong steer about the kinds of things that learning power might comprise. I've offered you a tentative framework. But second, I have immediately asked you to be critical and creative in your reaction to it. I've positioned you as co-researchers, if you like, into the nature of learning power. If the exercise worked for you, you will have engaged a very different set of learning muscles than if I had presented the framework as the tried and tested outcome of a lot of scholarly labor. In the first case you would have been thinking, talking, discussing, creating new possibilities, and making use of your own experience to test the framework. In the second case, you would have been trying to understand and remember it. Same content; very different mental exercise. We will meet a lot of examples of this kind of shift as we begin to look more closely into the learning-powered classroom.

# Why Does Learning Power Matter?

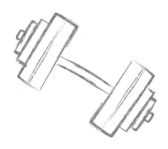

## 5

*10 Good Reasons for Pumping Those Learning Muscles*

Since we cannot know what knowledge will be needed in the future, it is senseless to try to teach it in advance. Instead our job must be to turn out young people who love learning so much, and who learn so well, that they will be able to learn whatever needs to be learned.

John Holt[1]

OK, you might be saying to yourself, I see that there are small tweaks I could make to my teaching—but why should I bother? Life as a teacher can be difficult enough, coping with all the demands of classroom life, as well as all the external pressures to raise standards. Why should I be making my life still more stressful by trying to change my own behavior? Especially if you already have good discipline, and are getting good results, you might be tempted to think that it ain't broke, so what am I supposed to be fixing? In this chapter I hope to persuade you—if you are not already persuaded— that something like the LPA is not just possible, but urgently needed. We need to start by thinking about the deep-down purpose of education in the 21st century.

---

First, let's be clear that there is no such thing as good education. World-class schools, best practices, and even "excellence" don't exist. Why? Because all such notions don't mean anything until you have specified what the aim is. Excellent at what? World-class in terms of what criteria? Best practice for achieving what goals? What counts as "good" depends on where you are headed.

- Good for producing 19th century–style factory workers?

- Good for producing people with high grades but who are selfish and callous?

- Good for developing dinner-table erudition?

- Good for turning out people with the rhetorical tricks to win an argument but who lack the ability to tolerate uncertainty and think deeply?

- Good for ensuring that people will live adventurous and principled lives, so they will, when the time comes, be able to die without regret?

We don't know what is good until we have first decided what the desirable outcomes of education actually are. Only when we know where we want to go can we think about the optimal ways of getting there.

Everybody knows that examination scores are not enough. We don't just want young people to be able to churn out an A-grade essay; we would like them to be literate, to enjoy literature. Simply being able to do math and calculate correctly won't suffice; we would like them to be able to think flexibly and creatively, as real mathematicians do. Being able to recapitulate conventional interpretations of history is not a preparation for life. We want young people to have learned the lessons of history: to be willing to inhabit with sympathy the worlds of different places, times, and peoples, and know that there are many sides to every story. If I can knock out a little essay on the origins of impressionism, does that mean I can also revel in the artistry of Monet and Cezanne? Not necessarily (though knowledge and understanding may enhance that pleasure). We want education to cultivate character as well as knowledge, real-world inclinations as well as academic expertise—don't we?

Many schools, and many education systems around the world, don't seem to understand this simple truth. They think there is no need for all that philosophizing. Improving education, they think, is just a technical matter of getting better grades, and especially getting better grades for poor kids so more of them can get to college. Many statisticians and politicians tend to value what they can measure and to discount that which can't be measured easily. But, as we shall see, grades capture some of what we would wish for the next generation, but not all. And if we neglect the development of character simply because it is tricky to measure, we shrink and pervert education to fit our narrow conceptions of value, and do young people a disservice and an injustice.

All those who espouse a learning power approach are aware of this risk, and unwilling to accept it. We want to tackle the hard question of how to prepare youngsters properly for life in a tricky world—and that means all of them: not just those who by temperament or good fortune are destined for Stanford, Harvard, Oxford, or Cambridge. Admission to high-status universities is not the gold standard by which we should judge all of education. The world needs only so many professors; it needs more plumbers than eggheads. I know of no evidence that scholars are happier, kinder, more honorable, more socially responsible, or more fulfilled in their lives than anyone else. If one talented hairdresser, footballer, dancer, or cartoonist comes out of school feeling like a failure, we should look again at our teaching.

Making the LPA a reality in your classroom or your school takes time, effort, and ingenuity. To be willing to embark on the journey, as an individual teacher or, even better, as a whole school—you have to really want to. Changing any habit is hard. Researchers have found that even changing a small dietary habit—like snacking on a piece of fruit rather than a chocolate bar—takes two months of effort before it becomes second nature. And one of the main things that keeps you going is commitment. It is especially difficult to change your habits if you don't feel the need to. The LPA asks teachers to change their classroom habits—gradually, bit by bit, but, again, they have to really want to. So understanding the purpose of the LPA, and being keenly aware of its benefits, is an important ingredient of the change process. Here are 10 good reasons why any teacher should be interested in the LPA, and take it seriously enough to be willing, little by little, to change their ways. If even just one of these reasons gets under your skin, that might do the trick.

# 1. Because Life Is Complicated

Our world is complicated, uncertain, and fluid—personally, socially, communally, nationally, and globally. Being alive in the 21st century is mentally demanding. Just think of all those bank or savings accounts, monthly bills to pay, all those passwords to keep track of, all the smart phone updates, the junk e-mails, the scams and viruses to be detected, the social media accounts, conversations with hundreds of people to be remembered, gadgets to be worked, games to be played, holidays to be planned, children to be taken care of. And that's just our day-to-day personal lives.

"Work hard at school; go to a good college; get a well-paid job; be happy" is not a story line that parents can confidently spin to their children any more. Even 10 years ago, more than a quarter of the young people who

## 10 Reasons to Take the Learning Power Approach

1. Learning powers help us make sense of a complex, ever-changing world.

2. Learning powers increase empathy.

3. The LPA develops confident, competent learners.

4. People who have learning powers are more successful in life.

5. Employers are looking for employees with learning powers.

6. Powerful learners do better in school.

7. Powerful learners do better in college.

8. The LPA makes teaching more rewarding.

9. Tackling challenges with learning powers makes us happier.

10. Learning powers help us deal with stress and lead healthier lives.

graduated from college were without a full-time job three years later. Some big international companies such as Pearson, PricewaterhouseCoopers (PwC), and Ernst and Young are no longer interested in the nature or level of your degree, or even in the university you went to. They have found that the ability to be a diligent student does not predict the kinds of agile intelligence that their companies are looking for. The global head of learning at Google rang me up a while ago because he wanted to compare my work on learning power with what they are calling "learning agility"—flexible thinking in the face of major new challenges—which they prize much more than academic achievement, or even IQ.

Currently, more than 12 million skilled people worldwide are finding work by posting their credentials on upwork.com, where more than 5 million registered clients are looking for skilled freelancers to work on their projects. Last year the website brokered more than 1 billion dollars' worth of work. In such a world, it's your ability to do the job that counts, not your degree. When a member of Google's Future think tank—a group of very smart people trying to predict the world 30 years hence—was asked if he could offer any advice to today's school leavers, he replied, "I can't tell you much . . . but I would strongly advise them against going into medicine or the law." Sharp intake of breath! If these gold-standard careers are at risk of digital automation and international outsourcing, what are parents to tell their children to aim for?

The ability to deal well with what is called the VUCA world—volatile, uncertain, complex, and ambiguous—to be a powerful learner—is not a luxury for tomorrow's citizens; it's a basic necessity. Education has to work to expand young people's capacity to think clearly and calmly about complicated, important matters, and to strengthen their inclination to do so. Filling their heads with uncontroversial facts, and teaching them how to knock out an A-grade essay, is not adequate preparation for modern life. Of course you have to know things to function, but just "knowing" them doesn't of itself create the mental agility and precision people will need. It is increasingly a learning-powered world out there.

> Education has to work to expand young people's capacity to think clearly and calmly about complicated, important matters, and to strengthen their inclination to do so.

## 2. Because Learning Power Makes the World a Safer Place

If we feel like we are drowning in this complexity, it is no wonder that some of us are tempted to latch on to whatever simplistic solutions come our way. To counter uncertainty, we might yearn to turn the clock back to a past where things seemed more secure and clear-cut. Joseph Tainter, University of Utah historian and anthropologist, author of *The Collapse of Complex Societies*, says, "The simpler past seems more attractive than today's complex reality, so people vote for . . . simplicity over complexity, and [local] identity over internationalism. Politicians promote themselves by giving voice to this."[2] But it does our societies no good to give up on thinking and learning, and sign up to hokum and snake oil. So it is not just a matter of personal security or fulfillment. Learning power makes the world a safer place.

Our job as citizens, you might say, is to act, to the best of our ability, in ways that increase harmony and security—not just for ourselves but for our families, our neighbors, our countries, and our planet. That means being aware of and doing our best to evaluate all the relevant factors, thinking through the likely consequences of different courses of action, imagining how others will react, listening to different voices, and being willing to revise our opinions.

We have to bring to new situations the wisdom of our personal experience and of our cultural knowledge, yet be alive to the possibility that old solutions and historical precedents may well not be adequate to meet the complex needs of the present and future.

In the 21st century, schools need to be places where young people learn to make better judgments than their predecessors—seeing more clearly, weighing up situations more carefully, understanding complicated things more deeply, learning more powerfully—and therefore are able to act more intelligently.[3] The overriding aim of the curriculum should be to build minds that are rich and supple enough to cope well with such demands. People with strong minds are more likely to contribute to building a world that is peaceful and secure.

You can even see these differences in the brain. Faced with difficulty, shallow thinkers show greater fear-driven activity in the amygdala, while more thoughtful people show greater activity in an area known as the anterior cingulate cortex, which, the authors of the study say, "is a region of the brain that helps people cope with complexity."[4] The tendency toward black-and-white, judgmental thinking is found in extremist groups all over the world, so you end up with simplistic thinkers squaring up to each other, threatening to escalate tension by their impulsive actions, and thus rendering the world more dangerous and volatile. In a recent speech, Professor Louise Richardson, the vice-chancellor of the University of Oxford and an expert on terrorism, said,

> Any terrorist that I have ever met through my academic work had a highly over-simplified view of the world, which they saw in black-and-white terms. Education robs you of that simplification and certitude. Education is the best possible antidote to radicalization.[5]

Actually, she should have said *good* education *should be* the antidote—because, sadly, it isn't always. Scarily, these dangerous black-and-white attitudes can actually be strengthened by education. Instead of making young people more tolerant of difficulty and better able to think carefully, they can become less so.

As a powerful case in point, one study looked at the education of Islamic extremists in the Middle East and North Africa region.[6] An extraordinarily large number of such people opt for university courses in hard-nosed subjects such as engineering, science, and medicine, and many of these courses are taught in a fact-based, true-false, right-wrong kind of way, with no room for discussion of difficulty or nuance. Such courses, with their black-and-white methodologies, seem to appeal to people who already have that narrow need for certainty, and their education actively reinforces that mindset. Seeing this, many universities are introducing compulsory courses for trainee engineers in the arts and humanities, precisely to make them engage with zones of experience where simplistic thinking just doesn't work.[7] And it is not just "them" who can suffer this disabling effect. It could be happening, as a result of any form of ideological extremism, in a school near you, in your leafy suburb of Cambridge, Massachusetts, or Cambridge, UK.

## 3. Because We Won't Always Be There

If we see education as a preparation for life for everyone, rather than a preparation for college for some, then we have to think about a lasting legacy of those long years in school that is over and above the grades. The investment has to be enabling rather than disabling, especially for those who are not going to get the grades. Yet—as I said in the introduction—for many young people, including myself, one of those legacies was a kind of dependency on our teachers. We got used to being told what to learn, how to go about it, what counted as a good answer, and how well we had done. But we are not going to be followed around by a kindly teacher for the rest of our lives, organizing, marking, and rescuing us when we meet things that challenge and stretch us. We are going to have to do it for ourselves.

So it seems pretty obvious to me that we need to teach tomorrow's youngsters—all of them—to become competent, confident learners in their own right. As I've said, you do not learn how to organize your own learning by constantly being organized, nor to evaluate the quality of your products and solutions by always being told how good they are by someone else. We don't learn the strategies of self-discipline, nor discover its benefits, by being constantly disciplined by someone else. To suppose otherwise is just bad psychology.[8] The research shows, for example, that young children don't learn to rescue and soothe themselves by being rescued and soothed by an (over)caring mother at the very first signs of distress. They build their resilience by being gently weaned off their reliance on their caretakers to do all the caring. So if we are going to help young people develop those important attributes of resilience, self-management, self-discipline, and self-evaluation, we have to teach them in a particular way—and that is what the LPA aims to do.

## 4. Because Good Learners Are More Successful in Life

In a 2013 report to the Organisation for Economic Co-operation and Development, the OECD, Nobel economics laureate James Heckman and colleagues summarized a major body of work on what predicts success in life.[9] By "success" they meant a whole variety of socioeconomic indicators: income, job satisfaction, home ownership, stable relationships, health, and self-reported happiness; and as indicators of a lack of success, they looked at unemployment, drug use, trouble with the law, delinquency of children, money troubles, and so on. They found that academic achievement is a weaker predictor of these later-life outcomes than what they call in their report "non-cognitive skills." What they mean by these non-cognitive skills are "such qualities as perseverance, conscientiousness, self-control, attentiveness . . . resilience to adversity, openness to experience, empathy [and] tolerance of diverse opinions."[10] They found that conventional tests of achievement are worse predictors of life success precisely because they do not capture these critical qualities. They argue that, for this very reason, current attempts to improve young people's life chances just by racking up their test scores are misguided, and doomed to fail. The assumption that "achievement tests capture the important life skills . . . misses important dimensions of human flourishing," they say.[11]

This insight also makes sense of another curious but important research finding: that success in life depends more on the sheer number of years you have spent in school than on the grades you obtained on those high-stakes tests. It is as if the ability to stick with education, keep turning up, keep handing in those assignments, keep trying even though your performance may not be very good, matters more than the ability to retain and display knowledge to a required level. As with Heckman's research, it looks like the "non-cognitive" capabilities needed to keep going with school (such as resilience, conscientiousness, and attentiveness) outweigh the narrower cognitive skills of comprehension, retention, and manipulation of knowledge.

> What am I looking for in those I employ? People who show initiative, tell me about problems they've solved, look for opportunities that I've missed, work well with other people, and make me feel that they're enjoying what they do.
>
> A UK employer

Heckman and his colleagues also conclude that the deliberate attempt to develop the wider attitudes and habits of learning can be highly effective. The evidence is especially strong for certain approaches in the early years, such as Tools of the Mind (www.toolsofthemind.org) and for targeted interventions with adolescents who come from disadvantaged backgrounds.[12]

## 5. Because Employers Want to Hire Powerful Learners

The Confederation of British Industry, the CBI, is the major employer organization in the UK, representing nearly 200,000 businesses of all types and sizes. In 2012 the CBI published a report called *First Steps: A New Approach for our Schools*.[13] Supported by McKinsey & Company, and based on detailed discussions with a wide range and number of business leaders and educators, *First Steps* concluded, "The system is currently too much of a conveyor belt. . . . It is the narrow definition of success we give schools at each stage of development . . . that encourages this approach." The key recommendation was for "the development of a clear, widely-owned and stable statement of the outcome that all schools are asked to deliver. This should go beyond the merely academic, into the *behaviors and attitudes* schools should foster in everything they do."[14]

The CBI report quotes the World Bank's 2020 education strategy: "Education [should] enhance people's ability to make informed decisions, be better parents, sustain a livelihood, adopt new technologies, cope with shocks, and be responsible citizens and effective stewards of the natural environment."[15] And it notes approvingly the recent changes in the Singaporean education system, which has consistently topped the international league tables while "shifting the balance of teaching to reduce the amount of subject matter taught and to increase the learning of life-long skills, [and] the building of character and competencies such as critical thinking and creativity."[16] Clearly there is no necessary conflict between high levels of achievement and a broader set of valued outcomes. Hard-headed business leaders around the world agree that developing qualities of mind such as learning agility, resilience, imagination, and collaboration is a vital aim for 21st century education, is achievable with a shift in teaching methods, and is entirely compatible with the development of knowledge, understanding, and better grades.

> [Attitudes and] behaviors can only be developed over time, through the entire path of a young person's life and their progress through the school system. Everything that happens in a school should embed the key behaviors and attitudes.
>
> Fothergill, *First Steps*, p. 32

The report acknowledges the importance of getting the language right. It says,

> In the past, the CBI has tended to discuss many of these areas in terms of "employability skills." This terminology was misleading, giving the impression that they could be taught separately in the curriculum. That is not the case—[attitudes and] behaviors can only be developed over time, through the entire path of a young person's life and their progress through the school system. Everything that happens in a school should embed the key behaviors and attitudes.[17]

And what are these precious mental habits? Among those that employers consistently say they value are the dispositions to see things through, work independently, resist distractions, allow others to speak, explore new things, be willing to try new experiences, develop new ideas, respect the feelings of others, and show appreciation of others. Clearly, this agenda maps tightly onto the LPA.

## 6. Because Powerful Learners Do Better in School

Even if we narrow our sights to conventional grades, students who know more about the process of learning, understand what it takes to be a good learner, and have help with developing their learning strengths get better grades. So even teachers who might be skeptical about the grander aims of education, and simply want to help their students master more knowledge and do better on the tests, become more effective if they adopt the LPA. In a very useful paper published in 2010, British educator Chris Watkins summarizes a wealth of evidence that shows that, in his words, "learning about learning enhances school performance."[18]

For example, Chris notes, "For nearly 25 years it has been known that students with more elaborated conceptions of learning perform better in public examinations at age 16."[19] There are still a few teachers, I find, who don't know what that means. The phrase "more elaborated conceptions of learning" doesn't connect with the way they think about their classrooms and what they are trying to achieve. But increasing numbers do understand, and are keen to help their students develop those richer understandings. In particular, Chris shows how to make learning itself an object of attention, of conversation, and of reflection in the classroom. We can help students become more aware of how learning happens and what good learning looks like. We can help them build a rich vocabulary for talking about the processes, strategies, and attitudes that underpin powerful learning. And we can make time for them to review their own strengths and weaknesses as learners, and to design activities and targets for themselves that will help them to improve.

Thinking and talking about learning benefits lower-achieving students, and those from lower-income families, disproportionately. For example, the graph in Figure 5.1 shows the effect of a Learning to Learn (L2L) intervention on the achievement of students in a British high school.[20] You will see that the percentage of students hitting or exceeding their target grades is higher in the L2L cohort, but that the improvement for students from disadvantaged backgrounds (identified in England as eligible for extra funding called the Pupil Premium) is significantly greater: so much so that their relative underachievement is all but obliterated.

One explanation for this dramatic effect has been suggested by New Zealand educator Graham Nuthall in his remarkable book *The Hidden Lives of Learners*. On the basis of many years of his own research, Nuthall concludes that many of those who perform badly in school do so not because they lack either innate ability or motivation, but because they simply haven't figured out the tricks of the trade of learning. They may even not have realized—for a variety of reasons—that learning is something that it is possible to get better at. So a classroom culture that opens up the idea that learning itself is learnable, and is abuzz with talk by both teacher and students about how it is possible to get better at learning, is of particular benefit to them. Instead of feeling inadequate or defeated, they can now become interested

FIGURE 5.1 Effect of Learning to Learn Teaching
on School Performance

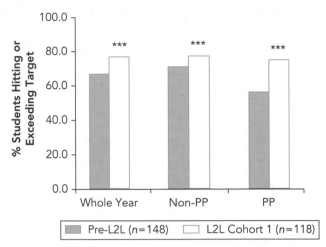

Students' attainment after three years: Learning to Learn (L2L) cohort versus pre-L2L control group. Notice that the L2L intervention is of particular benefit to students from poorer backgrounds (entitled to the Pupil Premium, PP)—so much so that the difference in attainment between them and students from better-off homes is virtually eradicated.

*Source:* Mannion & Mercer (2016); figure courtesy of Dr. James Mannion

*** Statistically significant differences versus control group; $p \leq 0.001$.

in how to improve. Carol Dweck, in her book *Mindset*, movingly describes the reaction of one disenchanted adolescent boy in a New York school to the news that "learning was learnable." He slowly raised his head, blinking as if emerging from a dark place into the light, and said, "Mrs. Dweck, you mean I don't *have* to be stupid?"

# 7. Because Powerful Learners Do Better in College

Surrounded by skillful, effective, caring teachers, very many students are able to achieve the grades necessary to get into college. Continually coaxed, coached, and corrected, they can meet the criteria. Unfortunately, in the United States at least, such intense cultivation does not prepare them with the skills and strengths they are going to need when they get there, and around three-quarters of them fail to complete their course. As Paul Tough puts it in *How Children Succeed*:

> The United States does not so much have a problem of limited and unequal college access; it has a problem of limited and unequal college completion. Among the thirty-four member countries of the OECD, the U.S. still ranks a respectable eighth in its college enrolment rate. But in college completion—the percentage of entering college freshmen who go on to graduate—the U.S. ranks second to last, ahead only of Italy. Not long ago, the U.S. led the world in producing college graduates; now it leads the world in producing college drop-outs.[21]

Some people suggested that the reason for this is that students, especially from low-income backgrounds, may choose the wrong courses, or the wrong colleges, and struggle and lose heart because the work is too hard for them. Students themselves may believe this and keep chopping and changing their courses before finally giving up. But a University of Chicago research consortium found that that wasn't it. It is the lack of those learning strengths that is to blame. More specifically, it is the kind of teaching that raises achievement, but does so without building those strengths. Here is the conclusion of the Chicago report:

> The essential question is not how to change students to improve their behavior but rather how to create contexts that better support students in developing the critical attitudes and learning strategies necessary for academic success. . . . Teaching adolescents to become learners may require educators to shift their own

beliefs and practices . . . to support student learning in new ways. *Academic behaviors and perseverance may need to be thought of as creations of school and classroom contexts rather than as personal qualities that students bring with them to school.*[22]

In fact, the final paragraph of this report could be taken as a plea for the widespread adoption of the Learning Power Approach:

Teaching adolescents to become learners requires more than improving test scores; it means transforming classrooms into places alive with ideas that engage students' natural curiosity and desire to learn in preparation for college, career, and meaningful adult lives. This requires schools to build . . . the strategies, behaviors and attitudes that allow [students] to bring their aspirations to fruition.[23]

Positive mental attitudes toward learning, complexity, and uncertainty are not just relevant to students who are from poor or disadvantaged backgrounds, however. It is a mistake to see the cultivation of these attitudes as a kind of compensatory education for those who are not destined to be natural-born winners at the grades game. When wealthier or more successful kids go on to Yale or Stanford, their social safety net is often dramatically weakened. When they are away from home, taking subjects that their parents and friends couldn't help with even if they were available, feeling like a small fish in a much bigger pond, with a backlog of assignments piling up, greater resilience and resourcefulness will be needed. If they have not been helped to develop those qualities at school, such seemingly well-favored students can often crash and burn, feeling like failures because they are not coping.

# 8. Because It Makes Teaching Easier and More Rewarding

In Greek mythology, there was a character called Sisyphus who was king of Corinth. He displeased the gods, Zeus in particular, by trying to be too clever, and he was punished by being made to roll a big boulder laboriously uphill every day, only to watch it roll back down before he got it to the top, and continually having to start over again. Teachers can sometimes feel as if they are condemned to such a cycle of effort and frustration, having to exert all their energy and ingenuity to engage disaffected students, only to find that almost nothing has stuck.

Yet all children are born curious. Babies and toddlers are naturally inquisitive and resilient in their trial-and-error attempts to predict and control their world. But if this inherent learning power has been weakened, when they get into a classroom they are no longer "pulling" at the learning from their side, so it seems as if the teacher is forced to do all the "pushing." This continual need to find ever more ingenious ways to entertain and capture students' attention quickly becomes tiring and dispiriting. At a time when many teachers are experiencing high levels of stress due to pressures to "perform" (and, in England at least, to push children

> Involvement with Building Learning Power has had a huge impact on the way learning happens in my classroom. My students have amazed me with their ability to drive their own learning—working independently, questioning with confidence, taking risks, and setting their own targets: all great life skills. Teaching is more enjoyable and also more challenging as the students make greater progress; they are pushing their own limits every day and are motivated and enthusiastic; it is a really positive approach.
>
> Elaine Humpleby,
> Sprowston High School

through a content- and assessment-heavy curriculum that is prescriptive and exhausting), anything that makes students more enthusiastic and adventurous can only help.

The alternative to becoming an entertainer, or a martinet, is to try to rekindle students' own curiosity and determination. That is the LPA. If we can reawaken students' willingness to be intrigued, and rehabilitate the innate optimism that investing their own effort in learning will generally pay off in competence and satisfaction, then teaching becomes easier and more fulfilling. Instead of rolling rocks up a muddy hillside, being with a room mostly filled with confident learners feels like just giving the boulder a nudge and then watching it roll itself along.

The very first school I worked with to develop practical approaches to building learning power was a primary school in a country town in the west of England. After a year of trying out new approaches to teaching, many of the teachers, as well as some of the parents, and one member of the board of governors, wrote their reflections.[24] Here are a few of them.

A teacher who had just come back from a challenging study trip to New Zealand wrote,

> Becoming a conscious learner again has made me aware of the sometimes frustrating, chaotic, recursive but ultimately exhilarating nature of learning. Facts and knowledge themselves are useless without the skills to make connections, think, and apply what we know appropriately—to be active learners. Our children live in a constantly changing world. . . . I had to travel half way round the world to rediscover what had been hidden under a mountain of curriculum documents: the most important lesson of all is to learn what it is to be a learner.[25]

One of the parents wrote,

> It is so exciting because it is not just what the children
> learn but how they learn that matters. As parents
> we are very grateful [to the school] for enabling
> our children to face the uncertainty of the 21st
> century with a confidence and a Ready-Brek Glo [an
> advertising slogan at the time] that I am sure we all
> wish we had had as 11-year-olds.[26]

The chair of the board of governors' curriculum committee
was quoted in the local newspaper. She had noted a marked
difference in her own 10-year-old daughter's attitude toward
learning since the project had started:

> The way she tackles her homework has changed.
> Before, she would panic, get cross, saying "I can't
> do that," and we'd have to leave it. Now she'll come
> home and say, "Mum, this maths looks hard this week.
> Can I run through it with you and then have a go?" If
> she makes a mistake she doesn't mind. I'd have loved
> to have those skills. I've had to wait till the age of 40
> to get that kind of confidence![27]

## 9. Because People Are Happier When They Are Learning

Learning is one of the most readily available forms of
happiness there is. In a simple experiment, psychologist
Mihaly Csikszentmihalyi gave thousands of people a note
pad and a bleeper. The bleeper would go off at random
moments during the day, and when it did, they simply
had to note what they were doing at the time and how
happy they were. He found that the most everyday kind
of happiness occurred when people were engaged in

doing something challenging but that they considered worthwhile, when they felt they were making progress (even if slowly), and when the challenge was so engrossing that all their other cares and worries fell away and they were just totally engrossed in the present activity.[28]

It is as if there is only so much brain power available, and when we are really absorbed—Csikszentmihalyi calls it being "in flow"—all those mental resources are rounded up and dedicated to the task at hand, and there simply isn't any left over to service the usual background feelings of fallibility, regret, overload, or anxiety. One of the participants in his study said,

> It happens when I am working with my daughter, when she is discovering something new. A new cookie recipe that she has made herself; an artistic work that she has done and she is proud of. Her reading is something that she is really into, and we read together. She reads to me and I read to her, and that's a time when I sort of lose touch with the rest of the world. I am totally absorbed in what I am doing.[29]

The mother is completely engrossed in the mysterious challenge of being with her daughter, trying to see the world through her eyes, and to track and respond quickly to her thought processes. This is a demanding task, rather like that of professional dance partners in training who are keeping moment-to-moment contact with each other's moves, so their own moves engage seamlessly with their partners'. In order to do this, to be so totally in tune, everything else has to fade into the background. There is not enough brain power to go around.

So there is a direct link between stretching ourselves to meet a challenging goal and being full of happiness or well-being. And this connection is available to everyone—provided we have the confidence and capacity to immerse ourselves fully in the learning process. If we lack the requisite optimism and concentration, then the most common source of human happiness is denied to us. So if we want to raise young people to be happiness-prone, we have to ensure that they develop the attitudes and capabilities that underpin powerful learning.

## 10. Because Young People's Mental Health Depends Upon Their Learning Power

Students are reporting unprecedented levels of stress. The decline in the mental health and well-being of children and young people, even in affluent countries, is a major concern. In the UK, *The Independent* reports that " rates of depression and anxiety among teenagers

For me as a primary school teacher, the two most important reasons for the LPA are engagement and well-being. (1) Engagement of students—this is what gets me so excited about learning power teaching—the children LOVE coming to school and get excited about learning. Parents regularly comment on the change they have seen in their children. (2) Mental health issues—which are getting worse/more common. I just need to look at my amazing but struggling teenage nieces and nephews to personally worry about this, but it's obviously a worldwide problem as well. Children seeing a real purpose to going to school is absolutely key to getting to the root of this problem. It is no use training teachers just to deal with mental health symptoms—like a doctor who sends you away with a pill rather than trying to get to the root of the problem. The LPA deals with the cause and engages children from the word go.

Annie O'Donnell,
Westway Primary School

have increased by 70% in the past 25 years. The number of children and young people turning up in hospital accident and emergency departments with a psychiatric condition has more than doubled since 2009, and, in the past three years, hospital admissions for teenagers with eating disorders has also almost doubled. In a 2016 survey, 93% of teachers reported seeing increased rates of mental illness among children and teenagers, and 90% thought the issues were getting more severe, with 62% dealing with a pupil's mental health problem at least once a month and an additional 20% doing so on a weekly or even daily basis."[30]

Social, emotional, and commercial pressures account for some of this rise, but schools add to it significantly. *The Independent* notes, "Research by the mental health charity Young Minds has found that exams are a significant trigger for mental illness in young people.[31] Under pressure to get the best possible results, schools are inclined to give teenagers the impression that they have only one shot at tests that will determine the rest of their lives (even though this is not true). According to Julie Lythcott-Haims, former dean of freshmen at Stanford and the author of *How to Raise an Adult*, examination anxiety is having a direct impact on young people's mental health, as parents as well as teachers strive to maximize their children's accomplishments."[32] Things are, if anything, worse at college. *The Independent* also found that "the American College Health Association surveyed 100,000 college students at 53 U.S. campuses and found that 84% of U.S. students feel unable to cope, 79% are exhausted, 60% feel very sad, and more than half are experiencing overwhelming anxiety."[33]

What is stress? It is the toll that life takes on body and mind when the demands on us exceed the resources we have to cope. So stress can be reduced either by reducing the level of demand, or by increasing our capacity to respond effectively. Some people are more resilient—better able to cope with pressure—than others, and we know that resilience is like a muscle that is capable of being exercised and strengthened. It is also a resource that can be weakened and depleted. Likewise, we know that mindfulness—the ability to see your thoughts as thoughts, and not the unquestionable truth about situations—is also a powerful antidote to stress that can be built up by deliberate practice. School ought to be a place where such mental and emotional resources are being deliberately increased, so that young people leave education feeling more equal to the demands and uncertainties of life, rather than defeated by the enormous pressure of examinations and expectations. It is the noble aim of the LPA to build those resources, so that youngsters feel more confident about their ability to cope with nonacademic, as well as academic, challenges.

---

So there are my 10 good reasons why the LPA is highly desirable. Being a powerful learner seems, according to the evidence, to help you do well in school. It prepares you for life at college or university. It equips you for the world of work. It makes you less likely to want to blow the world up, or to retreat into a narrow, predictable cocoon spun out of your own habits and opinions. And it makes for a more interesting, fulfilled, and happy life. What's not to like?

I hope you are convinced, because commitment to a valued goal helps give you staying power—in this case, when making the effort to develop your style and your habits as a teacher.

## Wondering

Do you agree that education ought to be about more than grades? If so, how do you articulate what you think that "more" should be? How confident do you feel talking about these deeper purposes? Where do these values come from?

Whose job do you think it is to decide on the purposes of education? Superintendents? School principals? Individual classroom teachers? Parents? Politicians? Academics? Students themselves?

In the schools that you know, how clearly are the purposes of education specified? What do they say they value, and what do they act as if they value? Is there any gap between the two? How big is it? How can you tell what a school acts as if it values? What are the telltale signs?

Which of the 10 arguments for the LPA do you find the most convincing? And which the least? Can you explain why you think that?

## Notes

1. John Holt, *How Children Fail*, p. 173.
2. Quoted in John Harris, "A Society Too Complex for the People Risks Everything."
3. Of course good thinkers need to turn their thoughts into actions and not get paralyzed by complexity. If situations are urgent, they need to come up with the best course of action in the time available, implement it, and keep watching to see how it is doing. We will come back to this aspect of the intelligent mind later.
4. For more on this research, see Nigel Barber, "Conservatives Big on Fear, Brain Study Finds," and Ryota Kanai, Tom Feilden, Colin Firth, and Geraint Rees, "Political Orientations Are Correlated With Brain Structure in Young Adults."

5. Louise Richardson, addressing the Going Global conference, London, June 2, 2015. Quoted in Martin Rose, *Universities, the Job Market and the Jihad* (unpublished).

6. Diego Gambetta and Steffen Hertog, *Engineers of Jihad*.

7. Martin Rose, *Immunising the Mind*.

8. For a very good review of this research, see Lynne Murray, *The Psychology of Babies*.

9. Tim Kautz, James Heckman, Ron Diris, Bas ter Weel, and Lex Borghans, *Fostering and Measuring Skills: Improving Cognitive and Non-Cognitive Skills to Promote Lifetime Success*.

10. Kautz et al., p. 9.

11. Kautz et al., p. 11.

12. See the two excellent books by Paul Tough, *How Children Succeed: Grit, Curiosity and the Hidden Power of Character*, and *Helping Children Succeed: What Works and Why*.

13. James Fothergill, *First Steps: A New Approach for Our Schools*.

14. Fothergill, pp. 7–8.

15. Fothergill, p. 10.

16. Fothergill, p. 28.

17. Fothergill, p. 32.

18. *Learning About Learning Enhances Performance* was the title of an earlier version of Watkins's 2010 paper, *Learning, Performance, and Improvement*.

19. Watkins, p. 9.

20. James Mannion and Neil Mercer, "Learning to Learn."

21. Paul Tough, *How Children Succeed*, p. 150.

22. Camille Farrington, Melissa Roderick, Elaine Allensworth, Jenny Nagaoka, Tasha Keyes, David Johnson, and Nicole Beechum, *Teaching Adolescents to Become Learners*, p. 74.

23. Farrington et al., p. 77.

24. This and the following quotes are taken from a record of the school's journey edited by the head teacher, Peter Mountstephen, *Primary Tales: Learning by Heart*.

25. Mountstephen, p. 63.

26. Mountstephen, p. 56.

27. Mountstephen, p. 11.

28. Mihaly Csikszentmihalyi, *Flow: The Psychology of Happiness*.

29. Quoted in Maria Allison and Margaret Duncan, "Women, Work, and Flow," p. 131.

30. For a review of this research, see my book *What's the Point of School?* See also Geraldine Bedell, "Teenage Mental-Heath Crisis: Rates of Depression Have Soared in the Past 25 Years."

31. Guy Claxton, *What's the Point of School?*

32. Julie Lythcott-Haims, *How to Raise an Adult.* See also Geraldine Bedell, "Teenage Mental-Heath Crisis: Rates of Depression Have Soared in the Past 25 Years."

33. Information from Geraldine Bedell, "Teenage Mental Health Crisis: Rates of Depression Have Soared in the Past 25 Years."

# 6

# What Is Learning Power Made Of?

> It should be the responsibility of schools to make children aware of our information environments. . . . We must teach our children, from a very young age, to be skeptics, to listen carefully, to assume everyone is lying about everything. (Well, maybe not *everyone*.) Check sources. Consider what wasn't said. Ask questions. Understand that every storyteller has a bias—and so does every platform.
>
> Andrew Postman[1]

An effective sports coach has to know what it takes to excel at her sport. She has to have a rich vocabulary for talking about the expertise that is required. It is no use saying to an Olympic champion, "Just go out and run around for two hours." You need to say, "Today we are going to work on your speed off the blocks," or "your backhand slice," or "your upper-body strength," or "your peripheral vision." The same is true for designers and coaches of learning. Learning itself is a sophisticated craft, and a competent coach has to understand what goes to make up a powerful learner. Having established your classroom as a safe and engaging place for young learners to be, the next step is to develop greater fluency in speaking the languages of learning power. So in this chapter I'm going to describe in more detail the suite of beliefs, values, attitudes, and habits of mind that go to make up learning power, and explain how they fit naturally together.

**Being Your Own Learning Power Hero**

*Source:* By kind permission of TLO Ltd

Let's be clear: Learning power isn't a new "thing" that has just been discovered. It is a way of packaging a whole variety of mental habits, beliefs, and attitudes that all contribute to the overall sense of being optimistic and resourceful when it comes to tackling things that are hard or strange. Think of it like the name of a successful orchestra such as the New York Philharmonic. An orchestra is just a collection of instruments playing in concert. To sound good, all the instrumentalists need to play well, but they also need to play well together. When we are learning, we don't get a series of solos—first a burst of Curiosity and then some Resilience or a passage of Reflection. We get a dynamic interplay between all the instruments playing in harmony. Nevertheless, when we are thinking about coaching the development of learning power, it is useful to be able to pick out the different "instruments" in order to recognize the unique contribution of each one, and sometimes to practice each separately.

How do we know what the instruments of learning power are? There are several sources of information that I have blended together. First, there are a number of previous attempts to map this general terrain that have generated and synthesized a wealth of research. For example, there are Art Costa and Bena Kallick's *Habits of Mind* program, Robert Marzano's *Dimension of Learning,* and the rich survey of creative learning habits that Robert and Michèle Root-Bernstein referred to as *Sparks of Genius*. Ron Ritchhart has developed a framework for what he calls *Intellectual Character*. Christopher Petersen and Martin Seligman's monumental work *Character Strengths and Virtues* is a vital source book of a wider set of character traits that includes many of those that contribute to learning power. My own *Building Learning Power* offered an earlier mapping that I have tried to improve on in the present description. (A lot of experience and research has been gathered in the last 15 years, and it is time to refresh and enhance my first attempt.)

Second, there is now a wealth of more fundamental research in the cognitive and social sciences that has affirmed the learnability of many aspects of learning power, especially those to do with resilience and grit,[2] growth mindset,[3] concentration,[4] and intuition.[5] Third, there are now many more outcome studies showing the effects of different learner attributes on school performance. (See, for example, the books by Paul Tough in the reference list at the end of the book.) And finally, I have gathered 15 years' worth of conversations with school leaders and schoolteachers in many countries around the world to capture their impressions of what goes in to making up a successful learner.

And all of this work builds on a long tradition of research and practice in education, developmental psychology, and the study of intelligence. Alfred Binet, inventor of the IQ test, did not believe that children's mental ability was fixed. In a much quoted passage from a 1909 book, he railed against what he called the "brutal pessimism," entirely without foundation, inherent in "the view that intelligence is a fixed quantity, a quantity that cannot be increased." He thought that children would benefit from what he called "mental orthopedics." "Before exercises in grammar they should be exercised in mental orthopedics; in a word, they must learn how to learn."[6] He particularly thought that children who struggled at school would benefit from this approach; we now know that all children, even the high fliers, do. In 1975, Arthur Whimbey wrote a book called *Intelligence Can Be Taught,* and in 1999 Lauren Resnick, past president of the American Educational Research Association, published an article called "Making America Smarter," in which she described intelligence as "the sum total of one's habits of mind." Perhaps the best summary of this tradition is David Perkins's excellent book *Outsmarting IQ: The Emerging Science of Learnable Intelligence.* Learning power builds on the work of such pioneering intellectual giants.

# The Elements of Learning Power

So with that introduction, let me introduce you to my current version of the Orchestra of Learning Power. It has eight sections, with several instruments within each.

## Curiosity

The spurs to learning are interest, intrigue, and surprise. It is the feeling of curiosity that makes learning attractive. The launchpad for learning is not-knowing and wondering. It is curiosity that creates engagement with things that are currently strange, unpredictable, or problematic. To be a powerful learner, you have to be open to novelty, and keen—or at least willing—to find out about it. Babies and toddlers are incredibly curious—they are drawn to things that are just out of reach, physically and cognitively. Yet so often curiosity is dulled by school rather than sharpened. In the first month at primary school, the number of questions children ask each day drops by around 90%. When you are constantly being told what it is you need to learn, your faith in your own inquisitiveness can easily become undermined, and proactive curiosity replaced by passive compliance or just plain apathy. Schools that want to turn out powerful learners have to balance the requirements of the curriculum with the deliberate stimulation of children's and young people's own appetite for learning.[7]

There are different aspects to curiosity. They include elements such as these:

> The launchpad for learning is not-knowing and wondering.

- **Wondering:** Having an inquiring mind; wondering about the world; being keen to learn; being willing to have your curiosity aroused by a math problem, a rainbow, or a new classmate. Without the inclination to wonder about things, life loses vitality and sparkle.

You can miss out on the excitement and satisfaction of learning new things.

- **Questioning:** Asking how come things are the way they are. "Why is the sky blue?" "Why do you have to soak the beans before you boil them?" "Why do bad things happen to good people?" Puzzling about things and seeking possible explanations. Without the disposition to ask your own questions, you are at risk of being towed along by other people's enthusiasms, and losing the driving force of your own curiosity. You miss out on the funds of knowledge and experience that the people around you possess.

- **Exploring:** Being up for an adventure and a challenge, and willing to hang out on the margins of your own comfort and control. As a powerful learner, you are willing to take the risk of going into the unknown and having your brain stretched by the effort to come to grips with something new. Without the willingness to explore, any interests you might have remain latent and passive. To be a powerful learner, you have to be adventurous (though not reckless).

- **Experimenting and Tinkering:** Actively grappling with new or difficult ideas or struggling to develop new forms of mastery. To be a powerful learner, you have to engage in trial and error: to *do* something different from usual, notice what happens, and keep adjusting your responses till they deliver the results you want. Experimenting and tinkering are more focused than exploring: You are working at the edge of your competence in order to expand or improve it. Without the willingness to get your hands dirty and maybe make a fool of yourself, to make mistakes and "fail forward," your curiosity won't translate into real competence.

These learning habits can be made stronger, broader, and more sophisticated by the way the teacher behaves, or they can be weakened and marginalized. It is our choice, and it is one we need to make consciously.

## Attention

From a psychological point of view, the main prerequisite for learning is attention. Attention acts like the pipe that connects your intelligence to the object of your learning. You have to focus on the thing that is problematic or difficult. Without this connection, without locking on to the bit of the world you want to find out about, no learning can take place. Learning changes the way you react in the future, and it does so by modifying the connections that already exist in your brain. Powerful learners are inclined to lock on to interesting bits of the world so change can come about. Unless your brain is fired up and ready to connect the new information with your existing networks, those changes are not going to happen. Attention puts the relevant bits of your brain into "learning mode." When attention is foggy or haphazard, not much learning can happen. The quality of your attention determines the quality of your learning. Attention has different elements, such as these:

> I have not failed. I've just found 10,000 ways that won't work.
>
> Thomas Edison

- **Noticing:** Being attentive to details and patterns in your environment. Learning often depends on noticing telling details or incongruities. Powerful learners have to be able to zoom in with their attention and be really observant, or the significance of what is out there may be missed. The difference in appearance between a harmless snake and a venomous one can be quite subtle. You also need to be good at distilling out patterns and trends from a variety of "noisy" experiences. Babies are expert pattern detectors, but perception can get more sloppy or slapdash as we grow up. Perceptiveness needs protecting and developing.

- **Concentrating:** Being able to resist distractions. A big part of what academics call "self-regulation" or "executive function" is the ability to stay focused on things that matter, even if they are taking some time to figure out, and even if there are temptations and distractions around. Powerful learners tend to have all sorts of techniques, both practical and psychological, for blanking out distractions and staying on track with learning that matters to them. They know what suits them, and take trouble to get the conditions of learning right.

- **Contemplating:** Taking the time to let information sink in. In some learning you have to keep looking or listening for a while before "what's there" becomes apparent. It takes time to let one of those 3D "magic pictures" form in your brain. You may have to stand and look at a painting for some time before it begins to reveal itself to you. Powerful learners know when they need to slow down, stop trying to figure things out with their conscious minds, and let impressions form in their own time. Without that ability, much of the depth and meaning in life can be lost, and the hare loses out to the tortoise.

- **Immersing:** Being lost in what you are doing. Learning happens best when you are so engrossed in what you are doing that everything else drops away and time flies by. That means that all the attention that your brain has is dedicated to the focus of learning, rather than being spread around in coping with all kinds of background worries and concerns. Successful students enter the state of absorption more often and more deeply than less successful ones. Without the capacity for absorption, learning is slower and more laborious, and an important source of well-being is denied to us.

## Determination

Learning means engaging with something you can't do yet, or don't understand yet. So learners constantly run the risk of being surprised, confused, frustrated, or disappointed. They don't get it right the first time. They can't instantly look good or successful. If you are allergic to these feelings and experiences, then, to avoid them, you are likely to bail out of learning, and miss out on its benefits. To be a powerful learner, you need to be able to tolerate—perhaps even enjoy—the feelings that go along with being exposed as not yet perfect. There is a form of deep pride or satisfaction that comes only from having hung in there, grappled with something really challenging—and having made it in the end. Many psychologists have written about the quality of mind that underpins determination. It goes by names like resilience, grit, self-efficacy, and optimism. It is Carol Dweck's "growth mindset." They all agree on two things: that it is a powerful predictor of success in life, and that it can be cultivated and strengthened. We might identify some different forms of determination:

- **Persevering:** Staying intelligently engaged with tricky things. Powerful learners don't give up at the first setback. They understand that not-good-enough-yet and not-clear-enough-yet are just normal when it comes to learning. Instead of getting upset and giving up, they keep calm and think of things they could do to help. They know things they could try when they don't know what to do. When confident learners of reading meet an unfamiliar word, they can sound it out, read on to try to guess the meaning from the context, go and get a dictionary, or look at the picture to see if that helps. They know it is no use just blankly staring at the page feeling miserable.

- **Recovering:** Bouncing back from mistakes and mishaps. The fashionable word for this quality is *buoyancy*— the ability to recover quickly when your learning has gotten derailed. Athletes, for example, know how to psych themselves up or calm themselves down in order to regain their poise and focus. They know that there are kinds of self-talk that are helpful and some that are definitely unhelpful, and they learn to replace negative thoughts with more positive ones. They invest energy in figuring out what works best for them, and young learners similarly can be helped to develop their own strategies for "getting over it" quicker.

- **Practicing:** Putting in the time to master a tricky skill. David Perkins in his excellent book *Making Learning Whole* talks about "practicing the hard parts." If you are a powerful learner, you are perceptive enough to identify what it is that is holding you up—a tricky bit of fingering in your cello piece, maybe, or a particular concept in chemistry you don't understand—and determined enough to devote time to zooming in on that bit and wrestling with it. Working on the hard parts may not be much fun, but powerful learners feel confident that it will be worth the effort in the end.

## Imagination

Often learning founders because we are stuck for an idea to try out. Our first attempt proved unsuccessful, and we can't think of anything else to do. Being a powerful learner means being able to rescue yourself from this impasse by coming up with a reasonable suggestion that you can then get to work on. It might not work out in practice, but it is a good basis for some more experiments and tinkerings. "Maybe if I swap green for blue, I might be able to see a way forward." "Maybe if I try supposing that $x = 1$, that might help me to see how the equation could be solved." So being able to come up with a good guess is an important way of kick-starting your own learning. And *imagination* is the name of the family of strategies and plans that helps us come up with those fresh possibilities. Without imagination, learning grinds to a halt much more often, or the solutions we do come up with are more limited or stereotyped.

- **Connecting:** Making interesting links between different ideas. Clues as to how to move forward in learning can often come from deliberately searching our memory banks to make fruitful connections between ideas. We go looking for prior experiences that might suggest what to try. We make use of analogies, similes, and metaphors to find verbal connections between superficially different concepts and ideas. Powerful learners know how to maximize the creativity that is already latent within their own knowledge.

- **Playing With Ideas:** Allowing the dreamy mind to come up with associations. The purposeful mind makes sharp assumptions about what will be "relevant"; it keeps its knowledge in separate silos. In reverie, when we are more relaxed but still alert, those boundaries soften: More ideas can be actively in play at the same time, and they can combine and recombine in more playful ways. While dropping off to sleep, surfacing in the morning, showering, or driving to work, possibilities just pop into our heads. Sometimes our wandering minds come up with garbage, but often they find fruitful connections, ripe for testing, that we would not have thought of deliberately.

- **Visualizing:** Using mental rehearsal as a way of developing expertise. Our brains are capable of running possible scenarios of input and reaction offline. We can watch ourselves performing in our mind's eye without actually moving. A wealth of research has shown that such mental rehearsal is powerfully effective at helping to build fresh skills and strengthen existing ones. Expert athletes, musicians, and even bankers make effective use of this kind of visualization to support their learning.

- **Intuiting:** Paying attention to hunches, inklings, and promptings from the body. Successful scientists, artists, and entrepreneurs know the value of intuition— connections and directions that come to mind not through clear thinking nor through imagery but through bodily feelings. When we feel touched or moved by something, it has meaning for us even if we cannot say why. Powerful learners pay heed to these promptings, not as surefire solutions or insights, but as promising suggestions worthy of investigation.

## Thinking

Critical and creative thinking go hand in hand, but they use the mind differently. Creativity and imagination often need a more patient, less focused attitude; good, clear, hard thinking needs a more constrained and disciplined attitude. Creative thinking generates interesting or fruitful ideas; critical thinking probes them and tests them out. Powerful learners have to be able to choose the right mode and know (often intuitively) when to switch from one to the other. Being able to think clearly, dispassionately, and critically about complicated matters is a vital asset, and it is not easy. We all know the mischief that egotistical and sloppy thinking can do. In *Outsmarting IQ*, David Perkins distinguished between four kinds of very common "bad thinking," which he calls *hasty*, *narrow*, *fuzzy*, and *sprawling*. We need to help young people develop the ability and the inclination to think carefully when that is what is needed.

Without this, their knowledge and beliefs are always likely to be flaky and fallible. Here are some aspects of careful thinking in a little more detail.

- **Analyzing:** Clear, hard, precise, logical thinking. This is the kind of thinking that philosophers do. It requires careful articulation—choosing the words that have exactly the meaning you want—and stitching them together into arguments that will withstand rational scrutiny. Powerful learners talk and write in ways that are convincing and make sound use of evidence and argument to underpin their knowledge and beliefs. This is the form of thinking that schools seem to espouse above all others, though they often fail to embed the habits of sound thinking to the point where they become second nature.

- **Deducing:** Creating plausible explanations and drawing reasonable inferences and implications. This is the scientist's way of generating sound knowledge, by creating rational conjectures about why things—particles, organisms, football crowds—behave the way they do, and then drawing observable inferences that act as tests of those conjectures. But we all make use of this so-called hypothetico-deductive thinking in everyday life. Done well, it delivers ever-more-reliable ideas about how the world works (though all theories are works in progress!).

- **Critiquing:** Taking a skeptical stance toward thinking—other people's and your own. The world is awash with dubious claims and propositions, and young learners need what the great writer Ernest Hemingway called a "built-in, shock-proof crap-detector" in order to stay safe and see off shysters of all kinds. The Internet is a dangerous place for the unwary, full of silly, dangerous, and manipulative nonsense, and it is vital for

21st century citizens to be inclined to say, "Hold on. Who is telling me this? Why do they want me to believe their claims? How can I check they are who they say they are, and be sure that their claims hold water?"

- **Systems Thinking:** Expanding the aptitude for thinking that does justice to complex situations. The world is made dangerous by people who are incapable of thinking complexly about complex matters. If you can't, you are vulnerable to radicalization, fundamentalism, and extremism of various kinds. Religion, economics, health, and the weather are all complex systems. It is hard to hold in mind more than three or four factors that are interacting in complicated ways—but people can be helped to get better at it, and the world will be a safer place as a result.

## Socializing

Much of our learning happens in interaction with other people. In a good conversation, we spark off each other, and our thinking becomes productively intertwined. We develop our own ideas through trying to explain what we think to others, and through bouncing off their thoughts. Cambridge University's Professor Neil Mercer has done a great deal of research on the value of what he calls *interthinking*.[8] Several heads are often better than one. But sometimes you think and learn better if you go off somewhere quiet by yourself. Brainstorming comes up with better ideas, for example, if participants have time to think quietly about the issue before the storming begins. Powerful learners are able to make good choices about how they learn and who they learn with and from. They are able to balance being open-minded with being able to stick with their own ideas even when they are in a minority. A few people are effective learning-hermits, but to a very large extent learning is a social affair. Here are some of the social aspects of learning in a little more detail.

- **Collaborating:** Being a good team player. Being inclined to listen carefully to others, to build on their contributions, and to disagree and to give feedback and suggestions respectfully. Powerful learners are supportive of others' learning and generous with their own insights and discoveries. They know there is a time to hold back and listen, and not to get carried away with their own brilliance and enthusiasm. They know that people who they would not naturally spend time with are often valuable collaborators precisely because of their different perspectives.

- **Accepting:** Being open to ideas and feedback. Powerful learners know that other people can offer reflections and make suggestions that help them improve their own learning. They tend to react positively to these suggestions rather than taking them personally. Open-mindedness is a great aid to learning, as are patience and a degree of humility.

- **Imitating:** Picking up good ideas about how to learn and problem-solve from other people. The research shows that we are natural-born mimics. We watch how other people do things that we want to be able to do, and then try to emulate their methods, while weaving them into our own natural styles. Powerful learners know that imitating involves more than just copying; it requires thoughtful customization. Being open to other people as role models of effective learning, and, if necessary, going looking for the best people to imitate, are powerful ways to amplify our own learning.

- **Empathizing:** Being able to adopt different perspectives. Research shows that the ability to look at a situation through different people's eyes boosts memory. Shown a scene of someone's living room, and later asked to recall the objects in the room, people's memory gets a second wind if they are told to imagine they are the householder, and then to shift to the perspective of, say, a burglar. Asked to put themselves in the shoes of a historical character, students' imaginative writing becomes richer and more memorable. In addition, teams work better if their members are inclined to see each other's points of view.

- **Leading:** Playing a role in developing the teams and groups they belong to. Powerful learners are inclined to maximize the harmony and productivity of their teams. They are perceptive and encouraging in getting the most out of other team members and in suggesting ways in which the group might improve its learning performance.

## Reflection

Powerful learners need to be able to think strategically, monitor their own progress and performance, and know themselves reasonably well—especially their own strengths and weaknesses as learners. Reflection involves thinking about how you are doing what you are doing, and adjusting your approach in the light of unfolding events. Reflection involves the deployment of a particular kind of awareness, one that is able to stand back from the learning fray and notice what is going on. In his book *The Reflective Practitioner*, philosopher Donald Schön distinguished between on-line reflection-*in*-action, and retrospective reflection-*on*-action. Both are useful. While busily playing our "learning instruments," we sometimes become the conductor or coach of our own learning—observing our own thinking and behavior, and think about how we might be able to make use of our minds and resources better.

Some people use the words *metacognition* or *mindfulness* to refer to this capacity. The list below includes some of the varieties of reflection. All of them taken together contribute to an important disposition that Ron Berger, founder of Expeditionary Learning, calls *craftsmanship*: a voluntary commitment to producing the best product or solution of which you are capable, even if it means having to change tack, take more time, ask for some feedback, or go back and redo things that you thought were OK.

- **Evaluating:** Standing back and appraising your progress and the quality of your work. You are able to become your own critic, guided by a real sensitivity to what "quality" would look or feel like. Rarely, in real life, is learning only about getting the right answer. Usually, there is also pride in getting a solution in an ingenious, elegant, or satisfying way. When struggling to express yourself in words or paint or music, you are paying heed to an inner sense of satisfaction or dissatisfaction that guides your efforts and tells you when to persevere or revise and when to stop.

- **Self-Evaluating:** Taking stock of your own strengths and weakness and building an accurate picture of your own "learning character," and how you could improve it. In self-evaluation, it is your own nature that is the focus of attention, not the external project on which you are working. To evaluate yourself, you need to build up a rich vocabulary—such as the one we are exploring here—and also the perceptiveness and honesty to look at yourself in the mirror and describe what you see.

- **Thinkering:** Blending doing and thinking. This is the kind of thinking that emerges while you are in the process of tinkering and experimenting—*thinkering,* as the author Michael Ondaatje called it.[9] For many people in the real world, their best thinking happens in the real-time context of constructive activity—planing a piece of wood, concocting a meal, during their hockey training—not before (planning) or afterward (reviewing). For example, I don't know clearly what I am going to say until I sit down to write; my meaning emerges in a dance between what my fingers are typing and what my eyes are reading.

- **Witnessing:** Observing your own thoughts without judgment. This is the skill that is taught through the practice of mindfulness meditation: being able to observe the stream of your own experience without either jumping in and buying it, or criticizing it and trying to edit or improve it. Witnessing enables you to see your own assumptions and beliefs more clearly, and thus have a fresher and more dispassionate view of the world—that is, a more accurate basis for learning.

## Organization

To be powerful learners, we need to be able to organize, design, and plan our own learning. We need to work out our revision schedules, put our lecture notes into a coherent order, book the rehearsal studio, organize our computer files and folders. We need to be methodical as well as opportunistic and imaginative. We need to think about what we need to learn and how best to resource it and pursue it. Powerful learners are intelligent managers and designers of their learning lives. Here are a few aspects of organization.

- **Learning-Designing:** Putting together your own learning activities. As I said earlier, you are not going to be followed around for the rest of your life by a helpful teacher, telling you what you need to do to make the grade. You will need to figure out for yourself— individually or with others—what you need to learn and how you are going to go about it. Many sports coaches now involve their athletes in helping to design their own training; there's no reason why you couldn't do something similar in your math or English lessons.

- **Planning:** Anticipating the learning journey. All explorers—at least the ones who live to tell the tale—plan their expeditions carefully. Before setting out, they think about what they might need on the way, and make sure they have it. They anticipate how long the journey is likely to take, and manage their time accordingly. They anticipate what kinds of hurdles or difficulties they are likely to meet on the way, and create contingency plans, so, if those pitfalls appear, they will be less "thrown." It should be easy to build the inclination to do the same kind of planning in a classroom.

- **Resourcing:** Creating the environment for learning. Every skilled worker has a toolkit or a well-equipped workshop. All writers have their banks of resources in their studies and on their laptops. Everyone who takes on a challenge benefits from creating a supportive environment, full of useful resources—their smart phone, their list of contacts, their sketchpads. David Perkins says that learning nearly always involves what he calls Person-Plus, not Person-Solo.[10] So we should get our students thinking about how best to kit out their own learning niches.

Put these qualities together (see Figure 6.1), and I think you will agree that you have a profile of a powerful learner—a person who is naturally confident and competent when it comes to dealing with things that are difficult, challenging, and complicated. We have a provisional blueprint for the kind of person who will deal well with life's challenges, surprises, and setbacks. If we could help to develop these strengths in our students, we would have a world of young people who are agile, thoughtful, resilient, and resourceful: people not thrown by uncertainty; not defensive or apathetic; not easily hoodwinked by specious nonsense,

**FIGURE 6.1   The Elements of Learning Power**

**Curiosity:** Having an inquisitive attitude toward life

*Wondering:* Being alive to puzzles and incongruities

*Questioning:* Seeking deeper understanding

*Exploring:* Actively and adventurously investigating

*Experimenting:* Trying things out to see what happens

**Attention:** Locking your mind on to learning

*Noticing:* Being attentive to details and patterns

*Concentrating:* Maintaining focus despite distractions

*Contemplating:* Letting perception unfold

*Immersing:* Being engrossed in learning

**Determination:** Sticking with challenges that matter to you

*Persevering:* Staying intelligently engaged with difficult things

*Recovering:* Bouncing back quickly from frustration or failure

*Practicing:* Mastering the hard parts through repetition

**Imagination:** Creatively exploring possibilities

*Connecting:* Using metaphor and association to leverage new ideas from what you know

*Playing With Ideas:* Allowing the mind to bubble up with possibilities

*Visualizing:* Using mental rehearsal to refine skills and explore consequences

*Intuiting:* Tapping in to bodily based hunches and inklings

**Thinking:** Working things out with clarity and accuracy

*Analyzing:* Reasoning with logic and precision

*Deducing:* Drawing inferences from explanations

*Critiquing:* Questioning the validity of knowledge claims

*Systems Thinking:* Thinking about complex states of affairs

**Socializing:** Benefiting from and contributing to the social world of learning

    *Collaborating:* Being an effective and supportive team member

    *Accepting:* Being open to ideas and feedback

    *Imitating:* Being permeable to other people's good habits

    *Empathizing:* Adopting multiple perspectives

    *Leading:* Playing a role in guiding and developing groups and teams

**Reflection:** Standing back and taking stock of learning

    *Evaluating:* Appraising the quality of your own work

    *Self-Evaluating:* Knowing yourself as a learner

    *Witnessing:* Quietly watching the flow of your own experience

    *Thinkering:* Blending doing and thinking together

**Organization:** Being methodical and systematic about learning

    *Learning-Designing:* Creating your own learning activities

    *Planning:* Anticipating the needs and pitfalls of the learning journey

    *Resourcing:* Building your bank of learning resources

whether political or commercial; but proactive, engaged, critical, and creative. I think that would be a better world. I can't think of a more noble or fulfilling calling than to be such a teacher.

It is extraordinary that it has taken education so long to develop a good vocabulary for talking about effective learning and powerful learners. We have long had rich languages for talking about teaching, curriculum, and assessment but, until recently, only a very impoverished one for describing what is going on at the learners' end. In some countries, like the UK, all we have had were the opaque and problematic notions of "ability"/"intelligence" and "effort"/"motivation," sprinkled, sometimes, with some "study skills" and strategies such as "mind maps" and mnemonics.[11] Now we can talk with greater confidence about the capabilities and inclinations that underpin powerful learning; we can specify more clearly what the desirable residues of those 13 years of schooling ought to be—in addition to literacy, numeracy, general knowledge, and a clutch of certificates.

The framework I have outlined provides such a specification. But it is already quite complicated, so remember the "starter kit" that we looked at in Chapter 4. Feel free to start working with just a few of these muscles, and then gradually build up the complexity when your students, and you, are ready for it. We have found that sharing this vocabulary with students is very empowering, provided they really understand and feel the import of the concepts. (It is no use them just learning to parrot back some dry definitions.) But it is overwhelming to be presented with the whole framework all at once. So use your own judgment about which ideas you would like to introduce first, and which can be revealed later on, or only with older students.

## Wondering

Think about the framework I have offered you in this chapter. Compare it with your own conception of what it means to be a powerful learner. Which bits of my framework do you find the most plausible, and which bits the least?

Consider the two ideas of being a "powerful learner" and being a "successful student." Can you think of a young person you know who is a successful student—who is well-behaved, is liked by her teachers, and gets good marks—but is not a very powerful learner—who is dependent, conservative, and anxious, say? Alternatively, do you know anyone who is a powerful learner (adventurous, inquisitive, and determined in some areas of life), but is not a very successful student?

# Notes

1.  Andrew Postman, "My Dad Predicted Trump in 1985," p. 17. Andrew's father was Professor Neil Postman, author of *Amusing Ourselves to Death* and many other works of social criticism.
2.  See Angela Duckworth, *Grit: The Power of Passion and Perseverance*.
3.  See Carol Dweck, *Mindset*.
4.  See Daniel Goleman, *Focus*.
5.  See Guy Claxton, *Intelligence in the Flesh*.
6.  Alfred Binet, *Modern Ideas About Children*, pp. 105–106.
7.  Here especially the LPA owes a great deal to approaches to early childhood education such as that of Reggio Emelia. See Carolyn Edwards and Lella Gandini, *The Hundred Languages of Children*.
8.  Neil Mercer, *Words and Minds: How We Use Language to Think Together*.
9.  Ondaatje coined the term *thinkering* in his novel *The English Patient*.
10. See David Perkins, "Person-Plus."
11. The recent book by Ken Richardson, *Genes, Brains and Human Potential*, is a brilliant account of just how problematic the common conception of intelligence is.

# 7

# Learning Power in Action

## Some Classroom Illustrations

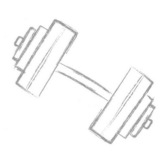

After all that conceptualization, it is time to get back into the classroom and take a more detailed look at the Learning Power Approach (LPA) in action. I'll describe a series of lessons and draw out their "learning-power-ness," so you can deepen your sense of how the approach works and the difference that it can make.

The first example comes from Becky Carlzon's mixed Year 1/Year 2 class at Christ Church Infants School in Bristol, England. Becky writes a blog at www.learningpowerkids.com, and this is one of her recent posts about encouraging her children to become better editors of their own writing. On January 7, 2017, Becky wrote,

I love the start of the new year, after the Christmas break. I always feel like this is the time to introduce new ideas because the children seem more settled, ready, and open. So this week we have taught the children how to reflect on and edit their own and each other's writing. The children already have a basis of understanding that (a) mistakes are good opportunities to learn, and (b) it is good to try to improve your learning. On our Superpower Learners wall, one child came up with, "Superpower learners say, 'I wonder how I can make this even better,'" which we referred to while teaching the children about editing.

We started by talking to the children about peer marking. To explain how (and very importantly, why) they might peer mark, we used one child's writing as a model, showing the children how to spot really good things about their friends' writing and things their friends might want to improve. In our school, we use green pens to notice good writing (green to be seen) and pink to improve mistakes (pink to think), so the children were told they would have their own green and pink pens to mark their friends' writing. We discussed as a class how you might give feedback positively and sensitively (therefore developing social skills and empathy). To do that, I gave a bad example ("Haha! I can't believe you made that mistake! That's rubbish!") and got the children to give me a more positive one. Finn suggested, "Maddie, I don't know if you noticed, but you forgot a period there." We talked about how those two different versions would make your partner feel.

Before the children went off to mark their friends' writing, we spent some time thinking with the children about how to choose their feedback partners. As we always do, we emphasized choosing a partner who wasn't a close friend, but someone who they thought would give positive feedback. The emphasis, as always, was on choosing someone new (and after three months of encouraging this, the children are getting very relaxed and good at it). Apart from developing collaboration skills, the purpose of this is to give children the opportunity to think about what helps them learn best. Because of having made this decision themselves, they were totally absorbed in the process of marking their friends' writing.

The children organized themselves to take turns and carefully notice the positives and areas of improvement in each other's writing. Some children were in threes and organized themselves by putting the "hot seater" in the middle, who read out their piece of writing; a "noticer" with a green pen, noticing good writing on one side; and an "improver" with a pink pen on the other side, spotting mistakes. The children were totally on board and very perceptive. They noticed mistakes a tired teacher marking 30 books at the end of the day would never have spotted. For example, one girl got really fussy about how her partner wasn't writing on the line well enough and gave him a next step to make sure he wrote on the line. We had just learned how to spell "ed" words, so one child noticed his partner had spelt a few "ed" words incorrectly, and so needed that as a next step.

The children whose writing was being marked had "purple polishing pens" to use to correct their mistakes. (The idea, of course, is to raise the profile of learning from and improving your writing.) All of the marking was meaningful to the children because it had come from a peer. I know this partly because, when given the chance to practice something they wanted to improve in their writing that afternoon, many children chose to practice the exact thing their friends had picked up on.

Seeing the children mark each other's writing was one of the most exciting lessons of the year for both me and my teaching assistant. I am excited to continue to find ways to develop the children's skills at choosing good editing partners and feeding back effectively and positively. Most important, I want to see if peer marking translates into a greater willingness, and perceptiveness, when it comes to the children editing their own work. I'm hoping this strategy of starting with peer critique will develops the children's reflectiveness, feedback skills, and willingness—in fact enthusiasm—to learn from their mistakes: triple learning power! I am now going to think about how to develop the same depth of reflection and feedback in math.

*Source:* By kind permission of Becky Carlzon

Becky's description of this lesson speaks for itself. Many elements of the LPA are evident: her intention to help the children become more independent, her ingenuity at devising activities that stretch several different learning muscles at the same time (in this case reflection, noticing, collaboration, and giving and taking feedback), her constant willingness to involve the children (even five-year-olds) in thinking about learning and designing their own learning activities, her use of displays to capture and reinforce learning messages, and her relentless desire to look for the next step. "OK, that went well in English; now, how could I extend that capacity into other areas, for example, mathematics?"

---

The next example is from a fifth-grade mathematics workshop at Anser Charter School in Boise, Idaho. Anser is an EL Education school; *EL* previously stood for Expeditionary Learning. The spirit of the school is well captured in the way it presents itself on its website (www.ansercharterschool.org). It talks of "challenging students to meet rigorous academic and character standards" and of helping them "learn to take responsibility for achieving their personal best," while also "developing perseverance and self-discipline." The school describes its methodology as "harnessing the power of adventure and discovery."

> At Anser, Giselle Isbell teaches math to fifth graders. Giselle is using one of the key EL lesson formats called "Workshop 2.0." (You can watch this lesson on the DVD that accompanies the excellent book about EL Education, *Learning That Lasts* by Ron Berger and his colleagues.) Today's topic is dividing decimals by whole numbers. The workshop begins with students working independently on a "grapple problem" designed by Giselle to build on what they already know, but to stretch that

understanding in a new way. Today's grapple problem involves dividing a 2.58-acre garden into six plots of equal area, so the gardener can grow six different crops. For five minutes, students work individually, trying different ways to extrapolate from their existing understanding of division (working with whole numbers), for example, to make sure that they get the decimal point in the right place. This "makes their brains hurt," but one of the students, Raven, explains why it is a good idea to start with this struggle. "I think it is good to try something before you get taught," she says, "because there are pieces of the math problem that you kind of have to piece together, and if you just learn how to do that just one way, you can't piece them all together, and [through grappling] you understand the problem better." Giselle circulates asking questions and, where a student is stuck, offering a general clue or a hint about what the student might try.

After five minutes, Giselle asks if they are ready to Pair-Share, and the students buddy up to explain what they have been doing and what worked and what didn't during the grapple time. After a few minutes, the whole table of five or six students compare notes. As they talk, they refer to the "anchor chart" the whole class has made earlier, posted on the classroom wall, that has helpful prompts to guide productive discussion: sentence starters like "How did you . . . ?," "Have you tried . . . ?, "Could you explain . . . ?," "I see a connection between . . ." and "Now I'm wondering. . . ." Again Giselle moves around, eavesdropping on these conversations to get a feel for what insights, ideas, strategies, and misunderstandings her students are coming up with. Another student, Kaelyn, explains the value of this conversation. "I think it's important to work as a group [after you have struggled on your own] because even if another person got it wrong they might give you a hint, and then you're like, 'Oh, I see how to do this now,' and then you can help them."

Following the group discussion, the workshop moves into its third phase, the focus, where Giselle offers some explicit guidance to the whole class based on what she has been hearing. She emphasizes the central objective of the lesson and introduces the idea that there are a range of strategies for solving the problem but that some of them may well be more powerful, economical, or elegant than others. Raven suggests that "kids don't mind if they get the grapple problem wrong because [as a result of grappling] you learn more when Giselle explains it and you really get the hang of it, and become able to figure it out for yourself." Giselle gives the class a range of further problems to solve, challenging them to see if they can find more efficient strategies, and students move into the application phase of the workshop, dispersing to work either individually or in small groups. Finally, the workshop concludes with a review in which the students reflect on how successful they have been in grasping and applying the main point, and also on the effectiveness of their own learning processes and strategies. They offer their thoughts about the structure of the workshop, making suggestions for possible improvements, and they look forward to where this topic might be heading, and what the next step in difficulty might be.

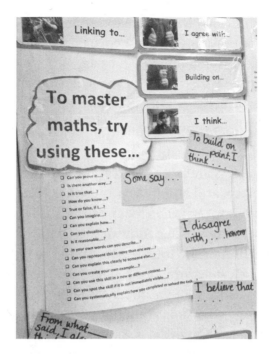

Examples of Anchor Charts for Students to Refer to as They Talk

This is a lesson that aims to do two things: to enhance students' mathematical competence, and to stretch their learning muscles. If we were to check the muscles off against the framework on pages 122–123, we would see a pretty good all-around mental workout going on. There is *questioning, exploring,* and *experimenting.* The students are *noticing* and *concentrating.* They are certainly practicing *persevering* and *recovering.* They are *connecting* what they already know to the current challenge and playing with ideas. They are clearly *analyzing* and *deducing.* They are *collaborating*: They are *accepting* feedback and ideas from each other as well as some nudges from the teacher when they need them, and they are sharing their strategies and discoveries in a way that enables and encourages *imitating.* They are *evaluating* their own success, and they show impressive levels of *self-evaluation* for 11-year-olds. This is not just good teaching. It is teaching that is deliberately targeted, in a very sophisticated way, at the development of transferable learning dispositions. It is not just engaging; it is designed to stretch specific learning muscles in exactly the same way that a good sports coach would consciously design a training session to develop particular strengths and skills.

Note that this teaching style is neither stereotypically progressive nor traditional. It is both. It is progressive in the sense that students are taking a great deal of responsibility for their learning, and also in that there is much less "teaching" than normal. The focus part of the lesson—the only part where the teacher addresses the whole class—takes up only a fraction of the total lesson time. The rest involves students doing the learning for themselves, both individually and in groups. Only when a student is failing to grapple productively with the subject matter does Giselle intervene, and even then, her intention is to do as little prompting as is necessary to get that productive grappling going again.

But the lesson is also traditional in the sense that there are clear goals, a purposeful curriculum, and no lack of either rigor or respect for demanding content. There is no question of throwing out the mathematics in order to do something nebulous called "developing thinking skills." On the contrary, this lesson achieves a deeper and more flexible understanding of mathematics: one that will stand students in better stead as they go on to university and out into the world, and will also help them get the grades they need to get to college or university. The dual concerns with mastering content and developing process are woven together (as warp and weft) through the way the lesson is structured and the way the teacher behaves.

Let's look at the template that Giselle is using in more detail, and focus in on the kinds of skills that she needs as a teacher to teach this way. First, she has to create a good grapple problem: one that is relevant to the topic of the lesson, but that is carefully designed to be just beyond the students' current level of competence. Too easy or too hard, and nothing new will be learned. To do this she has to look and listen carefully to the class, to know where their current limits are.

The lesson begins with students wrestling on their own with the grapple problem. They are thrown into the deep end, so to speak, but they don't mind because they are used to it. They have gradually been coached to experience challenge as productive rather than as an anxiety-provoking invitation to fail. For many classes, that might take time, care, and a willingness on the teacher's part to keep explaining why she is stretching their ability to learn this way.

Then students talk about their strategies, and share what worked and what didn't. There is a lot of process talk like this in an LPA classroom. To increase the productivity and the focus of these discussions, Giselle has, in a previous lesson, gotten the students to brainstorm a variety of sentence frames that they have graphically represented on what she refers to as the anchor chart, and she deliberately reminds them to refer to the chart as they are talking. Again we see the mind coach at work, deliberately creating and offering training devices that scaffold the development of the learning strengths that the school values (in this case collaboration).

Giselle circulates during this period, eavesdropping on students' conversations, and only then, in the light of what she hears, is she formulating the "teaching" part of the lesson, the focus. Here she clarifies the main learning intention of the lesson, and tees the students up for the application phase, where they work on a series of problems with the intention of discovering for themselves strategies that have wider ranges of efficiency and elegance. Most groups work productively on their own, freeing her up to spend time with students who need more help. But even then she resists the temptation to do too much telling, preferring to offer questions and hints that enable them to experience, as much as possible, the pleasure and satisfaction of figuring things out for themselves.

The lesson ends with a good length of time for synthesis and review. Students reflect on the extent to which they have achieved the mathematical learning target, but they also discuss the learning strategies that they have found to be productive. Giselle invites their comments on the lesson structure—"Was that a good grapple problem?" she asks—and also gives them opportunities to offer suggestions for improvement about timings, groupings, and the focus content. By doing this, she is not only modeling being a good learner herself—always looking for ways to fine-tune her own teaching—but also inviting the students to become more conscious and critical consumers of their own education. Inviting them to critique the lesson lays the groundwork for them to be able to design learning for themselves.

———————

My third example comes from the work of British educator James Nottingham. James is perhaps best known for his concept of the "learning challenge" (see Figure 7.1). Trained in a teaching approach called Philosophy for Children originally developed by U.S. educator Matthew Lipman, James has created a lesson format designed to get students—even quite young ones—into a state of cognitive confusion about some concept, and then to learn to rescue themselves from the discomfort of being in the "learning pit" by figuring their own way out of the confusion.[1]

> In this example, he poses to a class of primary children the question, "What is 'real'?" He puts a "real" apple and a plastic apple on the table and invites the students to consider whether the three apples are equally "real." First they protest that there are only two apples, but James says no—there is an imaginary one as well, which he can see perfectly well in his mind's eye. He pretends to pick it up, inspect it carefully, and describe its color and shape.

FIGURE 7.1  The Learning Challenge

The Main Steps in the Learning Challenge

**Concept**
Find a concept worth exploring that you know a little bit about.

**Question**
Find the problems, the nuances, and the exceptions to your concept. You can do this by comparing your concept with another, considering if it always applies, or trying to find a definition that works in all cases.

**Cognitive Conflict**
If you've uncovered lots of examples and exceptions to your concept, and realized how complex your chosen concept is, then you are in the pit! This is where deep learning really gets going.

**Construct**
Identify patterns, relationships, and meanings between all the ideas you've uncovered. Distinguish between them by sorting, classifying, grouping or ranking. Use your findings to create a more precise understanding of your concept.

**Eureka!**
Eureka, you found it! The feeling of enlightenment and discovery you feel at this stage is the ecstasy of learning. This is what makes the learning journey so worthwhile. Congratulations for persevering!

**Consider**
Look back at your learning journey. Which strategies worked best? What would you change next time? How can you apply your new understanding to different contexts?

Easy Learning / Deep Learning

The Pit

Adapt / Apply / Transfer / Review

Challenging LEARNING

*Source:* Nottingham (2017). Reprinted with permission.

James continues to act like a latter-day Socrates, raising awkward questions that make the students challenge their own thinking. "Are you saying that things are only real if you can see them? I can't see my dog at the moment; does that mean he isn't real? What about atoms or the Great Wall of China: I've never seen them, so are they not real?" A student says, "But you have seen photos or diagrams of them," to which James says, "The pictures might have been photoshopped. The model of the atom might be wrong. Lots of things that don't exist can be made to look real online. Lots of scientific ideas have been disproved. . . ." And so on. "Is the plastic apple real? If you think not, then what about this plastic chair: Is that not real?" "If you dreamed an apple, would it be real?"

"Are toys real?" He might use stories such as Margery Williams's delightful tale of *The Velveteen Rabbit: Or How Toys Become Real*. (You may remember that the Velveteen Rabbit asks his friend the Skin Horse to explain to him what is real. "Real isn't how you are made," the Skin Horse replies. "It's a thing that happens to you. When a child loves you for a long, long time, not just to play with, but REALLY loves you, then you become Real." He goes on, "Generally, by the time you are Real, most of your hair has been loved off, and your eyes drop out and you get loose in the joints and very shabby. But these things don't matter at all, because once you become Real you can't be ugly, except to people who don't understand.")[2]

Once the students are thoroughly confused, they are in the learning pit. Confusion is a condition that people are generally keen to escape from, so students are motivated to think and discuss more deeply, in order to resolve the conflict. They challenge each other, come up with their own test cases, discover patterns and make links, refine their conceptualizations, and identify similarities and differences between different test cases. So now James stands back and lets the conversation develop, intervening only to keep students on track and prevent them sliding off into too many unproductive deviations. He might offer them a visual tool (such as a Venn diagram) for organizing their developing thoughts, but he doesn't rescue them or hint at any right answers. Usually students make good progress at refining their thoughts about "reality" and making more subtle distinctions with which they can be (provisionally) happy.

The lesson ends—as did Giselle Isbell's—with a good few minutes to review the learning journey of the lesson. What have they learned? What strategies did they use? Which proved useful, or unhelpful? How might they pursue the inquiry further? Who else might have pondered the nature of reality, and what resources might they be able to find? How could the challenge have been improved?

Notice again what is being asked of teachers who want to teach this way. They have to be willing to both go with the flow of the suggestions and ideas the students come up with, and at the same time be able to steer the discussion in a productive direction. This is more subtle, but no less purposeful, than a "stand and deliver" approach that revolves centrally around the direct transmission of a predetermined body of knowledge that is to be understood and accepted. The latter is good for some purposes: nothing wrong with it in principle. But it is not so good for the development of learning strengths such as thinking, disciplined argumentation, or reflection. Again, which method is better depends on the valued outcomes. If you want to produce children who are accurate and uncritical knowers, then "stand and deliver" is good. If you want to produce children who are critical, creative, and curious thinkers, then James Nottingham's way is better.

My next example comes from a school in Australia that has been experimenting with the Building Learning Power (BLP) framework. It is one of a small group of schools forming a research project that I ran in collaboration with Independent Schools Victoria from 2013 to 2016.

Prue teaches German at St. Leonard's College in Brighton, a seaside suburb of Melbourne. She is frustrated that her Year 10 students do not seem to be progressing as well as they should. One of the reasons, Prue has noticed, is that they seem to pay little attention to the corrections she makes to their written work. They attend to the mark, but not to the information she provides to help them improve. So she wonders how she could get them to take her feedback on board. In fact she wonders out loud, at the beginning of a lesson. "What do I need to do to help you learn German?" And then she switches the question to, "What do *you* need to do?" She explains that she will push as well as she can from her side, but that the students will need to pull from their side as well.

She gives them each a notebook that she wants to be their learning books. She explains that she is not going to correct everything from now on, but is going to use a range of codes that indicate the general kind of mistake she has spotted. It will then be up to the students to figure out exactly where the mistake is and what it is, and to note down both the mistake and the correction in their notebooks. She explains her thinking behind this shift, hoping that this will make them more active and thoughtful, and, as she puts it, will make them "try to stretch their noticing and self-evaluating muscles." Then she writes an example on the board:

"Er möchtet eine Jeansjake kauft."

There are three different kinds of mistakes, to which she gives the codes *SV, SP,* and *V.* Prue asks the students to work in pairs to find the mistakes, and try to decipher the codes. Eventually they produce the correct sentence:

"Er mochte eine Jeansjacke kaufen."

And they also figure out what the codes mean. Prue suggests that they would write in their notebooks something like:

SV: Er möchtet → Er mochte

When Prue asks for questions and reactions, the students seem interested and engaged. One comments, "But if you write the wrong version down in your notebook alongside the correct version, that might serve to stamp the wrong one in your brain as well as the right one, and you'll get confused." Prue encourages the class to consider this objection to her proposal, and after some discussion they agree to start using her method, but to keep it under review. Finally she gives them back the homework she has marked with her new codes and gets them to work in pairs to find and repair their mistakes.

At the end of the lesson, Prue asks for feedback, and then challenges the students to see if they could (over the next few lessons) refine or develop her initial way of categorizing their mistakes. She also asks if they think this kind of training could be useful in other subjects.

Notice that, with these older students, it is possible for the teacher to be very open about what her goals and frustrations are, and why she is altering the classroom procedure in the way she does. But she is also ready to involve them as intelligent critics, co-constructors, and monitors of their own experience. She is genuinely interested in their thoughts and reactions, and willing to modify her ideas along the way. She is also inviting them to stretch their ability to think about deeper or more creative ways in which they could develop her proposed strategy. And she asks them to see if they can imagine useful ways of applying the same principle in other contexts and subjects. She is training them to be more self-aware, self-diagnosing, and capable of their own learning design. And she is also turbo-charging their learning of German.

The final example comes from another school in Melbourne, Bialik College, which has been working not with the BLP framework but with David Perkins and Ron Ritchhart's ideas of Visible Thinking.[3] In Visible Thinking, students use a variety of Thinking Routines to stimulate and stretch different learning strengths. Each Thinking Routine is a way of framing the way that students are to bring their minds to bear on the subject matter of a lesson.

> Nicky Dorevitch teaches a creative writing course, and today her fifth graders are exploring the topic of poverty. She was concerned that they were not really delving into the subject, and were just spouting clichés such as "make poverty history," so she decided to use a Visible Thinking Routine called the Circle of Viewpoints to encourage them to go deeper, and hopefully to find a more individual voice for their writing. In Circle of Viewpoints, students are asked to respond to a complex stimulus by stepping inside the perspectives of a range of different characters in the stimulus. Nicky's stimulus was a photo of a large Mongolian family crammed into a battered old car. The car looks as if it is on its last legs, and what could well be the entire contents of their house is strapped precariously to the roof. The car sits in a barren landscape completely devoid of buildings or vegetation, except for a few tufts of grass. Clearly the family is in considerable hardship, though their faces show little obvious emotion.
>
> The students take time to look carefully at the photo, noticing every little detail, and then identify the different perspectives there might be: those of different family members, the car itself, the dark threatening sky, and so on. Each student then chooses one perspective to adopt, and they start to write notes in answer to a series of questions such as:
>
> • What do these persons or things observe from their perspectives?
> • What do they know or believe?

- What do they care deeply about?
- What are they wondering or questioning?
- What are they feeling?
- What do they want to do?

Having immersed themselves in their chosen perspectives, the students start to write. One student, who had chosen the mother's perspective, wrote,

> Oh, my husband is so good, trying to keep the kids so calm when all of us are scared. With not even butterflies in our stomachs, they are more like leeches. I hope we have enough fuel to make it to the next village before nightfall, so we can find food. I have a whole family to feed and I can't bear to see them suffer. If any of us has to go hungry it won't be the children. . . . Oh no: The enemy is catching us up; I must engage the children in something so they don't look back. I see my husband's face as he bashes down the accelerator and now I know it's bad.

This "split screen" lesson is seeking to develop students' creative writing ability, but it is doing so by inviting them to stretch a variety of learning capacities. They are learning to take their time and look carefully. They are experiencing the delicate interplay of attention and imagination. They are stretching their empathy muscles by trying to adopt a range of different perspectives—even those of inanimate objects. In short, they are learning the mental attitudes and strengths that underlie the work of real novelists and poets.

They could go on to explore the reflective and autobiographical writings of writers, to go deeper into the intricate workings of the creative mind. Nicky could, for example, give her students a *Harvard Educational Review* paper by American poet Anne McCrary Sullivan called "Notes From a Marine Biologist's Daughter: On the Art and Science of Attention" to study. In the article, Sullivan develops the idea of "aesthetic vision." Here is how she describes it.

> Aesthetic vision engages a sensitivity to suggestion, to pattern, to that which is beneath the surface, as well as to the surface itself. It requires a fine attention to detail and form: the perception of relations (tensions and harmonies); the perception of nuance (colors of meaning); and the perception of change (shifts and subtle motions). Aesthetic vision . . . may seize a moment in order to stare at it and see more fully, more deeply.[4]

A group of bright 11-year-olds might—if their teacher judges them rightly—be ready to explore their own capacities for attention in this way. And as they do so, they are not just learning *about* things; they are learning to *do* subtle and important things too.

---

These four examples should, I hope, have given you a more detailed idea about how the LPA comes alive in a variety of different classrooms. Critically, teachers are not just dressing up their material in an attempt to create greater engagement. They are all, in a variety of different ways, training learning attitudes and capabilities that will be of real use beyond the confines of formal education—and getting better grades at the same time.

## Wondering

What reflections on your own teaching are prompted by these examples? Do they help you see possibilities for deepening learning in your classrooms that you might not have been aware of at the time?

Whatever age or subject you teach, are there any ideas that you think you could take away and try out?

Take one of those examples, and imagine what the teaching trajectory might have been that got students ready and able to make good use of these opportunities they are being given. If you were that teacher, where do you think you might go next? What is a good next stretch that the students might be ready for?

Refer back to Figure 6.1, the summary table of the learning powers (pages 122–123). Then consider each of the vignettes in this chapter, and see in detail which learning muscles are being engaged and which are not. (I have given you some examples in the text of this chapter, but there are many more that you could discover.)

Look carefully at these examples, and see if you can extract whether there is a template or a set of design principles that the teacher is using. (I have done most of this for Giselle's lesson in my commentary, so try one or two of the others.) Imagine how this template might be used with children of a different age, or in a different subject. What are the limits of the template: Where do you think it would not be applicable (or appropriate)?

# Notes

1. James Nottingham, *The Learning Challenge*.
2. Margery Williams, *The Velveteen Rabbit: Or How Toys Become Real*.
3. Adapted slightly from Ron Ritchhart, Mark Church, and Karin Morrison, *Making Thinking Visible*.
4. Anne McCrary Sullivan, *Notes From a Marine Biologist's Daughter*.

# Design Principles of the LPA Classroom

The medium is the message.

Marshall McLuhan

Having had a look at a few detailed examples of the Learning Power Approach (LPA) in action, let's stand back again and get a more general idea of what these teachers are up to. In this chapter I am going to draw out some of the design principles that underpin what goes on in an LPA classroom. We have found that teachers are hungry for "worked examples" of what LPA looks like in practice, such as those in the previous chapter. But it doesn't work simply to try to replicate them in a different school with different kids. As 11-year-old Raven said in the last chapter, if you learn just one way of doing something, you lose flexibility and creativity, and you are likely to give up if your one way isn't working. In fact LPA teachers often say that they think they have cracked it with one class, only to discover that next year's class behaves quite differently, and they have to go back to first principles. So understanding what those principles are helps all teachers to customize their teaching in a way that keeps the spirit of the LPA fresh and appropriate.

Remember in Chapter 2 I suggested the metaphor of the classroom being like a river, with learning of different kinds going on simultaneously at different depths. Quick and visible on the surface is the content: the subjects and topics that students are learning about. Below the surface are the kinds of expertise that enable students to access that content and make good use of it; students are learning what it is like to think like a mathematician, a historian, a scientist, or a writer. But deeper down, less easy to notice and track but just as important, more general attitudes toward learning itself—the elements of learning power—are slowly being formed.

These different layers of learning respond best to different kinds of teaching. If you just want retention of the content, then old-fashioned chalk-and-talk, provided it is engagingly presented, clearly explained, appropriately pitched, and regularly checked, will do nicely. That will enable students to do reasonably well in traditional examinations. If you want more fluent expertise, however, then your students will need a more varied diet of problem-solving, so they can understand the content more deeply and begin to master the rules of the game in the different knowledge disciplines. (The conventions that determine what counts as "good writing" are very different in chemistry, history, and psychology, for example. I remember the first undergraduate psychology essay I wrote being dismissed by my tutor as being in entirely the wrong voice. "Perhaps when the *Radio Times* [a UK weekly radio and TV listings magazine] starts publishing psychology, Claxton, you might have found your audience," he said, witheringly.) To grow these different literacies, the teacher needs to allow more discussion and experimentation. "Just one way" doesn't cut it.

But if you want to grow the habits and attitudes of powerful learning more generally, then you need to think about the whole environment you, the teacher, are creating in the classroom. These strengths (or weaknesses) are not so much taught, or even directly trained, as cultivated. In biology, a *culture* is a nutrient medium that is conducive to the growth of a plant or an organism. (You may remember growing bacteria in biology lessons at school in a shallow Petri dish of a nutrient medium called agar jelly.) The whole classroom has to be configured as a culture that invites and supports the development of independence, resilience, collaboration, imagination, and so on.

So the way you talk matters. How long you talk for matters. (Remember Giselle making herself keep the focus part of the lesson short.) How you comment on students' successes and failures (both informally and in written marking) matters. What you notice and appreciate, or ignore or censure, matters. The way you design activities matters. What you pin up on the walls matters. Your attitude toward the use of erasers matters. How you arrange the furniture matters. How you organize group work (or let the students organize it for themselves) matters. Whether you invite feedback from your students about their experience of your lesson (or not) matters. How you set the scene at the beginning of the school year matters very much.

So when you start paying conscious attention to the cultivation of learning strengths, down at the lower levels of classroom learning, you become not so much a teacher as a *learning designer* and a *learning coach*. Coaches are people who have been lent some power by other people, happy to adopt the role of learners, who want help achieving their goals. The learners let the coach boss them about a bit, because they have faith that, by doing so, they will be helped to advance those long-term interests. Your coaches work with you to design a regime that will get you where you said you wanted to go—the Olympics, the playhouse, the university, the world-class school, the Little League team, the apprenticeship, whatever. Their experience and knowledge enable them, so you hope, to construct a better regime than you could have constructed by yourself. They work with you to design potent activities that will stretch and strengthen the capabilities you want to acquire. They push you when you are tired or confused—because you asked them to and gave them permission. They help set targets so you can keep achieving personal bests—in swimming, in mathematics, in maintaining concentration, in collaborating with people who are not your friends. They celebrate your progress and encourage you when you are down. They create a feeling of camaraderie among the squad (the class), so learners are generous with their own knowledge and expertise and supportive of each other's journeys.

> A coach is someone who tells you what you don't want to hear, and has you see what you don't want to see, so you can be who you have always known you can be.
>
> Tom Landry, U.S. football coach

> Probably my best quality as a coach is to ask a lot of challenging questions, and let the person come up with the answers.
>
> Phil Dixon, British Olympic mountain bike coach

With these thoughts in mind, let me suggest some of those design principles for building up a learning-powered classroom.

# 1. Create a Feeling of Safety

Learning is demanding. It makes you think. It requires attention. You have to try things out you don't know you can do well yet. To learn is to be vulnerable: to run the risk of being—and being seen to be—ignorant or incompetent or just plain wrong. In order to be curious, inquisitive, and take risks, children need to feel a sense of well-being and security at school. If they are tired, hungry, anxious, preoccupied, or frightened of their classmates or their teacher, those needs and feelings compete with and often suppress learning. So making the classroom a safe place for students to be learners isn't a matter of being soft; it is just good educational sense. To have a roomful of adventurous spirits, teachers need to understand this vulnerability and do their best to respect it. Teachers need to retain their ability to empathize with young people who are finding learning hard. We don't protect students from difficulty; we show them a warm and encouraging respect for engaging with it.

Faced with something strange or tricky, toddlers take their cue from their mothers. If they see from her expression or hear in her tone that she is warm, relaxed, and encouraging, they are more adventurous and inquisitive. If she looks or sounds anxious or disapproving, they are more likely to shrink back. (Child development experts call this *social referencing*.) Gradually children learn to be more judicious and resilient for themselves, but very few of us entirely grow out of the fear of looking a fool in front of a potentially hostile audience.

Teachers set the tone in their classrooms. Students quickly pick up on "what goes around here," and what doesn't. So to make the classroom a safe place to be a learner—as we saw earlier in the example of the no-put-down zone—it is our job to ensure that students never jeer at each other for making mistakes or venturing half-baked opinions. We have to be vigilant and reliable wardens, making it very clear that dissing other students for being learners is unacceptable. Again, this isn't about being nice or soft. If you want all the students in the room to commit their intelligence to tricky matters, it is smart to make it safe to try to risk.

At the same time, the LPA teachers' basic craft of the classroom enables them to create a calm, orderly atmosphere and consistently convey a clear set of expectations about behavior. Children—especially those whose own learning power is not yet well developed— cannot learn in a chaotic or constantly disrupted environment. After more experience of the LPA, they will be better at maintaining concentration despite some disturbances, for example, and more inclined, both individually and as a class, not to leave it to the teacher but to take responsibility for creating good learning conditions. But earlier on, they will benefit from a more orderly atmosphere being maintained by the teacher. As students build up stronger learning habits, they become able to handle more responsibility and benefit from a looser, more collaborative and conversational culture. Good discipline is not, in the LPA, an end in itself. We don't think it is a good thing *per se* to see children sitting quietly in rows. Order is just the launchpad for more diverse and imaginative forms of classroom organization.

## 2. Distinguish Between Learning Mode and Performance Mode

Students—like all of us—behave very differently depending on whether they are in learning mode or performance mode.[1] When we are performing, we want to look our best, to impress, to get the best marks, to win the match. We rein in our creativity a little. We are less adventurous. We privilege competence over experimentation. We don't try out, on stage on the opening night, the kinds of odd-ball interpretations that we explored in rehearsals. We don't make the same jokes in a high-stakes job interview that we would venture in the pub. But if we are confused, or if the director, the coach, or the teacher is a sarcastic perfectionist, we might quickly learn to treat every rehearsal, every training session, every lesson, as if it were a performance, and try to look good and get it right rather than explore, question, and tinker. If performance mode becomes our locked-in style, our learning power is diminished. Both modes are necessary, and it is very useful to be able to switch between them.

In England, children take high-stakes examinations at the end of Year 6 (Grade 5). They are called the Key Stage 2 SATs. Some teachers, keen that their students get the best possible marks, treat the whole year as if it were about performance. They let performance mode become the default. They and their students become stressed and anxious. Learning becomes focused on rapid correctness rather than imaginative thinking and discussing. But not in Sarah Jackson's Year 6 class at Christ Church Primary School in Wiltshire. Learning mode is alive and well most of the time. But every so often, to get them ready for the exam, Sarah gives the children a test and tells them to "put their Test Face on." They have to sit separately, not talk to each other, look earnest and effortful, and do their best. And then, at the end of the test, they relax and talk to each other again about what Test Face feels like, and whether they think it helped or hindered their actual performance. When the big day arrives, the children are used to adopting performance mode—they have rehearsed it—and are less wound up. After the exam they talk to each other not nervously about the answer to Question 5, but about how interesting or challenging the questions were. They bounce back immediately into learning mode. They are, actually, accomplished question setters. During the year, they have looked at and discussed past examination papers, and had fun writing harder questions for each other. By the way, their actual marks on the test have improved year on year under this kind of teaching.

Ironically, performance mode often has a negative effect on performance (if students haven't learned to see it as a "mode"). A classic study by Cheryl Flink and colleagues at the University of Colorado compared the test performance of two groups of fourth-grade students, one who had been taught by teachers who had been told that their job was to "facilitate the children's learning," and the other by teachers who were told, "Your job is to ensure the children perform well." The latter group felt more pressurized, used more controlling classroom strategies, and gave their children less choice or responsibility for their learning than did the first group. Not surprisingly, children in the second group did significantly less well on the tests.[2]

Conversely, Jane Leo at St. Mary's Primary School in the west of England tried an experiment with her Year 6 students after they had done their Key Stage 2 SATs tests. She gave them the Key Stage 3 SATs math paper, designed for 14-year-olds with three more years' schooling behind them. She said it was for "a bit of fun" and told the children that, though they had not studied many of the topics, "by applying your thinking and using what you already know, you ought to be able to have a go at much of the paper." When she marked their papers, she found that every student in the class showed a "magical" improvement in their performance, all but five achieving at the level expected for the 14-year-olds. In learning mode, they were able to bring their learning power to bear on things that they "oughtn't to be able to do." Jane wrote to me:

> I believe that their willingness to have a go stemmed from a year's worth of teaching them how to learn and knowing themselves as learners. Through Building Learning Power they now know how to tackle a challenge; what questions to ask themselves; how to apply what they know to new situations; how to be flexible in their thinking, not always taking the expected route and being comfortable with that; knowing when to move on to something new and let their brains reflect on a problem while working on something else.

With older students especially, it is important for the teacher/mind coach to clarify the nature of the contract that both parties are signing up to. The coach needs to be open with her students about what she is trying to help them become, and why, so they understand why it is in their own best interests to turn up and try hard, and cede that power willingly. Not everyone in the room may buy in immediately. You may have to keep at it. And a few may never come on board—but it is a false economy not to do your best to get that buy-in. With what sociologists call the widespread "decline of deference," today's students, even quite young ones, respond well to being treated as intelligent consumers of education, entitled to know why they are being asked to engage with what the teacher is offering. Just to say "because I say so," "because it is on the curriculum," or even "don't be cheeky" isn't very smart. (Many teachers skip this stage and are disappointed when they meet resistance from young people who may not have a clue why they are made to attend school.)

# 3. Organize Compelling Things to Learn

Unless a learning invitation grabs the learner's attention, any learning that takes place is likely to be superficial and feel like hard work. When learners are engaged, their attention and motivation are focused on the matter at hand, and learning proceeds more deeply and more agreeably. Engaged learners bring their learning power and their learning stamina to the party, and the more fully engaged they are, the better the learning. As I said earlier, engagement is not an end in itself; it is the precondition for learning. "OK, you've got my attention. . . . Now what?" Once learners are engaged, then more interesting things can happen. They can be stretched and challenged in a variety of ways, and they will rise to the challenge. If learners are not engaged, or engaged only to avoid sanctions or embarrassment, then whatever the teacher does is likely to feel effortful: All the energy has to come from the teacher. You end up having to be a cross between a prison guard and an entertainer, and over time, both those roles can be draining.

So engaging your learners is vital. But engagement can't be engineered by a teacher; it can only be invited. So how do you issue strong invitations that are likely to engage as many of your class as possible, as fully as possible? Some mixture of the following seems to work.

Your invitation can be intriguing in its own right; you set out to puzzle or disconcert your students so they want to find out the answer, or to develop the skill that they are frustrated to realize they lack.

It helps if you can explain to your students the personal value of what they are learning. Some things clearly have practical use: reading, calculating, digital technology, and so on. Others have long-term value for the majority of students—understanding health, economic, political, and ecological issues, for example—but may need selling to students who do not immediately see their use. And there are other topics that may not have obvious relevance or utility, but that make good "exercise machines" on which to develop useful skills and habits of mind. (David Perkins's book *Future Wise* is a really thought-provoking exploration of what's worth knowing for most students in the 21st century.)

Many schools, where possible, involve students in such authentic learning: work that has genuine value for themselves, their classmates, or their communities. In schools like High Tech High, or the EL Education schools, learning is mostly done through extended projects that result in products or solutions that genuinely matter. There is a special kind of pride that comes with having wrestled with a difficult problem that is of real importance, and come up with something novel (at least in that context) and useful. Ricky Gervais, the British comedian and actor responsible for *The Office*, said in a recent interview that it was not until he was working on those scripts in his mid-40s that he learned to experience what he called "the joy of the struggle." And he wished he had discovered it earlier. Finding out that a major investment of effort, resilience, imagination, and reflection can result in that deep inner glow of pride is transformative for many young people, especially those for whom traditional schoolwork does not come easily.

## 4. Make Ample Time for Collaboration and Conversation

In LPA classrooms, much of the time, there is a buzz of engaged conversation between students. That is where most of the thinking happens. Of course the teacher floats around eavesdropping on those conversations—as Giselle Isbell was doing in her math workshop at Anser Charter School—making sure that misconceptions don't become embedded in students' minds. But letting them figure things out for themselves builds confidence that they can do so. In her Year 1/Year 2 classroom, Becky Carlzon builds that confidence and capability in her children every day. From the beginning of the year, she trains them to turn and talk to whoever happens to be near them, so they don't get stuck on one "learning buddy" and feel helpless if he or she isn't available. Becky's children don't have their own special place to sit in the classroom; again, she is training them to get used to feeling that they can all help each other. She wrote to me in an e-mail a couple of days ago,

> Kids love the idea that they can use their friends as a learning tool. Building in collaboration creates an immediate culture change and, I have found, an immediate positive impact in attitudes to learning. Collaboration is a skill that can easily be built up throughout the year. It also opens the door to risk taking, self-instruction and being resourceful as children can learn from their peers.

In an LPA classroom, students are guided to feel that the whole class is a learning resource—not just the teacher. They discover that working with someone who is not a friend can be more productive, and that people different from you may give you fresh perspectives and new ideas to help your own learning. Students become generous with their own learnings and discoveries, so they are keen to share their insights with others. Remember Kaelyn in Giselle's workshop saying that someone in a group might say something that acts as a clue to spur your own learning: "And you go, *Oh, I see how to do that now.*" And she immediately adds, "And then you can help them." In the "network" classroom (see Figure 8.1) students are vital resources for each other, and the teacher is one—albeit a very important one—node in that network.

Is collaboration "cheating"? Not in most workplace teams, and there is no reason why it should be seen as such in school. A group of six-year-olds were discussing the value of imitation in their Building Learning Power (BLP) classroom, and their teacher asked, "But isn't that just copying?" The children thought, and then one said, "Copying is when you just do what someone else did without thinking. Imitating is when you take their idea, try it out, and make it your own." That's a pretty nifty understanding for a six-year-old.

Learning how to have productive discussions—developing the skills of collaboration and what Neil Mercer in Chapter 6 called "interthinking"—is at the heart of the LPA.

FIGURE 8.1    The Centralized Versus the Network Model of the Classroom

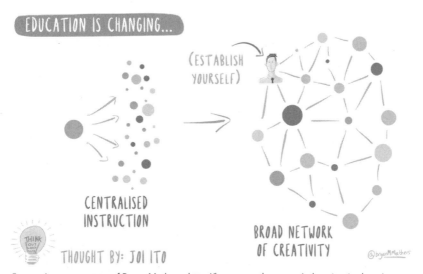

Source: Image courtesy of Bryan Mathers, http://bryanmmathers.com/education-is-changing

# 5. Create Challenge

Learning means mastering something new. First you don't understand it or can't do it; then you wrestle with it, flounder intelligently, and begin to get some ideas about how to do it; and then you consolidate, hone, and broaden your competence through practice in varied settings and contexts. So LPA teachers have to gradually (but relentlessly) get their students used to going into "the pit" and having "grapple time." In a culture that confuses intelligence with the easy delivery of approved answers, students will not like to grapple, because they interpret grappling as evidence of lack of brightness. But in an LPA environment, they enjoy the process of grappling with tricky challenges and don't mind if they make mistakes or have to struggle. They know that it is through struggle and effort that worthwhile achievements and personal development arise. (The British Royal Air Force motto is *per ardua ad astra:* "The way to the stars is through struggle.")

To do that, you have to know your students. An LPA teacher is very attentive to what they (individually and collectively) can currently do, and what they are finding difficult, so that she can create good learning challenges and grapple with problems. This enhanced attentiveness to students is also advocated in Dylan Wiliam's Formative Assessment and John Hattie's Visible Learning, but in both those systems the aim is for the teacher to help students close the gap between their current performance and that needed for good examination grades. In the LPA the primary aim is to inform the design of suitable challenges that stretch students' ability to manage and evaluate learning for themselves. In a classroom where students are developing their learning power, keen to stretch their learning muscles through grappling with a range of topics, the examination performance tends to look after itself.

Of course, creating a good challenge is always a matter of informed intuition, and you might misjudge it and make it too hard or too easy. So inviting feedback from students helps to strengthen that intuition. It is also good modeling. Students like to be around teachers who are visibly keen to keep improving their own performance. Becky Carlzon wrote to me,

In a classroom where students are developing their learning power, keen to stretch their learning muscles through grappling with a range of topics, examination performance tends to look after itself.

> It is good for teachers to model making their learning too tricky or too easy and talking to the students about how that felt. In my classroom there is a photo of me and all the adults in our classroom, as well as all the children, on our "learning ladder"—the image we use to show publicly how "risky" our learning is. I often put my face on "high" on the learning ladder if I am teaching in a way I haven't tried before. It models to the children that I am a risk taker in my teaching. It also takes the onus off them if the lesson doesn't quite go to plan: "My fault!" I'll say—and then review with the children how I could adjust the lesson for next time.

Carol Dweck has reported a recent study in which video game designers developed two versions of some math software. Both gave students batches of problems to do, and both were able to monitor how much smart effort and time students put in, as well as their overall success in solving the problems—but the feedback in the two versions was different. In the first, quick success was rewarded with 10 "brain points" and some praise. Slow performance with errors got nothing. In the second version, fast success was greeted with a sad face and an apology from the computer. "I'm so sorry; I gave you problems that were much too easy for you, didn't I? Shall we try something more interesting? No brain points for you today." It was those who struggled but managed to make some progress who got the smiley face. "Well done! You worked really hard at those problems. 10 brain points for you!" The results were clear. After the initial shock to the system for the high achievers, all students, whatever their current level of performance, showed greater engagement and greater progress with the second reward structure than the first. Yet the first is far more common in classrooms.

A similar result came from an analysis of recent OECD math data by the UK National Foundation for Educational Research. Fifteen-year-olds who said that their teacher "always or often" gave them problems that made them struggle and think showed higher levels of achievement and progress, as well as greater engagement and enjoyment of math. They also found that, while all students benefit from such teaching, "pupils with low and medium socioeconomic status (SES) profit most from having high levels of cognitive activation in their math lessons. Yet lower-achieving pupils report undertaking such activities less often." Why? Because "their teachers may not believe lower ability pupils are able to cope with the cognitive demand." Through a misguided assumption, the students who would most benefit from an LPA approach are being deprived of it.[3]

Notice the use of language, by the way. Giselle Isbell might have said to her students, "Today I am going to give you something to do that most of you will fail at"—but she didn't. Her talk of "grappling" and "grapple problems" sounds more positive and engaging. Becky Carlzon talks to her first graders about doing "tricky" things. *Tricky* is a word they like; they feel proud when they have managed to do something tricky. James Nottingham's language of the "learning pit" (see Figure 8.2) may sound forbidding, but most students like its connotations of mystery and danger. Simple changes of terminology like this can make a huge difference in the mood and culture of the classroom.

FIGURE 8.2   The Learning Pit

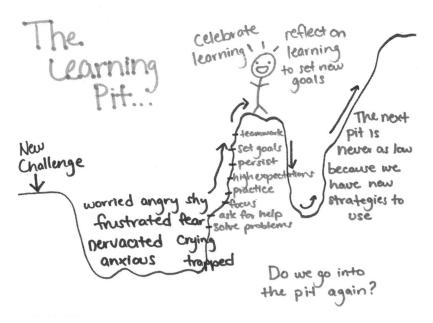

This image of the learning pit comes from the Year 4 class at Prospect Primary School in Adelaide, South Australia. I like it because it was generated by the children themselves. The words and the strategies are theirs. They were especially pleased to come across the word *nervacited,* which is a much more interesting and positive word for how you feel when you are in the pit than *anxious* or *trapped.*[4]

*Source:* By kind permission of Anna Weinert

# 6. Make Difficulty Adjustable

Classrooms are full of people with different levels of capability (in anything you'd like to name). So how do you create problems that are suitably stretching for everyone in the room? The first answer is to create a menu of different degrees of difficulty. Remember Becky Carlzon's "chili challenges." Traditionally, the teacher might have been responsible for who chooses what out of such a menu, but better, in LPA terms, is to train up the students to make their own selections. If they get it wrong and it turns out to be too easy or too hard for them, no face is lost; they just adjust the choice up or down. Through being given this freedom to choose, students get better at choosing: better able to predict what will be a productive grapple problem for them. In principle, they are capable of knowing best where the sweet spot of learning is for them at any moment.

Remember the young footballers from Sunderland who had been trained to monitor their own sweet spots, and change the level of difficulty for themselves when they were finding their learning too easy or too difficult. They were not just selecting from a menu of options of preset difficulty; they were creatively customizing the activity, in the light of their own ongoing experience, so that they derived the maximum learning from it.

In Becky's classroom, I watched a pair of children who had chosen a four-chili challenge—and nailed it. They went to her and asked what they should do next. Becky pointed out another pair who had also successfully answered the four-chili challenge, and suggested that the two pairs might like to see if they could design a *five*-chili challenge for each other. Their eyes lit up at the idea that they might now be able to be their own teachers and design suitable learning activities for themselves or for each other. That's the LPA in action, right there.

Remember in Chapter 4 we talked about a BLP tool called the *riskometer*. It's a simple scale that looks like a thermometer but measures degree of challenge or riskiness rather than temperature. There is a strip of Velcro up the middle on which children can stick a small picture of themselves to indicate the level of challenge they have chosen. An English teacher at a high-achieving girls' high school liked the idea of the riskometer, but thought (probably rightly) that it would be too simple for her bright, sophisticated Year 10 class. So she adapted it. When setting a homework assignment, she discussed with the girls several different ways they could tackle it, which represented different degrees of familiarity, and therefore risk. They could do it as a straightforward piece of descriptive writing, or as a screenplay, or as a Socratic dialogue, or as a graphic cartoon strip.

Together they devised a scale, from 1.0 to 1.9, which would represent their judgment about the degree of difficulty they had selected, and they would indicate this when they handed their piece of work in. 1.0 = "familiar and pretty certain of success"; 1.9 = "really unfamiliar and very uncertain of success." The teacher then explained that when she marked the work, she would first mark it according to the success criteria of the rubric, but then she would multiply that by their "tariff of difficulty" to make their final mark—thus incentivizing risk-taking and adventurousness. Now the girls who liked to be top of the class could only achieve it by tackling something outside their comfort zone. (Of course, this will only work with a group that is already mature enough to make honest judgments, and not to cheat by inflating their tariff.)

The LPA classroom is like a fitness center or gymnasium. Activities are like the pieces of equipment in the gym. Each one is capable of being customized by the individual user to suit her current level of ability. It doesn't matter that the Olympic rower on the machine next to me is doing something way harder than I could possibly attempt; we are both adjusting the activity so that we find our own sweet spot. Our goal, in training, is not to beat each other, but to keep reaching for a new personal best for ourselves (though a bit of healthy competition, within this LPA spirit, is no bad thing).

# 7. Show the Innards of Learning

There is a resurgence of interest in making. The Maker Movement in the United States is growing in strength. The course on "How to Make (Almost) Anything" is one of MIT's most oversubscribed. But making isn't just about 3D printers and home-crafted beer or jewelry; it is about finding elegant solutions to math problems and getting a piece of writing to sparkle. What is interesting about making is the process. In the LPA classroom, learning broadens from an exclusive concern with the quality of the *product* to include a real interest in the *processes* whereby those excellent products arise. Young people are keen to learn about the "how" of learning—the ways in which their performance in algebra or basketball can be improved—so we need to show them many rich examples of how other people go about tinkering, improving, and problem-solving.

Read the sleeve-notes to Paul Simon's album *Stranger to Stranger*, and find out where his songs and rhythms come from. Watch the last 10-minute "diary" section of David Attenborough's recent natural history films like *Planet Earth II,* and see how much time, effort, ingenuity, patience, and ability to tolerate frustration lie behind those amazing wildlife images. Read the biographies of sportsmen and women like Simone Biles or Usain Bolt, and discover the sophisticated rigors of elite training and the tricks of the trade that make their practicing more effective than other people's. Look at the notebooks of scientists, poets, or artists, and see the

> LPA lays bare the innards of the learning process so that young people will get an accurate insight into how learning really happens, and not fall prey to the stupid idea (so common in schools) that academic "ability" means getting it right fast, the first time, always, preferably without breaking a sweat.

half-baked thought processes that eventually led to their amazing discoveries and accomplishments. LPA lays bare the innards of the learning process so that young people will get an accurate insight into how learning really happens, and not fall prey to the stupid idea (so common in schools) that academic "ability" means getting it right fast, the first time, always, preferably without breaking a sweat.

### Isaac Newton's Lab Book

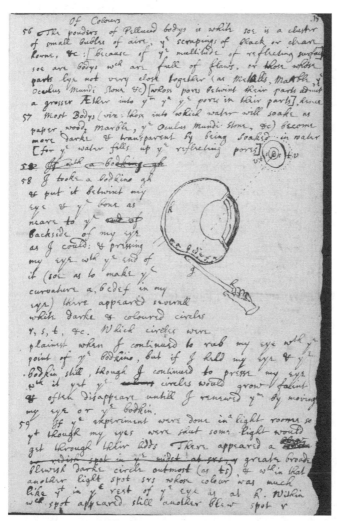

*Source:* Reproduced by kind permission of the Syndics of Cambridge University Library

# 8. Make Use of Protocols, Templates, and Routines

The LPA classroom is full of activities and strategies that deliberately stimulate and structure learning. Take the protocol called Workshop 2.0 that Giselle Isbell was using, which is widely used across all ages and all subjects in the EL Education schools. Starting with the grapple problem builds independence, resourcefulness, and self-confidence. It produces, over time, children who are not afraid to enter the confused, uncertain state called learning. Then an activity like Pair-Share develops strength in discussion, debate, and collaborative problem-solving. The injunction to go looking for more efficient and elegant strategies spurs students' imagination and adventurousness. The synthesis or review at the end of the lesson exercises students' ability to reflect on their own performance, to critique their own educational experience, and to give constructive feedback to teachers. EL Education has developed many such lesson formats that provide neat, flexible templates for designing mind-stretching lessons.

James Nottingham's lesson, "What is 'real'?" draws on a template for creating challenging learning that he calls the Learning Challenge. The challenge involves four stages: Concept, Conflict, Construct, and Consider. First he introduces a rich concept—in this case "reality"—to focus students' thoughts. Then, via skillful questioning, he gets them to realize that things are not as simple as they thought, and to experience the confusion and frustration (Conflict) that energizes the third phase, Construct, where he gets them to surface their intuitive reactions, assumptions, and beliefs. Finally the Consider phase involves animated dialogue and discussion between students, which leads to a deeper, but still provisional, understanding.

In the BLP framework, teachers use an approach called Split-Screen Teaching. Here, two complementary objectives are explicitly woven together: the goal of advancing students' knowledge and understanding of a particular topic, and the goal of stretching a specific learning strength. This dual focus is made clear to the students, and the structure and the activities of the lesson are designed by the teacher accordingly. For example, Andy Carpenter, a Year 13 chemistry teacher, realized that his students had become too passive and dependent on him, and he needed to rehabilitate their ability to evaluate for themselves where their understanding was strong and where it was weak. Exams were coming up, so his dual objectives were "to build your questioning muscles and concentrate on how you revise" and "to review and evaluate your knowledge and understanding of organic chemistry."

To achieve those two aims together, the task he set was this: "Please spend the first lesson working in groups, analyzing and reviewing your work. You MUST put up on the board at least two questions that will concentrate on an area of misunderstanding." As a result of using this strategy with the class for two or three weeks, Andy found that he had indeed rehabilitated their willingness, collectively and individually, to honestly and astutely self-evaluate their level of understanding, and, as a result, their performance on the anticipated test of organic chemistry exceeded his (and their) expectations.

Split-Screen Teaching is a very good way of training yourself, as a teacher, to pay greater attention to the learning muscles that students are using, and become more creative at designing activities that will stretch those muscles, one by one. "I'm teaching my class to add fractions; how can I do that in a way that also stretches their ability and willingness to find and fix their own mistakes?" "I've got a history topic coming up; how could I use that as a way of building the students' disposition to put themselves imaginatively in other people's shoes before making judgments about them?" "In my art lesson, how could I get them to develop a sense of craftsmanship, reflecting on their own products and finding ways to make it even better for themselves?" (It is important not to rely on only the most obvious connections here—"math = reasoning," "art = imagining," "team sports = collaborating"—but to explore less obvious pairings: ways that math might stretch imagination, art develop self-critique, or science improve collaboration.) Of course, the longer-term goal is for all the learning strengths to weave naturally and seamlessly together in the course of wrestling with interesting challenges, but splitting them up and focusing on one at a time is a good training exercise for both teachers and students. As everyone gets more used to using the language of learning power, so the different strengths dissolve back into spontaneous competence.

Within lessons, the Thinking Routines (developed by Ron Ritchhart's Visible Thinking team) offer a variety of ways to stretch different mental muscles. Giving them easy-to-remember names such as Think-Pair-Share or See-Think-Wonder, and using them frequently in different contexts, enables students to enrich their own repertoires of learning habits, and store them so that they easily come to mind when they might be needed. In the lesson at Bialik College, the teacher is making good use of the Thinking Routine called Circle of Viewpoints, which trains students in the skills of perspective taking and empathy. You can think of the thinking (or learning) routines as being like the focused exercises that a personal trainer might set for her clients in a fitness center, each activity being designed to work a different set of muscles. By varying the routines, interest is maintained, and over time, all-around fitness (whether physical or mental) is increased.

These ready-made templates and routines are also just to get you going. They are starter kits that demonstrate how the aim of strengthening students' learning capacities can be woven, without distracting from the content, into the fabric of "normal" lessons. But once you find your feet, you and your students can become more creative and think up different routines for yourselves. One group of fourth-grade students thought up a routine that they called Spider and Wider. They were used to using mind maps and spider diagrams to clarify the structure of their knowledge on a particular subject, but they realized that sticking to the "rules" constrained the kinds of questions they could ask. So they allowed themselves to add curly lines and clouds to their diagrams that drew attention to relationships between concepts that had ended up on opposite sides of the diagram, or to "holes" in their understanding that the traditional diagram couldn't display.

In another classroom, the teacher, Julie Green, had dreamed up a routine that she called ICT. Nothing to do with digital technology in this context, ICT stands for Independent-Collaborative-Teacher. Having explained an activity to the students, Julie used this routine to offer them a choice about how they wished to pursue it: on their own; in collaboration with a small group of other students; or in a group with her, the teacher. This routine was stretching students' ability to anticipate the demands of the task and make an informed guess about what kind of social context would best help them to approach it. At the end of the lesson, Julie invited her fifth graders to reflect in their learning journals on the pros and cons of the choice they had made, and to think about when, how, and why they might make different choices in the future.

## 9. Use the Environment

Many aspects of the classroom environment can be adjusted so as to support the development of learning power. The layout of the furniture either supports a teacher-centric atmosphere—with all eyes to the front, attention focused on the teacher and her interactive whiteboard—or invites greater dialogue between students. By changing the environment, you can shift from a centralized to more of a network model of the classroom (Figure 8.1). To support her use of the ICT strategy, for example, Julie Green lays out the tables and chairs in her room with some individual work stations around the edge, some ready for small group discussions, and some chairs clustered around her desk at the front. The Harkness table, a large round or oval table, big enough for the whole class to sit around, and with no "head" position, naturally invites (and stretches) the kind of whole-class discussion required in a James Nottingham Learning Challenge. Some teachers do away with their own privileged position at the front of the class entirely. Some, like Becky Carlzon, don't allow the students to have a set position or their own desk, in order to facilitate a greater camaraderie and confidence among the class as a whole. Some have bean bags or pods for quiet reading. And so on. No layout is neutral. The environment always assists some kinds of learning, and resists others.

Schools are sometimes praised for being "innovative" because they have a colorful or fashionable environment, but they lack any rationale as to how these eye-catching features are supposed to enhance learning. There are no obvious reasons why oddly shaped chairs and brightly colored bean bags should improve your math scores, let alone strengthen your empathy or determination. In the UK, a few years ago, there was a well-funded initiative to build new so-called Schools for the Future, but all too often they were simply schools for the past with a glass atrium stuck on the front. In an LPA classroom, these choices are driven not by the latest fashion, or by neon-colored cubes in a manufacturer's catalogue, but by a clear appreciation of what kinds of learner strengths and behaviors a school is trying to develop.

All kinds of classroom displays can support the development of learning strengths. Posters of inspirational quotations by characters that students naturally admire will remind them of the widespread value of determination, imagination, collaboration, and so on. Having supplied a few of these to kick things off, it is better if teachers encourage students themselves to source these quotations.

Learning Power Hero

*Source:* By kind permission of TLO Ltd

Students can make their own displays, like the one on the previous page, in which they nominate their chosen characters as "Learning Power Heroes" on the basis of the character's learning strengths. In the illustration above, a student, aged 5, has nominated motorcyclist Valentino Rossi, "because he has [had to] stretch his Perseverens Mucsele, [his] NotSing Mucsele and his Collaboration Mucsele." (This student was still working on his Speling Mucsele!)

You may remember that, as they were embarking on their small group discussions, Giselle Isbell drew her students' attention to the anchor chart on the classroom wall that summarized some ground rules and illustrated some helpful sentence forms. This display, produced by the students themselves, acts as a coaching device that helps them learn how to stay on track and interact respectfully and productively with each other. There are many such displays that LPA classrooms use to prompt good learning behaviors and build learning habits. BLP classrooms often make use of the Stuck Posters we looked at in Chapter 4, which are simply lists of hints about things that students could try to help themselves when they get stuck. By encouraging the development of such resourcefulness, these displays help students become less dependent on their teachers, and more able to rescue themselves when learning gets tough.

And then there is the choice of which examples of students' own work to showcase on the walls of the classroom or the corridors. Again, this choice is motivated by the attitudes that we are trying to cultivate. If we choose only the best examples, and ignore all the drafts and false starts—airbrushing them out of the visible culture of the classroom—then we are reinforcing attention to the excellence of the product or performance. It is as if the process of getting to those excellent outcomes had no relevance or interest. But if we choose to display some of the students' own drafts and jottings that they produced along the way, we are making the innards of learning salient and interesting. A six-year-old child can point proudly to the amazingly accurate reproduction of an image of a tiger swallowtail butterfly that he has managed to produce, but he can also show you, with equal pride, the amount of progress he has made—the fruits of his own resilience, determination, reflection, and creativity—by pointing to the series of drafts that sit alongside it. (If you haven't already seen it, I strongly recommend a YouTube video clip called *Austin's Butterfly*, produced by Ron Berger and EL Education, which beautifully illustrates that sense of pride in progress. You can use the QR code here to find it. If you have seen it before, reflect for a moment on how your teaching has changed as a result.)

https://youtu.be/hqh1MRWZjms

To read a QR code, you must have a smartphone or tablet with a camera. We recommend that you download a QR code reader app that is made specifically for your phone or tablet brand. Or you can just copy the URL into your browser.

## 10. Develop Craftsmanship

*Austin's Butterfly* illustrates another design principle of the LPA: the deliberate cultivation of what Ron Berger has called "an ethic of excellence." Austin was able to produce his impressive drawing because he had the courage, the imagination, the perception, and the support to have six goes at it, each one being subject to helpful and supportive critique by his classmates. Craftsmanship requires skill, but it also requires the motivation to persist and keep improving, until you end up with something of which you are justifiably proud. Because he was allowed to have several goes, and because he was supported by his teacher and by his classmates (and remember, they were only six years old), Austin was being encouraged to discover the joy of the struggle, to be unafraid of difficulty, and to develop that ethic of excellence. The EL Education schools share a deep conviction that all children, with the right encouragement and support, are capable of producing high-quality work—products of which they can be justly proud. And time is made for this to happen—unlike in many schools under pressure to hurtle from one superficial task to the next, falsely presuming that children's first go accurately represents their "ability"—what they are capable of.

Performance reflects a much richer set of influences than brute IQ. In their book *Learning Without Limits*, Susan Hart and her colleagues write,

> Explaining differences in terms of inherent ability is not only unjust and untenable, but also deprives teachers of the chance to base and develop their practice upon a more complex, multifaceted and infinitely more empowering understanding of teaching and learning processes, and of the influences internal and external to the school, that impinge on learning and achievement.[5]

This kind of craftsmanship matters in writing, mathematics, science—indeed in every subject of the school curriculum—and can be systematically developed in each of them. But it is perhaps most easily seen when students have time to make and improve physical objects and performances: in art, ceramics, dance, music, design technology (shop class), gymnastics, and sports. A Harvard project on Studio Thinking has mapped out in some detail the kinds of educational experience that build craftsmanship. There are targeted, stimulating inputs by experts that fire students' imaginations. There is training in the use of different tools and resources, and how to take care of them. There is the freedom to set goals that are meaningful and challenging. There is time to explore, experiment, muck about with ideas and material, and capitalize on serendipity. There are constant opportunities to stand back and reflect on one's own progress, and to seek improvements. And there is a collective studio atmosphere of support and critique. Students are coached in how to give feedback to each other in ways that are respectful, specific, and helpful, and how to accept criticism graciously and nondefensively. In *Austin's Butterfly* you see Ron Berger skillfully coaching different groups of students in the art of giving a good-quality critique. As a result of these teaching methods, students shift from seeing themselves as performers to becoming craftsmen and women, a shift that was neatly summed up by a senior at the Boston Arts Academy who said, "When I was younger I wanted to hear people tell me, 'Oh, you're doing so good. That's so beautiful.' And now I just want to grow. By just hearing the good things you don't grow."[6]

## 11. Allow Increasing Amounts of Independence

Some years ago I was visiting Glen Waverley Secondary College, a state school in Victoria, Australia. In the morning I was taking part in a conference with other visiting speakers, and in the afternoon we listened to students present the fruits of their independent studies. At that time, Year 9 students at Glen Waverley spent every Friday, for a whole semester, working in small groups on a research project of their own devising. (That's 10% of their lesson time over the course of the entire school year.) I was particularly struck by a presentation from three 14-year-old girls, Surabhi, Stephanie, and Fiona. Their research question concerned the inhospitable conditions under which asylum seekers and refugees were being kept. They wondered, Why do the conditions have to be like that?

They had researched the detention centers where these people were being held, conducted interviews with some people who had been detained there, and made inquiries into the necessity of these barbaric conditions. Their presentation was elegantly crafted and powerfully delivered. At the end, they spoke movingly about how much they had learned from the experience—research design and methodology, interview technique and analysis, PowerPoint presentation, as well as the stretching of learning strengths such as determination, curiosity, collaboration, and reflection. They also said that their focus of inquiry, which they intended to pursue, had evolved (as any good research tends to do) from the physical conditions themselves into a deeper question: As they put it, "Why do so many Australians feel the need to behave cruelly to desperate foreigners?"

I congratulated the girls on their presentation, and asked what they intended to do with such a useful piece of research. Sometime later I heard from their teacher, Adele Briskman, that they had sent a DVD of the presentation to the then Australian prime minister, John Howard, (they got no reply) and had also submitted it to an international conference on human rights due to take place in Melbourne the following year. Their paper was accepted, and three 14-year-old girls duly presented their findings to a roomful of academics from around the world. Three years later I got an e-mail from Surabhi about her plans to apply to Oxford to study, and expressing her appreciation of the fact that the project had dramatically expanded her confidence and her horizons, not to mention her intellectual competence and understanding. I thought, if such an outcome is not the core aim of 21st century education, then I don't know what is. If we hide behind curriculum requirements and administrative convenience as reasons not to provide such transformative experiences, then we have truly lost the educational plot.

Last year I spent some time at the Jakarta Intercultural School in Indonesia. I learned that a group of students—again in Year 9—had petitioned the head of year for an independent study opportunity. They all had developed interests and enthusiasms that they wanted time to pursue. And the school said yes. One boy was already an expert on theatrical lighting—he ran the light shows for school presentations and productions—and wanted to deepen his research into the effect of different lighting colors and effects on audience mood and response. Another was sure she was going to become a lawyer, and was already studying undergraduate-level courses in law in her spare time. Making time for students to follow their passions is not just a matter of being accommodating; it aids the growth of their learning prowess and independence.

Sugata Mitra is the Indian professor of education behind the famous "hole in the wall" computer experiments in Delhi. Illiterate street kids, given access to an Internet-enabled computer cemented into a wall in their neighborhood, turned out to be able to teach themselves how to use it. Within two months, without any tuition or instruction, they became digitally as competent as the average English secretary. After numerous experiments, Mitra concluded that "groups of four children, with a basic computer, internet access and an intriguing question, can teach themselves (almost) anything."[7] The social interaction that occurs around the screen turns out to be critical to their success. If there is one machine per person, the magic doesn't happen. Nor does it if a kindly adult intervenes to try to teach them. The formidable collective intelligence of the group dissipates like morning mist in the sunlight, and they turn into compliant students.

All this speaks to the formative power of well-designed project and inquiry work in schools. Of course, project work can be done badly and ineffectively—just as whole-class teaching, done badly, can be dull and dispiriting. If a project is not intriguing and engaging, if it is perceived by students as thinly disguised busywork, if it is so loosely specified and supervised that students just flounder listlessly, if it is overprescribed and overcontrolled, if students are unprepared for the degree of responsibility and maturity required to make it work, if they have not yet learned to work productively and respectfully together in a group—then inquiry-based learning can be, as some critics point out, a waste of time. But if some basic design principles are followed, and teachers navigate the middle way between being laissez-faire and being overcontrolling, so that students grapple productively with the challenges that arise, then its impact can indeed be transformative. Books such as Kath Murdoch's *The Power of Inquiry* are mines of information about how to do project-based learning well.

## 12. Give Students More Responsibility

As well as stretching students' ability to plan and organize their own learning, there are a range of ways to build their sense of ownership and responsibility for what goes on in the classroom and in the school more widely. Commonly this is seen as the role of the student council, but there are many ways in which students can become involved in creating, evaluating, and contributing to the improvement of the learning culture of the school as a whole. Here are some examples.

- In Landau Forte College (High School), students regularly review their progress in developing their learning strengths (as well as their achievement in their different subjects). As they go up through the school, from Year 7 to Year 13, so the complexity of the learning strengths framework they are working with increases, so that their understanding of what makes a powerful learner grows in sophistication. Students consult with their teachers and with each other to gain a good, all-around view of their progress. Older students use this preparation as a basis for the regular student-teacher-parent consultations, explaining to their parents the relationship between their academic progress and the development of their learning muscles. As a result of the review, all students are able to set learning targets for themselves for the coming weeks, some of which relate to their general behavior (such as punctuality), some to their progress in particular subjects, and some to a conscious effort to develop their concentration, collaboration, or effective use of imagination.

- The Harris Academies are a federation of state schools, mostly in lower-income localities in and around London. In 2008, the leaders of all nine schools created The Harris Student Commission on Learning. Around 200 students, ranging in age from 11 to 18, volunteered or were nominated to be commissioners. Their job was to seek out state-of-the-art information, from across the UK and around the world, about how to create the most effective learning environments. They read written sources, made school visits, and interviewed academics working in the area. The first I knew of this project was when I got a letter from a 13-year-old inviting me to present my research to a committee of commissioners. They listened politely and asked penetrating questions. At the end of the process, they produced a booklet, *A New Design for Learning*, that distilled everything they had learned into a set of practical "entitlements" for all students and teachers at the Harris schools. For example, "Every learner will be entitled to have opportunities for choice in what and how they learn; to undertake self-directed learning through extended projects tackling real-world questions and challenges; and to build learning partnerships with teachers to improve learning through feedback, co-planning and co-design."

These commitments were taken seriously. The booklet states, "The federation will ensure that senior leaders are held responsible and accountable for realising the entitlements. . . . Every academy will work collaboratively with students and teachers to develop plans for taking the entitlements forward." One of the school principals wrote, "In a school where there has been a lack of confidence and aspiration, the student commissioners have given their peers the confidence to demand more and better learning." Umu Lamina, a Year 10 student, wrote, "The chance to see our initial ideas in action— learning buddies integrated in our lessons, students delivering lessons, attending teacher meetings and planning schemes of work—has truly inspired and motivated me." Many students said how the opportunity to be involved in something so "real" and important, and so challenging, had stretched their confidence and their learning capacities in ways they would never have dreamed.[8]

# 13. Focus on Improvement, Not Achievement

In conventional schools, assessment measures achievement. And sometimes that is obviously necessary. Teachers and learners need to know if they have met external standards and criteria. And sometimes it is also useful to measure students against each other: to know who is top and who needs more help. But researchers such as New Zealander Terry Crooks and British academic Gwyneth Hughes have shown that, to help students learn better and faster, a third kind of assessment works best. Called *ipsative assessment,* it simply means measuring students' current performance against their own past performance. Focusing on improvement, charting the progress that each learner makes, is much more motivating and leads to accelerated learning. In the world at large, this kind of assessment is commonplace. In sports and athletics, for example, everyone wants to win, but the way to get there is to focus on the continual improvement of your personal best.

Gwyneth Hughes describes an occurrence in an amateur string quartet of which she is a member. Members of the quartet were reviewing a videotape of a recent concert of theirs, and her fellow players were full of self-criticism, focusing on all kinds of perceived inadequacies in their presentation and their playing. One player was so despondent that she even suggested they should give up altogether. But Gwyneth pointed out that they were implicitly—and unhelpfully—comparing themselves with professional performers, which they had neither the time nor the inclination to be. She reminded them of how far they had come since they started playing together two years ago, how the video actually demonstrated the dramatic increase in their ability to listen to each other, and nuance their playing accordingly, for example. When they started they would not have been able to play credibly in front of an audience, and now they could. In fact, the concert in the videotape was clearly a personal best for the quartet, of which they should feel justifiably proud. Reframing their assessment in this way completely altered their mood, and any talk of disbanding evaporated.[9]

Exactly the same shift occurs in an LPA classroom when the teacher's routine forms of assessment and feedback are couched in terms of personal improvement, and not as failures to achieve external standards of excellence. Paradoxically, excellence is more likely to be achieved when the focus is on improvement rather than achievement. (Remember the experiment I quoted by Cheryl Flink earlier in this chapter.) It takes a bit of effort for a school to reorient its standard methods of assessment in this way. It means that tests have to be designed to be cumulative, so that performance at a later time can be meaningfully compared to earlier performance. "No test without pretest," as one slogan puts it. But if you want a roomful of creative learners rather than anxious performers, it is well worth the effort.

In an LPA classroom, students are aiming at personal bests on two fronts: the subject they are studying, and the learning strengths themselves. They might be encouraged to keep a reflective journal or an e-portfolio that records examples of their developing strength and sophistication as team players or creative thinkers in different subjects, for instance. At Landau Forte College, as we have just seen, older students lead the periodic consultations between their teachers and their parents, and in preparation for these meetings, the students review their own progress in developing the learning habits. Discussion of this progress, and the evidence for it, forms a major part of the three-way conversation in the meeting.

A focus on improvement in learning habits can begin with young children. Becky Carlzon writes in her blog learningpowerkids,

> An example of focusing on progress is how we use assembly in Christ Church Infants School. Friday's

service is called "Celebration Assembly" and a few children from each class get to stand up and tell the school something they are proud of in their learning. The children are picked by the teacher and are chosen based on demonstrating that they have improved in [for example] their perseverance, collaboration or mimicking. I sometimes take this a step further and ask the children in my class who *they* think deserves to get up in Assembly. It's actually one of my favorite moments in the week because we spend time reflecting on the achievements and learning highlights of the week. Sometimes I already have someone in mind (and the children have often noticed this person too—so will mention them), but sometimes I wait to see what the children come up with and send those children up. Even if they don't get the certificate, the children feel really proud that their friends have noticed them being a good learner. It brings the class together and helps the children learn to be supportive of one another's achievements.

Many schools have developed their own "ladders" of progress in the different learning habits. In one secondary school I used to work with, they called these levels Asteroid, Moon, Planet, and Star. When students are ready, they present a portfolio of evidence to their class teacher, supporting their claim that they are now a Planet-Level Perseverer in their mathematics learning (or whatever it might be), and if accepted, they would get the appropriate badge. The incentive for students to seek this accreditation was an increase in the amount of independence they were allowed in the school. As they demonstrated greater maturity and responsibility, so they might be allowed more unsupervised access to library or computer facilities, or greater opportunities for independent study.

# 14. Lead by Example

It naturally fits with the LPA ethos I have been describing if the teacher is able to model being a learner as well as a knower. Students like to know that their teachers know their stuff, and are knowledgeable and reliable guides to the complexities of chemistry or English literature. But they also find it reassuring and encouraging to know that their teachers don't have to be right all the time, and are happy to make, and admit to making, mistakes and misjudgments. If you too are a visible learner, about both your subject and about teaching itself, your students can feel more relaxed about their own struggles and uncertainties. When Giselle Isbell asks her class, "Was that a good grapple problem?" and is clearly interested in and responsive to their feedback, she is presenting herself as an open learner, keen to improve her own practice, and not too proud to accept suggestions from her class about how she might do it better next time. When Becky Carlzon thinks aloud as she writes on the board—"Ooh, I wonder what word would go best here: this one or this one?" or "Oh! I've forgotten how to spell that word. I wonder where I would look to remind myself?"— she is showing the innards of her own thinking, thus demonstrating what it is like to be a learner "on the inside."

We know from the research of Vygotsky, Bandura, and many others that habits of mind are contagious.[10] We humans are biologically primed to imitate the behavior of those we interact with—especially if we are dependent on

> No printed word,
> nor spoken plea,
>
> Can teach young minds
> what they should be.
>
> Not all the books
> on all the shelves—
>
> But what the teachers
> are themselves.
>
> Rudyard Kipling

them, or consider them trustworthy or admirable. Young children pick up gestures, speech patterns, and accents from those around them, and over time, these patterns tend to become consolidated into habits and personality traits. So we as teachers cannot escape being role models for our students: role models of curiosity, good humor, humility, and tolerance of uncertainty; or of insecurity and infallibility. We teach who we are, as well as what we know, whether we are teaching young children or 17-year-olds. Of course we all vary from hour to hour and day to day, but we also have our tendencies and preferences, our "default settings," and it is these that children—fabulous little pattern detectors that they are—home in on and tend to replicate. So we need to reflect the habits of mind that we wish our students to develop in our own responses to difficulty, frustration, and uncertainty, as much as we can.

We as teachers cannot escape being role models for our students: role models of curiosity, good humor, humility, and tolerance of uncertainty; or of insecurity and infallibility.

## Wondering

As you have read through these design principles, what have you been aware of in the way you have designed your own lessons or classrooms? Think about

- How the furniture is laid out
- What you have on the walls
- What resources are available to your students and how they access them (do they have to ask you first?)
- When and how you model being a learner

*(Continued)*

(Continued)

- How you greet your students
- How you respond to bad behavior
- How clearly you distinguish between learning mode and performance mode

Ask yourself what messages these send to the students about their role and abilities as learners. Are these messages the ones that you wish them to receive, or are there any discrepancies between what you consciously wish for them and the messages of the medium?

What one small thing could you tweak next week? For example, how could you signal more clearly when you want your students to be in learning mode and when in performance mode?

## Notes

1. For a very good summary of this distinction, see Eduardo Briceño's TED talk, "How to Get Better at the Things You Care About."
2. Cheryl Flink, Ann Boggiano, and Marty Barrett, "Controlling Teaching Strategies: Undermining Children's Self-Determination and Performance."
3. Bethan Burge, Jenny Lenkeit, and Juliet Sizmur, *PISA in Practice: Cognitive Activation in Maths*.
4. Pinkie Pie, a character in *My Little Pony*, is credited with the invention of the word *nervouscited*. Subsequent usages differ in spelling.
5. Susan Hart, Annabelle Dixon, Mary Jane Drummond, and Donald McIntyre, *Learning Without Limits*, p. 17.
6. Lois Hetland, Ellen Winner, Shirley Veenema, and Kimberley Sheridan, *Studio Thinking: The Real Benefits of Visual Arts Education*.

7. Sugata Mitra, *Beyond the Hole in the Wall: Discover the Power of Self-Organised Learning*, TED Books; and Sugata Mitra, *The Future of Learning*. There has been some criticism of Mitra's work on the grounds that not enough of his studies have been published in peer-reviewed journals, and that he exaggerates the generality of his findings. But even if only a quarter of his research is right, it is still eye-wateringly important. The quote actually comes from a PowerPoint slide that Sugata used in a lecture at a conference in Buenos Aires where we were both keynoting in 2013.

8. Both Landau Forte College and the Harris Academies have undergone changes of leadership since these pioneering developments took place. I do not know to what extent the innovations I describe here have been maintained or developed.

9. Gwyneth Hughes (Ed.), *Ipsative Assessment: Motivation Through Marking Progress*. Terry Crooks, "The Impact of Classroom Evaluation Practices on Students."

10. See Anton Bucher, "The Influence of Models in Forming Moral Identity."

# What Is the Evidence for the Learning Power Approach?

As we have just seen, learning power is a complex and multifaceted concept. So it is a slippery beast when it comes to trying to find evidence that will help to answer three important questions. First, is the Learning Power Approach (LPA) effective in easing and strengthening the learning that happens in school? Second, can learning power itself be strengthened? For example, is it possible to help students, in the context of a math or history lesson, increase their natural inclination to be determined and resourceful? (You'll notice that this is a different question from "What can I do to capture their interest in the moment?") If it is capable of being strengthened, does the intention to do so have a demonstrable effect on the speed, depth, and engagement of their learning? And third, do any benefits of increasing learning power in one domain transfer to other domains? If I help my kids become more imaginative or adventurous in English, will those benefits show up in art or science, or even in their out-of-school clubs and activities?

As you might imagine, answering these questions is a huge research project that is only in its infancy. And it is difficult: The multifaceted nature of learning power means it is very hard to draw hard and fast inferences about the effects of each single strand. (A thick rope is strong because so many threads are woven together, and you can't easily detect the contribution that each individual strand is making.) Yet there are already some encouraging signs. Here are a few illustrations from the research literature.

## Does Curiosity Affect Learning?

Yes it does. Dr. Sophie von Stumm runs what she calls the Hungry Mind Lab at the University of London, where she researches the importance of curiosity. She and her colleagues have found that curiosity is as important as effort and intelligence in predicting students' academic performance. Effort and curiosity together have as much impact on how much and how well you learn as your IQ.[1] Curiosity predicts better grades in school, and also, importantly, predicts students' willingness to transfer knowledge learned in school into long-term interests and careers.[2] It makes sense. Your intelligence may strongly influence what you are capable of, but unless you apply it in real situations, when it matters, you won't be very smart at all. And what impacts on whether you do actually make the effort and apply your intelligence? It is your appetite to find things out, your enjoyment of puzzling about things till you get them, your determination to build your comprehension and your competence: in a word, your curiosity.

In fact, curiosity actually increases intelligence itself. Another study found that three-year-olds' curiosity led to an increase of 12 points in their IQ when they were 11 (compared with incurious children, regardless of their apparent intelligence when they were three).[3] The authors think that this is because "young stimulus seekers create for themselves an enriched environment which stimulates cognitive development." This is potentially very significant, as curiosity is something that can be actively stimulated and encouraged by parents and teachers alike, whereas IQ is often thought of as something that is relatively predetermined and beyond their control to change.

People vary in their curiosity enormously. Some are fascinated only by one small domain and are oblivious to all the other opportunities for wonderment that surround them. As John Dewey noted in his 1910 book *How We Think*, "In a few people, intellectual curiosity is so insatiable that nothing will discourage it, but in most its edge is easily dulled and blunted. . . . Some lose it in indifference and carelessness; others in a frivolous flippancy; [while] many escape these evils only to become encased in a hard dogmatism

> Curiosity actually increases intelligence itself.

which is equally fatal to the spirit of wonder."[4] Obviously curiosity is something that should be actively preserved and strengthened wherever and however possible.

# What About Concentration?

Consider what it takes to read a book or a story. As you read, you have to decode the visual symbols, turn them into meanings, and stitch the sentences together into a coherent image of the argument or the narrative. You have to connect the different bits of the jigsaw puzzle with each other, and also with the existing networks and models in your own mind, so that a new picture emerges that is distinct, but that makes sense in terms of all the other things you know. To do all this intricate processing requires concentration, especially when the plot or the argument is at all tricky. If our attention is only half on what we are reading, if our mind continually wanders off onto different trains of thought, or if there are distractions around us that we cannot ignore, the picture becomes degraded, hazy, or patchy.

So it is no surprise that the inability to spot when your mind has wandered and bring it back, or to resist the lure of external distractions, leads to less successful learning. Jonathan Smallwood at the University of York and his colleagues found that mind wandering, especially at critical junctures in the text, led to poorer comprehension and lower levels of attainment. This is obviously a particular problem for students who are preoccupied with distressing thoughts or worries, and for those with attention deficit disorders.[5]

A variety of classroom interventions seem to be effective both at preventing mind wandering and at enabling students to notice when mind wandering has happened and to try to refocus on the task at hand. U.S. educator Linda Lantieri, for example, has developed forms of attention (mindfulness) training that work even with children as young as four years old, and that have demonstrably beneficial effects on both behavior and school performance. In just five sessions with groups of four- and six-year-olds, their ability to concentrate and self-regulate were significantly enhanced.[6]

## Can Learners' Resilience Be Deliberately Increased?

Yes it can. Lisa Blackwell, Kali Trzesniewski, and Carol Dweck took a group of relatively low-achieving seventh graders, split them into two matched subgroups, and taught one group to think of their intelligence as being like a muscle that got stronger ("smarter") through effort. The other group had a similar series of sessions that taught them about study skills. Over the course of eight weeks, 27% of the students in the first group showed increased determination, with comparable academic improvement. In the second group, only 9% improved their motivation. Teachers made observations like these:

> Lamar, who never puts in any extra effort and doesn't turn in homework on time, actually stayed up late working for hours to finish an assignment early so I could review it and give him a chance to revise it. He earned a B—and he had been getting C's and lower.

> Maria was performing far below grade level. But during the past few weeks, she has voluntarily asked for extra help from me during her lunch period in order to improve her test-taking performance. Her grades drastically improved from failing to an 84% in a recent exam.

After the sessions, the overall school performance of the first group was significantly higher than that of the second.[7]

## Does Resilience Contribute to Raising Achievement in School?

Yes it does. The above study shows this, as—more dramatically—does another study from Dweck's lab. Susana Claro, David Paunescu, and Carol Dweck were invited to survey the entire cohort of 10th graders in Chile: That's around 148,000 students. They looked at a wide range of factors that might impinge on students' school performance: locality, ethnicity, parental education, family income, type of school, and so on. And they also assessed whether each student had more of a "growth mindset"—the belief that smart, effortful engagement with learning pays off—or a "fixed mindset"—the belief that how well you do depends mainly on a predetermined and fixed amount of intelligence.

Of many findings, one stands out. Children from poor backgrounds are less likely to have a growth mindset, and the resilience and determination that go along with it. However, the minority of poor kids who *do* have a growth mindset are performing in school at a level indistinguishable from that of kids from (and I'm quoting Carol Dweck here) "much, much, much wealthier families." To put it crudely, being brought up to believe that success comes not from being naturally bright, but through intelligent, effortful engagement, acts as a substantial buffer against the otherwise deleterious effect of poverty.[8]

## Does Imagination Improve Learning and Creativity, and Can People Get Better at Imagining?

Yes it does, and yes they can. There are many ways in which imagery and visualization have been shown to impact learning positively, and there has been a good deal of research into how imagery can be used to best effect.[9] For example, mental rehearsal of physical skills can accelerate learning in a wide variety of sports. It works better when done from a first-person perspective—that is, when the imagery includes the feelings and sensations from within one's own body—than from a third-person perspective, where one is visualizing oneself as a person moving about in the field of view. Neuroscientists have found that imagining a movement activates substantially the same circuitry in the brain as does actually making the movement. Repeatedly imagining yourself doing something more skillfully than you currently can really helps that skill to improve (though you have to do the physical practice as well). More experienced and successful athletes tend to use mental rehearsal more, and are better at it. With imagery, as with many things, the more you practice it, the better at it you get. You can make your imagery more vivid, more detailed, more multisensory, and more controllable, and all of those qualities add to its effectiveness as a learning aid.

So imagery can help you learn on the sports field and in the gymnasium, but what about the classroom, or the examination hall? Several studies have shown that training children in "making up pictures in your head" improves their reading comprehension, and helps them learn from a variety of texts.[10] Visualizing processes in science makes those processes vivid and helps them "stick." (Just imagine you are a bite of hamburger being mashed by hard teeth, then squeezed down a pulsating rubbery tube, and squirted with acid to break you up and turn you to slush. You may never forget it!)

> Repeatedly imagining yourself doing something more skillfully than you currently can really helps that skill to improve.

Imagery boosts learning power—but only if you use it in the right way. Students who spent time visualizing themselves having been highly successful on an upcoming exam actually did worse on the test, when it happened, than a control group. It seemed as if feeling assured of success made them work less hard for the test. But a third group who spent time visualizing themselves in the process of revising—imagining themselves settling down with their books and resisting distractions—actually improved their test scores by 8%. (That's information that any teacher and her class ought to find useful!)[11] Similarly, Angela Duckworth and colleagues showed that imagery that zooms in on possible obstacles to learning, and includes ways of coping with these obstacles, significantly improved the grade point average of a group of disadvantaged fifth graders. Duckworth's advice to students is not, "If you dream it you can achieve it," but "If you dream it you have just begun. Now imagine the learning and effort you will have to put in, and the obstacles you will have to overcome, to make it happen. Imagine ways around your obstacles, and get ready in your mind's eye for the journey ahead. And this will help your dream come true."[12]

> Being brought up to believe that success comes not from being naturally bright but through intelligent, effortful engagement, acts as a substantial buffer against the otherwise deleterious effect of poverty.

## Do Deliberate Attempts to Teach Students to Think Clearly Work? And Do They Improve School Performance?

Yes, they do. For example, a scholarly review of a wide range of published research by a team of British academics found, once they had weeded out all the badly conducted studies, that thinking skills interventions did improve students' achievement in school. The overall effect size was 0.64, which is quite substantial. The positive effects seem to be greatest for subjects like math and science. The report concludes, "When thinking skills programmes and approaches are used in schools, they are effective in improving pupils' performance on a range of tested outcomes. The magnitude of the gains found appears to be important when compared with the reported effect sizes of other educational interventions."[13]

As a specific example of teaching thinking, Keith Topping and Steve Trickey evaluated the effect of Philosophy for Children (P4C). A group of 10-year-olds in a British primary school engaged in one session of P4C a week, over a period of 16 months, learning how to think clearly and analytically and how to engage in productive debate. At the end of this period, they showed substantial improvement in their thinking ability, compared to a control group, and, what is more remarkable, this improvement had been maintained two years later, after their transfer to secondary school.[14] Not all attempts to teach thinking have had such lasting effects, and a lot depends on the context and the way the interventions are actually delivered; but it is clearly possible.

## What About Collaboration?

Collaboration involves students talking with and learning from each other. For this to work well, the talk between them, and the kinds of help and support they offer each other, has to be effective. And for this effectiveness to develop, it is usually necessary for teachers to explain, model, and coach the required behaviors. Explicit ground rules clearly explained and discussed with the class, together with timely prompts and commentary by teachers, all serve to scaffold the development of effective collaboration.[15]

In a widespread practice called Reciprocal Teaching, for example, children learn how to help each other with their reading. The goal is to strengthen their reading ability and especially their comprehension. The teacher first models several helpful kinds of support, in dialogue with the whole class, and then encourages and guides students to be able to use the same kind of talk in their conversations with each other. When due attention is given to this coaching process, Reciprocal Teaching has been shown to be a very effective method for boot-strapping children's reading comprehension. When teachers fail to invest in this coaching, and merely put children into pairs or small groups and tell them to "collaborate" or "talk," the effects are much more unreliable. Further research has shown that the benefit comes not from drilling a formulaic set of strategies into children, but from children's growing realization that they can, both individually and collaboratively, become more active and strategic in their approach to reading and its difficulties. And this applies whether a student happens to be playing the "learner" or the "teacher" role in any conversation. Student "teachers" learn at least as much from these structured conversations as their partners.[16]

One widely quoted review of research concludes that, when classroom activities involve well-designed collaboration between students, "there is considerable evidence that students will exert more effort to achieve, learn more, use higher-level reasoning strategies more frequently, build more complete and complex conceptual structures, and retain information learned more accurately."[17]

# Does the Same Apply to Empathy?

Yes it does. Several studies have shown a relationship between students' ability to see the world through other people's eyes and their school performance. It may well be that the ability to handle multiple perspectives—for example, on historical events—is an indicator of more general cognitive complexity, which in turn is related, not surprisingly, to intellectual achievement. However, much of this data shows only a correlation between empathy and performance, so we cannot conclude for sure that empathy is the driving factor in this relationship.

Stronger support comes from recent studies by Federica Bianco and Serena Lecce, researchers at the University of Pavia in Italy, who have shown that students' levels of empathy can be deliberately developed by teachers, and that when this happens, academic performance improves. In one study, eight- and nine-year-old children had four 50-minute lessons in which they read stories about complicated social situations, engaged in small group discussions about the different characters' perspectives, and then had to answer questions about who might be thinking what. Compared to a control group, these children showed significant improvement on tests of empathy that lasted at least as far as a two-month follow-up.[18] And, of course, it goes without saying that empathy has value in its own right, in addition to its effects on achievement.

# Does Reflection Aid Learning?

Yes it does, and quite substantially too—but only in the right hands. A recent review of research by the Education Endowment Foundation (EEF) found that getting students to think more clearly about their own learning can be a very cheap and effective way of improving their levels of achievement. On average, adopting this approach added the equivalent of an extra eight months of schooling to their performance. As we have seen before, the evidence shows that this effect is particularly marked for lower-achieving and older students. And reflection (or "metacognition") can certainly be cultivated. The EEF report notes that "these strategies are usually more effective when taught in collaborative groups so learners can support each other and make their thinking explicit through discussion."[19]

http://www.bbc.com/news/av/magazine-38407635/meet-the-kids-who-think-for-themselves

For a good illustration of children learning to be more reflective, and evidence that this actually helps learning, watch the video that links to the QR code here. In this video, Dylan Wiliam discusses the variability of the evidence. It clearly works well with some teachers and less well with others. We don't yet understand exactly what it is about their teaching that makes the difference.

## Does Learning Power Developed in One Context Transfer to Other Contexts?

The answer to this seems to be "Yes, but only if you teach in a particular way, and for a long time." If you try to teach "skills" or "strategies" in an abstract way, disembedded from specific subject matter, the benefits tend to be short lived and do not generalize to other contexts. Much of the early work on short-term, standalone interventions on "teaching thinking skills" had disappointing results, for example— despite the fact that students often enjoyed the lessons.

But more recent research has begun to unearth teaching methods that encourage the development of transfer.

If you deliberately exercise your skill or your learning disposition in a wide range of different contexts, as you are learning it, this seems to encourage the disembedding of the skill and make it more generalizable. If your history teacher, your math teacher, and your Spanish teacher are all designing activities that stretch your collaboration or self-evaluation, say, then those dispositions become peeled away from any particular wrapping and become more generic. Encouraging conscious reflection on the principles that underlie transfer—the "rules" as to when a learning strength is particularly relevant—also seems to promote transfer. Encouraging students to think about or imagine future situations in which the disposition would be relevant and useful also builds transfer. If all these factors are built into the way a teacher (or preferably a whole school) teaches, then transferability of learning becomes much stronger.[20]

A well-researched example of successful transfer is reported by British science educators Philip Adey and Michael Shayer, using their *Cognitive Acceleration Through Science Education* (CASE) project.[21] Year 7 and 8 students in eight schools in the UK were given a series of science lessons over two years designed to build their capacity for reflective thinking about their own learning, and looking for transfer. In follow-up studies two and three years after the end of the program, the students, when compared with a matched control group, were found to have better higher-order thinking ability and better achievement not only in science tests but also in standardized tests of English and mathematics as well.

Clearly there is much more research that could usefully be done. But these illustrations are encouraging. In many contexts, the strengths that underpin powerful learning are capable of being deliberately cultivated and deliberately broadened in their zones of application; and when that happens, learning improves, and there are wider benefits for quality of life both in school and beyond.

# What the Students Say

Perhaps the most convincing evidence for the LPA is what the students who have experienced it say about it. When a class of 10-year-olds in England were asked about their experience of the LPA, they said things like these:

"I never used to ask questions in class but now I am more involved and I ask questions all the time."

"Before our teacher changed, I wasn't able to finish my work. I was too fidgety and got distracted easily. Now I can pay attention better and I don't get distracted, and I finish what I am doing. I also notice more connections between things in the lessons."

"I like being more resilient. Now, if I don't really want to do something I will have a go anyway and see if I like it, and if I can do it."

"I used to kick off [lose my temper] a lot, but since I've learned about my imagining muscles, I can see that it makes life worse for me as well as everyone else so I don't kick off nearly so much now."

"I'm more resourceful. If I don't have a pen or something, I don't just sit and wait for the teacher to get me one; I go to the back of the room and get it myself."

"To start with, I didn't like being reflective, and I didn't see the point, but now I get it that it's better to look back and find your own mistakes and figure out how to put them right. I learn better that way. Also, being reflective helps me write better stories that have all the good things in."

"I still make mistakes but I am now used to editing my work and it comes out a lot better than I thought it would."

"Playing games, I used to be a sore loser, but now I just think how to win next time."

"I work better in a team now; I'm more fair and I let other people have a go. I don't always jump in and show off."

"I didn't used to be very good at collaborating. (I don't think any of us were!) But now when they're talking I listen and I don't talk, and when we play games I don't argue and I play by the rules."

"I wasn't very resourceful last year; I'd come in in the morning and wait to be told what to do. Now I just get on with it. And my Mum is pleased because in the morning I now pack my bag and think about what I am going to need for the day."

"Overall I think the Learning Power Approach has had a massive effect on me. It has made me a much better learner in school and generally."

And Year 11 and 12 students at an Australian High School said remarkably similar things:

"Sometimes you do it right; other times you learn."

"I used to be very unproductive in my work, but I have found that now I am able to make much better use of my time and be more mindful in what I am doing and focus much more effectively."

"18 months ago, I was more conscious about making mistakes as I would have preferred to get better marks compared to actually making progress in my English ability. Now I'm much more focused on deepening and improving my understanding."

"As a learner I have increased my independence in making sure that if I don't understand a concept I ask questions about it, and taking my own learning into my own hands. Through this, I have tried to capitalize on all my resources including my peers, my teacher and online resources."

"Recently I have begun persevering and setting small goals for myself to keep going and not give up, and then after completion being able to do something that I enjoy. This has meant that I have been able to get more work done and handed in on time."

"I am starting to question not only what I am being taught, but also my ideas about things, and why I think them."

"Capitalizing on outside resources is something I needed to work on more, and when I did push myself to explore them, the variety of perspectives that they provided were incredibly useful."

# And What LPA Teachers Say

To complement the voices of the students, here are some reflections from a group of teachers in a secondary school in Australia. You'll notice that they generally value the language of the LPA, which both enables them to talk more fluently with their students about the process of learning and how it might be strengthened, and also serves as an aid to reflecting on their own teaching practice.

"I find it very useful to talk to the class about perseverance. It helps me 'manage' their reactions to something they think is going to be difficult. Now they focus much more on what they do know, and how they can use that, rather than worrying about what they don't know."

"Students really appreciate the opportunity to review and improve their work, both on their own and through talking to each other."

"My language is slowly changing so my questions are more open-ended, and as a result the students are more engaged, more curious, and more willing to put their thinking caps on."

"Students are more self-aware now, and they can use the language to identify what is happening when they get distracted. Before I start an activity, I ask them to check whether they are focused, and to make sure there is nothing distracting them. . . . One row of Year 11 boys started the year sitting at the back and chatting, but now they are pride of place in the front row, regularly questioning and contributing to discussions."

"I wanted to let you know that my year 12 class last year really punched above their weight. 47% of the class got a 7 [the top grade], when only 25% had the previous year. The remainder of the class all got a 6. I was thrilled for them. They were not simply a more able class than my previous class, they just took more responsibility to own their learning and keep improving. The level of student agency in last year's class was much higher than previously and I think that made all the difference to their approach to learning and, ultimately, the results they got. I truly believe this improvement is because of my shift to an LPA culture with my classes. So thanks for showing me the way."

"I like the language—it is really clear, meaningful and powerful—and the students like it too. It has revealed much to me about them as individuals, and helped me to think about and modify my teaching."

Teachers in the same school were asked more formally how they felt their teaching had changed as a result of being involved in the LPA project, and their reflections are shown in the table presented here. They were using a Visible Thinking Routine called "I used to think. . . . Now I think. . . ," which highlights the ways in which their own attitudes and behaviors have changed over time.

## Teachers' Feedback on the LPA Project

**"How has your thinking about teaching and learning changed as a result of this project?"**

| I used to think. . . . | Now I think. . . . |
| --- | --- |
| As a teacher it was my responsibility to manage every aspect of students' behavior in class. | In the same way that students can be in charge of their own learning, they can take charge of their behavior. A particular example of this is talking about the matter of distractions and helping students to recognize and manage their own distractions. It helps them regulate their own behavior in class. |
| I wasn't sure whether students would be on board with a concept such as LPA. | Students are quite self-aware and keen to become more effective learners. They know that distractions get in the way, for example, and welcome the notion of taking charge of them. |
| It was important to stick to the curriculum I was teaching and students needed to stick to the focus target content (otherwise their work would be too inaccurate). | I think the LPA project has helped me to allow and encourage greater curiosity among the learners in my classes, even if this means they have strayed slightly from the topic or target language I have been trying to teach. What is important is to guide them on how to *inquire* effectively. |

| I used to think. . . . | Now I think. . . . |
|---|---|
| An assessment signalled the end of a unit, before moving on to the next thing. | Assessment should be used as a measure of the knowledge we have already, and what we need to know next. It is ok if the learning happens after an assessment. It is the learning that is important—not the grade. I try to remind students of this regularly so they can have the perseverance to keep going and keep trying. |
| Results are more important. | Students need feedback, not grades. |
| It would be hard to implement LPA in a Foreign Languages context. | It presented a good opportunity to implement aspects of LPA in the target language, which students learned and used appropriately. |
| That a noisy classroom was an unproductive one. | Now I think that noise often equates to productive, collaborative learning. |
| That I should only teach students how to solve certain problems *my* way. | That there are numerous *correct* ways to solve problems, it's just that some are more efficient than others. |
| That if I asked students to select their own questions, then they'd take the easiest option. | That students will often choose to challenge themselves if they understand the value of doing so. |
| That by senior school it would be hard for students to let go of a fixed mindset about their ability to learn in math. | That with time and effort and a conscious use of language, students' mindsets *can* shift in secondary school. |
| That students would be reluctant to talk about mistakes they'd made in front of the class. | That if mistakes are framed as awesome learning opportunities, then heaps of students are prepared to share their errors. |

## Wondering

What kind of evidence has the most impact on you? What would make you most likely to give something new a go? Is it research findings published in high-status journals? Case studies by other teachers in situations you can identify with? Simple vignettes and illustrations? Or direct testimony from students? How typical do you think your responses are of teachers in general?

When you read the table of teachers' "I used to think. . . . Now I think. . . ." reflections, which statements did you identify with most closely? Were you more with the comments in the left-hand or the right-hand column? Or a mixture of both? Has your own thinking about teaching changed over the last year, say, and if so, in what ways?

In the follow-up books in this series, we will give you lots of ideas about how you might monitor the effects of learning power tweaks in your classroom or your school as a whole. But for now, see if you can think up some low-tech ways in which you might tell whether your students are becoming more

- Curious
- Focused
- Determined
- Imaginative
- Thoughtful
- Collaborative
- Reflective
- Self-organizing

# Notes

1. Sophie von Stumm, Benedikt Hell, and Tomas Chamorro-Premuzic, "The Hunger Mind: Intellectual Curiosity is the Third Pillar of Academic Performance."
2. Todd Kashdan, *Curious?*
3. Adrian Raine, Chandra Reynolds, Peter Venables, and Sarnoff Mednick, "Stimulation Seeking and Intelligence: A Prospective Longitudinal Study."
4. John Dewey, *How We Think*, p. 33.
5. Jonathan Smallwood, Daniel Fishman, and Jonathan Schooler, "Counting the Cost of an Absent Mind: Mind Wandering as an Under-Recognised Influence on Educational Performance."
6. Linda Lantieri, Madhavi Nambiar, Susanne Harnett, and Eden Kyse, "Cultivating Inner Resilience in Educators and Students."
7. Lisa Blackwell, Kali Trzesniewski, and Carol Dweck, "Implicit Theories on Intelligence Predict Achievement Across an Adolescent Transition: A Longitudinal Study and an Intervention."
8. Susana Claro, David Paunescu, and Carol Dweck, "Growth Mindset Tempers the Effect of Poverty on Academic Achievement."
9. For a fuller treatment of this research, see Chapter 5 in Guy Claxton, *Wise Up*.
10. For example, Michael Pressley, "Mental Imagery Helps Eight-Year-Olds Remember What They Read."
11. Lien Pham and Shelley Taylor, "From Thought to Action: Effect of Process- Vs. Outcome-Based Mental Simulations on Performance."
12. Angela Duckworth, Teri Kirby, Anton Gollwitzer, and Gabriele Oettingen, "From Fantasy to Action: Mental Contrasting With Implementation Intentions (MCII) Improves Academic Performance in Children."
13. Steve Higgins, Elaine Hall, Viv Baumfield, and David Moseley, "A Meta-Analysis of the Impact of the Implementation of Thinking Skills Approaches on Pupils."

14. Keith Topping and Steve Trickey, "Collaborative Philosophical Enquiry for School Children."

15. Neil Mercer and Karen Littleton, *Dialogue and the Development of Children's Thinking: A Socio-Cultural Approach.*

16. Annemarie Palincsar and Ann Brown, "Reciprocal Teaching of Comprehension-Fostering and Comprehension-Monitoring Strategies." Annemarie Palincsar and Kristine Schutz, "Reconnecting Strategy Instruction With Its Theoretical Roots."

17. David Johnson and Roger Johnson, "Making Cooperative Learning Work," p. 73.

18. Federica Bianco and Serena Lecce, "Translating Child Development Research Into Practice: Can Teachers Foster Children's Theory of Mind in Primary School?"

19. *Education Endowment Foundation Toolkit.* See https://educationendowmentfoundation.org.uk/resources/teaching-learning-toolkit/meta-cognition-and-self-regulation, para. 2.

20. The best discussion of "the transfer problem" I know is Chapter 4 of David Perkins, *Making Learning Whole.*

21. Philip Adey and Michael Shayer, "The Effects of Cognitive Acceleration."

# 10

# Distinctions and Misconceptions

Intelligence plus character—that is the goal of true education.

Martin Luther King

So now you know the philosophy and rationale for the Learning Power Approach (LPA), and have an idea as to what it looks and sounds like in practice. Remember my image of the socket set: This book provides the conceptual "handle" onto which the following three practical "socket" books are going to fit. They will focus on primary teaching, secondary teaching, and whole-school culture change and leadership. There may be others, for example, on early childhood education, tertiary education, and teacher training. In this chapter I want to round up some of the critical features of the LPA, emphasizing where these differ from some other approaches that are superficially similar, and addressing some common criticisms and misunderstandings. To change the metaphor, this chapter reviews the launchpad for the LPA to ensure that you blast off in just the right direction. Though the LPA is quite easy to describe, we have found that it is also quite easy to get wrong, and for it to slide off track. So it is useful to highlight some of the key messages that have been woven throughout the book.

## Focus on Learning Power, Not Just Learning

It is important to keep talking about "learning power" and not just "learning." *Learning* is a very popular word at the moment, but it is slippery. Just relabeling students as "learners" doesn't change anything unless it signals *a genuine broadening of the range of valued outcomes of education to include the habits of effective learning themselves.*

Schools that use phrases like "high-quality learning" or "improving the quality of students' learning" may not have made that shift. In practice, they still talk as if learning refers to the *outcomes* of education, rather than to the *processes*, so they are inclined to take "improving learning" simply to mean "getting better grades." And, as we have seen, it is perfectly possible to raise students' achievement in a way that weakens, rather than strengthens, their learning power. Better test scores do not imply that students are growing in their independence and capability in the face of challenge and uncertainty. Helping children learn what they need to know to do well on school tests is not the same as helping them develop their broader ability to face new challenges with confidence and craft. In many schools and education systems, the habit of foregrounding knowledge acquisition and test performance is so strong that it is all too easy to slide back into seeing the LPA merely as a way of raising those outcomes. Consciously using the phrase "learning power" (or something similar) helps to resist that magnetic pull.

Central to the LPA is a vision of 21st century education. We think that a core aim of schools should be to turn out powerful, confident learners (not just people who can talk and write fluently about what they *already* know). When they meet tricky stuff, do they feel defeated and shy away, or trot out past solutions that do not really suit the new problem? Or do they roll up their sleeves, take a fresh look, and get stuck in? Broadly, which of those two attitudes they have developed will powerfully influence the rest of their lives—especially when the world is changing so fast? Remember the quotation from John Holt with which I began Chapter 5?

> Helping children learn what they need to know to do well on school tests is not the same as helping to develop their broader ability to face new challenges with confidence and craft.

> Since we cannot know what knowledge will be needed in the future, it is senseless to try to teach it in advance. Instead our job must be to turn out young people who love learning so much, and who learn so well, that they will be able to learn whatever needs to be learned.[1]

When Holt wrote that 50 years ago, a lot of people rolled their eyes and wrote him off as a child-centered romantic. And of course there is indeed knowledge all young people need to have that is best taught in school. Holt may be guilty of some exaggeration, but his main point is even more valid now than when he wrote it. Today I rarely meet anyone who doesn't think that the need for school to produce learners as well as knowers is just plain common sense.

(There are a few, but I tend not to meet them!) Learning power is what underpins Holt's love of learning, and confidence and capability at it.

## Learning, Not Thinking

Many people in education talk about developing students' ability to *think*, rather than to *learn*. They often use classroom activities that are designed to develop higher-order thinking skills, for example. But I see thinking as just one aspect of learning, and so prefer *learning* as the more inclusive word. It will have been clear that, when the LPA talks of preparing young people for a learning life, it is taking a pretty broad view of what learning is. People encounter a variety of kinds of learning in the course of their lives, and we believe that school should get youngsters ready for all of them. Sometimes, in life, you have to commit information to memory and be able to recall it accurately, to structure a written argument, or do the calculations for your tax form. But you will also need to learn how to get along with people from backgrounds and cultures that are very different from your own, how to master new technology, how to find your way around a new neighborhood, how to detect hokum, how to calm a fractious child, and how to approach complicated decisions.

Not all kinds of learning require deliberate reasoning or scholarship: Research shows that complicated decision making benefits from intuition as well as clear thinking.[2] And not all kinds of people—including perfectly intelligent and successful people—are bookish by inclination. So there is no good reason I can see why schools should focus so tightly on practicing the habits of *academic* learning, and neglect or marginalize the equally important habits of practical, social, and emotional learning. This is why, at least in my version of the LPA, I prefer to talk about learning rather than thinking. Though we can argue about semantics, to me, "thinking" has an intellectual feel about it, while "learning" embraces both reason and experience, mind and body, thought and feeling. Figuring things out neatly and rationally is only one tool in the learner's toolbox.

> Learning embraces both reason and experience, mind and body, thought and feeling.

This leads on to another characteristic feature of the LPA: It treats learning power as a matter of personal traits and dispositions as much as cognitive capability. How good a learner you are reflects much more than your IQ or "executive function." It reflects your social attitudes, your emotional tolerances and frailties, your capacity for "grace under pressure" as Ernest Hemingway called it, and your inclination to be reflective or self-aware. It also reaches right down into people's values and identities. How and when we learn may be powerfully guided by our gender, class, ethnicity, and many other facets of our character. We learn when we feel intrigued and stimulated, and also when feeling inadequate, uncertain, disconcerted, confused, disappointed, or frustrated. These aren't matters of knowledge or skill; they are matters of temperament and character. The LPA sees learning as a whole-person phenomenon.

## Learning Dispositions Are Malleable, Not Fixed

The LPA depends on the assumption that these attitudes and dispositions are, at least to some extent, malleable rather than fixed. We saw in the previous chapter that traits such as curiosity, determination, and collaboration can be strengthened—or weakened—by experience, both at home and at school. Angela Duckworth's Character Lab, for example, has amassed a good deal of research to this effect.[3] Carol Dweck has shown that even quite brief interventions can shift students from a fixed to a growth mindset.[4]

But this doesn't mean that you can just "teach" the traits as if they were another subject. Talking and thinking about resilience won't, by itself, make you more resilient. It will just make you more *knowledgeable* about resilience. These characteristics are (as Aristotle pointed out) habits that grow over time. Dispositions are just ways of behaving that you have gradually become more disposed to use, until they have become second nature: part of the way in which you naturally meet different kinds of situations. To be honest means to be generally disposed to tell the truth and hand in lost property. To be a determined character means to be generally disposed not to give up quickly when faced with difficulty. And so on. So while talking about the learning powers may help, they also need to be cultivated through the whole educational milieu in which young people are immersed.

Attitudes toward learning grow over time in two different ways. In *disembedding*, they may begin to be established in one subject or domain and then develop a growing range of applicability to include other domains, often being "customized" along the way. A child's growing confidence to ask her own questions (in school) may manifest first only in one subject, perhaps with a teacher with whom she feels a strong rapport, but then spreads to other subjects and wider domains of out-of-school learning. In *embedding*, an explicitly learned set of attitudes or strategies are discovered, by guided experience, to apply, again with modifications, to a particular area of study. Through the discovery of new or extended areas of applicability, an attitude can gradually become both more "generic" and more embedded within particular domains. In short, the generalizability of the learning strengths cannot be presumed, nor does this process occur automatically; but it can be deliberately fostered.

Unnecessary confusion has been caused by the contrary assumption that attitudes toward learning can be "taught" in abstract and then ought to magically pop up whenever and wherever they might be applicable. E. D. Hirsch, for example, says that "the conception that 21st century skills are all-purpose muscles that, once developed, can be applied to new and unforeseen domains of experience [is] an error that is fundamental and fatal."[5] He is right to critique the naïve view that "all-purposeness" is somehow automatically given, but he is wrong to reject the possibility that attributes like curiosity and imagination can be *helped to become more generic*. And the fact that these traits don't mean the same thing for a four-year-old as an 18-year-old, or to a historian and a mathematician, is entirely compatible with the idea that we can deliberately influence their growth. Yes, older children are capable of more sophisticated ways of maintaining concentration or collaborating, for example, than younger children. And curiosity obviously takes different forms in different subjects. But that is no reason to throw the baby out with the bathwater and dismiss the whole notion of cultivating general learning habits.

## Is the LPA "Traditional" or "Progressive"?

So we come to the vexed question of whether the LPA is "traditional" or "progressive." In many countries, including my own, the UK, pigeon-holing all approaches to education as one or the other still seems to be a popular pastime. Many who defend a traditional approach try hard to characterize anything that doesn't fit a narrow model of chalk-and-talk as laissez-faire, child-centered, and anti-knowledge—or "trendy nonsense," as our current minister for schools often calls it. A book by British researcher Daisy Christodoulou called *Seven Myths About Education*, for example, claims (following E. D. Hirsch) that any attempt to cultivate learning dispositions is flawed, because (a) it is actually impossible to separate "knowledge" from "skills," and (b) trying to teach "skills" competes with, and therefore distracts from, the central aim of education, which is to impart "knowledge."[6]

Such polarization is unnecessary and unhelpful. Was Giselle Isbell's math lesson traditional or progressive? It obviously combined—as 21st century teaching must—elements of both. The development of mathematical knowledge and skill were clearly central, and the success of schools like hers in getting students—many from poor backgrounds—good grades and admissions to prestigious colleges attests to their rigor. Yet Giselle's methods of teaching involved a good deal of exploratory talk and imaginative trial and error by students, with the explicit intention of building up their fortitude in the face of difficulty, their ability to contribute productively to discussion, and their confidence in working things out for themselves. The development and disembedding of useful habits of mind is cleverly woven into the ongoing fabric of the lesson, so the argument that knowledge suffers when skills are being addressed simply doesn't apply. Knowledge acquisition and skill development are not involved in a tug-of-war for time and attention; they are warp and weft of learners' everyday experience.

> Knowledge acquisition and skill development are not involved in a tug-of-war for time and attention; they are warp and weft of learners' everyday experience.

Over the last hundred years there have indeed been pioneering attempts to develop better forms of education that have turned out to be naïve or ineffectual, and there may be classrooms in which those early methodologies still persist. But that is not the state of the art. It is a weak (or ideologically blinded) form of argument that attacks its opponents' worst examples. The LPA represents a new middle way that manages to hit two kinds of targets at the same time: rigor *and* imagination; knowledge *and* mental development; respect for authority and tradition *and* creative and critical thinking. There is no necessary conflict, either conceptual or practical, between the two kinds of desirable outcomes for education. But it takes a subtle pedagogy to achieve both aims, and that is precisely what the LPA has been at pains to develop.

## Evidence, Not Measurement

Traditionalists sometimes disparage approaches like the LPA on the grounds that the development of learning habits cannot be assessed. They argue that there is no point in trying to cultivate them, because there is no way of knowing if the effort has been successful or not. While it is true that it is hard to think about how to evidence the development of resilience or concentration, and it is, to many people, an unfamiliar question, it is far from impossible. Much progress has been made in the last few years in developing ways of doing so. As I mentioned in the Introduction, back in 2002 my colleague Margaret Carr and I wrote a paper called "Tracking the Development of Learning Dispositions," which reviewed the pros and cons of a whole variety of possible approaches to the problem: student self-report questionnaires, teacher observation schedules, 360° appraisals, cumulative portfolios, performance tasks, and so on. We concluded—as do Angela Duckworth and David Yeager in a more recent revisiting of the issue[7]—that every method has it dangers and drawbacks, but that a basket of different types of data, taken together, can provide robust and reliable evidence. A mixture of quantitative and qualitative kinds of data avoids the pitfalls of both. (That is why I think it is better to talk about *evidencing* progress than *measuring* or *evaluating* it. It doesn't help to get locked in by language to only one kind of evidence.)[8]

Let me mention just two specific examples. (There will be much more detail on this issue in the follow-up books in this series.) Margaret Carr has gone on to develop robust methodologies for showing the growth of learning powers in young children, and her approaches have been adopted throughout her native country of New Zealand as well as internationally. One in particular revolves around the collection of what she calls "learning stories"—documented instances of individual children's personal bests in some aspect of their approach to learning. When they persist with difficulty for longer than they have before, or have collaborated well with partners who they would not normally have chosen, this can be quickly captured (often on a tablet or a smart phone) in a photo, a video, a sound recording, or a brief vignette written by an observer, displayed on their classroom wall, and added to a child's growing portfolio. Children can then be engaged in reflective real-time or retrospective conversations in which they learn to notice, articulate, and appreciate their own mental growth.[9]

The second example is the Effective Lifelong Learning Inventory (ELLI), a self-report questionnaire specifically focusing on the development of learning power, which my colleague Patricia Broadfoot and I developed at the University of Bristol with the help of our researcher Ruth Deakin-Crick. Extensive trialing showed that ELLI produced evidence that was both valid and reliable for Key Stages 2 and 3 students in the UK (7- to 14-year-olds), and could generate valuable conversations with students about their own attitudes toward learning, as well as convincing data of the success of a school's efforts to improve these attitudes. ELLI has now been extended to a wide range of other groups of learners, including ex-offenders, aboriginal adult learners in Australia, and corporate employees. As my co-originator Patricia Broadfoot has put it,

> Today, ELLI is associated with a range of development tools that help individuals address their learning needs. . . . What we now have is a language that makes learning itself much more "smart"; that puts the learner in the driving seat; that shows that the power to learn is itself learnable.[10]

## Precision About Language

As you will see, the LPA tends to be fussy about the language used to describe the traits of the powerful learner. (Art Costa, Bena Kallick, and I have recently written about this for the U.S. journal *Educational Leadership*.)[11] Many people, like us, believe that this challenge to education is critically important, so it is no wonder that there is a wide variety of terminology being used. Some people talk of *skills*— 21st century skills, noncognitive skills, soft skills, thinking and learning skills. Others prefer terms like *attitudes, aptitudes, habits of mind, dispositions, learning habits, mindsets, competences* (or *competencies*), or *character strengths*. What are the pros and cons of these different words and phrases? Though this may seem a bit academic, we don't think it is. We think that *how* we talk about these desirable outcomes of education really matters. Our vocabulary has practical effects on the mood we create in our classrooms and the ways in which our students respond.

To illustrate, let's look at the word *skill*. It is useful in emphasizing that educational outcomes such as "being inquisitive" or "persisting in the face of difficulty" are practical behaviors, responses to situations rather than decontextualized displays of knowledge. It reminds us that there is more to real life than being able to call facts quickly to mind, or checking the correct box on a test. In a fast-changing world, education has to prepare you to *act* intelligently when you meet the unexpected, not just to be able to trot out well-rehearsed performances of knowledge and understanding. However, "skill" usually goes along with the idea of "training," so it makes the development of these kinds of responses look like a technical matter. But encouraging the development of an attitude of curiosity or self-evaluation, say, is not like training someone to shoot a rifle or make a béchamel sauce. Curiosity has a skillful aspect, sure, but it also involves a deeper pleasure in finding out new things and an openness to novelty and challenge. To develop such inclinations, students need ongoing opportunities, encouragement, and guidance in a wide range of contexts, not just training. Attempts to train students in thinking skills have often been shown to be ineffective, because the skills do not last, they do not spread to new situations, and they do not come to mind when they are needed. As we have seen, to be a good collaborator, for example, you need to be ready and willing as well as just able.[12]

A skill also tends to be seen as something that students "can do," so it makes sense to ask, "Can they or can't they?" You can check a box to say that Bill is able to tie his shoelaces, use a spellchecker, or read to a certain level. But you can't do that with "collaboration" or "mental toughness" or "critical thinking," because they take a lifetime to develop. Which of us could honestly tick a box to say we have developed the disposition to "show empathy" or "consider multiple perspectives"? The truth is more complex, isn't it? It's more like, "Well, partly, on a good day, in some contexts, when I remember." So our methods and measures need to be correspondingly nuanced. For these reasons I tend to avoid using the word *skills* in the context of the LPA. It steers my thinking in unhelpful directions.

Some people prefer the word *habits*—I quite like it myself. I like the idea that what we are trying to do is help young people build habitual ways of responding to challenge or uncertainty, not just developing technical skills that they might or might not deploy in practice. The problem with *habit,* though, is that it has a knee-jerk quality about it. Habits are often things you do mindlessly or automatically, whenever the right trigger is pulled—and learning is too complicated to be reduced to a few reflexes. When I am reading a difficult book, I'm not just "persevering" like a robot. I am thinking and imagining and wondering and taking breaks and writing notes, as well as reading, and these learning activities are interwoven fluidly and dynamically, depending on the dictates of the moment.

Human beings are not collections of stimulus-response associations. That won't even do to describe the behavior of rats, let alone schoolchildren. We humans are more like floating clouds of inclinations that crystallize into actual behaviors freshly every moment, depending on what is going on. Just as rain starts to fall from clouds only when there is a particular constellation of temperature, air pressure, humidity, wind speed, dust particles, the shape of the land mass beneath them, and so on, so all our different traits and tendencies resolve themselves into actions— to lean in and investigate, or to turn tail and retreat, for instance—in complicated ways. That's why we have big brains, to do this integrating and sorting out, so we don't stay paralyzed by indecision (or not often). To signal this complexity, *disposition* tends to be the academic word of choice at the moment, but it sounds rather scholarly, so I often prefer *inclination* or *tendency.*

It is not that dispositions are different kinds of things from skills, by the way. We don't have to get tangled up worrying whether "questioning" or "self-evaluating" are skills or dispositions. As I've said, a disposition is just a skill that we are actively inclined ("disposed") to make use of. We want to help children, all other things being equal, to become *more inclined* to be inquisitive, imaginative, resourceful, and determined when they are struggling with learning: That's all.

While we are on the subject of language, you may have noticed that—as well as skills—some other familiar notions have been downplayed or ignored altogether in this book: creativity, motivation, problem-solving, and self-esteem, for example. Though creativity is clearly important, I don't think of it as a special kind of mental resource that people possess to differing degrees. If you look carefully, you'll see that creativity emerges from the well-orchestrated use of a number of the learning powers: imagination, certainly, but also reflection, self-evaluation, determination, curiosity, and frequently collaboration. So you can't cultivate creativity per se, but you can cultivate more specific members of the orchestra.

Motivation is similar. There is no kind of psychological fuel that "unmotivated" students lack. "How do we motivate them?" is the wrong question. Students may be disengaged from what their teachers are offering for a whole range of reasons. If Jo looks unmotivated to learn X, it can mean any combination of the following:

> Jo is not currently interested in X.
>
> Jo is interested in X but has competing priorities. For example,
>
> - Jo is tired or upset.
> - Jo is not confident in her learning; she doubts that her efforts and resources will be equal to the learning task.
> - Jo is frightened of what might happen to her at recess.
> - Jo is worried about her family or her friendships.
>
> There are distractions that are disrupting Jo's concentration, and/or Jo has difficulty concentrating.
>
> Jo doesn't like the person who wants her to learn X and wants to thwart him.
>
> Jo believes that becoming good at X will conflict with her image of herself, or jeopardize her standing with her friends.
>
> Jo believes that if she tries and fails at X, she will feel even worse about herself than she does already, so it is better not to try.

Just as there is no one medicine that cures all listlessness, so there is no nostrum that will cure "unmotivatedness." It is not smart to think so simplistically.

"Problem-solving," too, is too big a concept to be useful. I agree with Hirsch that there are no generic problem-solving skills. Not being able to solve a mathematical equation is a problem. Not knowing how to repair a precious relationship that has gone wrong is a problem. Being ill is a problem. But intelligent attempts to solve these three problems will have almost nothing in common. Again, it is better to go to a finer grain of analysis before trying to identify the learning habits and attitudes that people might benefit from.

And "self-esteem" is also problematic. It is a mistake to think that, as a parent or a teacher, you have to boost children's self-esteem before they are fit to learn. Constantly telling them how wonderful and talented they are is a sure way to undermine their resilience, for example.[13] And the research shows that the relationship between self-esteem and school performance goes in the opposite direction from the one commonly supposed. It is not that you have to feel good about yourself to learn. Rather, feeling good about yourself is more often the product of having struggled with something difficult and eventually having cracked it.[14]

## Learning Muscles and the Mind Gym

As well as being fussy about vocabulary, the LPA tries in general to use language that is down-to-earth and concrete, so that students and their parents—as well as hard-pressed teachers who don't have the time to read the research literature—can easily see what we are talking about. Some other approaches seem to think that we need long, unfamiliar, abstract concepts to talk about those desirable outcomes of education that are different from grades. And sometimes we may indeed need to use technical terms like *metacognitive strategies, self-regulation,* or *agency.* But if we get too stuck on such terminology, we risk making the whole enterprise seem alien to people's normal lives.

As you have seen, I often use the simple metaphor of "learning muscles" to get the idea of the learning dispositions across to people. Especially with younger children, this seems to work well. It helps them get the idea that how they learn is not just a matter of how bright or smart they are, as if there were some fixed-sized bucket of general-purpose mental resources inside their heads setting a limit on what they could achieve. Rather, learning depends on a host of well-orchestrated learning attitudes and abilities, each one of which can get stronger through being exercised. Thinking of your brain as being a collection of muscles is more beneficial than thinking of it as a fixed-sized bucket. Of course, brains are not made of muscle—it's just a metaphor—but it is a fruitful and appealing one. It is also more scientifically accurate to think of brains as collections of muscles than buckets of varying sizes. Lauren Resnick from the University of Pittsburgh, one of the world's most eminent researchers on intelligence, now says that intelligence is "the sum total of your habits of mind."[15]

The metaphor invites teachers to see themselves as mind coaches, constructing exercise programs for (and with) students that systematically stretch and strengthen different aspects of their all-around learning fitness. Teachers can encourage students to set targets for themselves and pursue personal bests, not in physical speed or strength, but in perseverance, empathy, or craftsmanship. Their classroom becomes a "mind gym" where students come to get their brains stretched. Topics, as well as being of interest or value in their own right, are seen as "exercise machines" that are suited to the development of different learning dispositions—and not only the obvious pairings like mathematics and reasoning, drama and empathy, or art and imagination. Perhaps—as Jerome Bruner suggested many years ago—science is well suited to the development of certain kinds of disciplined intuition.[16] Or—as Ron Berger's Expeditionary Learning schools have shown—vocational classes can be effective training grounds for skilled and sensitive critique.[17]

This "mind-training" perspective on education can also help school leaders think about the overall purpose of the education they are offering, and thus aim for greater coherence. Without a clear and committed sense of the *kinds of minds* we are trying to develop, it is hard to stop schools—especially high schools—from splitting into different subject silos. An average high school day requires youngsters to visit six or more parallel universes (English, mathematics, science, history, geography, Spanish, and so on) that seem to coexist but that are not connected. There is no overarching vision that makes it plain to students what all this compartmentalized knowledge adds up to. But when there is another set of desired outcomes of education—the learning muscles—that cuts across the pursuit of subject-specific grades, then greater coherence becomes a possibility. Those 13 long years amount to something more than just a sigh of relief (or despair) at getting (or not getting) the fistful of grades you need to enter the next phase of education.

> When there is another set of desired outcomes of education—the learning muscles—that cuts across the pursuit of subject-specific grades, then greater coherence is possible.

## Pedagogy Rules

The analogy of the river I used earlier makes it plain that learning in classrooms is going on at three levels simultaneously. Knowledge is being taught. Literacies and academic skills are being trained. And learning habits are being cultivated. Teaching, training, and cultivating are influenced by different aspects of the environment that the teacher creates. Teaching (the causes of World War I, for example) requires the teacher to show good understanding and clear exposition of her subject, and accurate marking. Training (the ability to structure a short essay, for instance) relies on the kinds of exercises and feedback that build competence. Cultivating (an attitude of craftsmanship, say) depends, as we have seen, on many facets of the students' environment: how the teacher talks, what she models, how she lays out the furniture and selects the displays, and so on. When it comes to building positive learning habits, it is the way teachers construct the overall ethos of the classroom that conveys the messages that are to be learned. In the LPA, as you have seen, we often talk about teachers as (co)designers of learning.

The LPA invites teachers to become more aware of these cultural messages and the ways in which they are conveyed, so that they can make more conscious choices about the kinds of attitudes that they are steering their students toward, and design the milieu accordingly. The LPA relies on tweaks to a range of small, apparently innocuous aspects of the ways teachers behave in the presence of their students. In fact, when it comes to the long, slow cultivation of learning habits, pedagogy trumps curriculum.

> When it comes to building positive learning habits, it is the way teachers design the overall ethos of the classroom that conveys the messages that are to be learned.

This is an aspect of the teacher's job that is not so often stressed and discussed in other approaches, some of which tend to focus predominantly (if not exclusively) on *what* is being learned, and *how well* students have mastered it. If there is little awareness of or interest in the longer-term development of mental character, then what is being learned in the depths of the river may be haphazard or even detrimental. Without meaning to, teachers may be encouraging students to become compliant, dependent, and conservative rather than robust, adventurous, and inquisitive. For example, draconian discipline can produce a cowed and slavish attitude, leading students to suppress their vitality, initiative, and sense of responsibility. But if discipline is viewed as a method of coaching the development of self-discipline, is framed and explained as such, and is gradually slackened over time so that students discover for themselves the pride and satisfaction that comes from effort and craftsmanship, there is quite a different feel. It may seem a subtle distinction, but its ramifications are dramatic.[18]

This emphasis on teachers as classroom designers may have tricky implications. If teaching style is so important to the development of learning habits, it cannot any longer be a personal choice. In traditional schools, teachers were largely free to teach as they felt fit, provided that students were treated well, behaved decently, and were making good progress on the tests. Indeed, teachers often prized their own personal style and fiercely defended their individuality. School principals may need to make time for staff to discuss this implication, and to agree on a working compromise between individual flair and some "pedagogical nonnegotiables": ground rules for creating the classroom milieu.

As coaches of the learning mind, schoolteachers are needed to help guide students' journeys into learning how to learn. Like any good coach, they will sense when to push and challenge and when to back off and reassure. They will have a good idea what the next step on the road toward becoming an elite-level learner might be, and how to present it to their students. But being an LPA coach is different from being a facilitator. A facilitator just helps individuals to go where they want to go, and largely foregoes their ability to "know better." But LPA coaches do believe that they know better than students what is in the students' long-term best interests, and they try to win students' agreement about the kinds of learning that are going to go on in the classroom. Students may not automatically understand why resilience, concentration, and self-discipline are important for a fulfilled life, but they are, and it is the job of LPA teachers to try to help their learners see that, and—if they haven't already—experience it for themselves.

## It's Not Just Classrooms; It's the Ethos of the Whole School

The LPA tries to knit together everything that goes on in a school. This is quite unusual. Commonly, the way a school works emerges from a mishmash of factors: the perspective of the principal or the local superintendent; the latest dictates of government; currently fashionable books, research, and ideas; a history of relationships and compromises; the opinions of strong personalities; the loud voices of a few parents; pressures and resistances from teachers' unions; received wisdom and unquestioned routines; the requirements of examinations; and so on. Because of these competing currents, there are often fudges and inconsistencies. We would love to do more project work—but the timetable just won't allow it (and the deputy or assistant principal in charge of timetabling is a powerful figure). The home page of the school's website talks grandly about preparing all our students to fulfill their potential, or become independent learners—but when you sit at the back of a routine lesson on geometry or history, it is hard to see how these inspiring values have changed anything. They don't flow through into the "minute particulars" (as visionary poet William Blake called them) of everyday teaching and learning. The practice and the vision have become dislocated. (And sometimes they are even at odds. I have been in schools that make a big deal of respect— but in practice it is very clear that this fine quality is only expected to flow one way—from students to teachers. Teachers treat students harshly or disdainfully, and seem not to notice the hypocrisy.)

**FIGURE 10.1**  How a (Vision) Magnet Produces
Coherence in a School

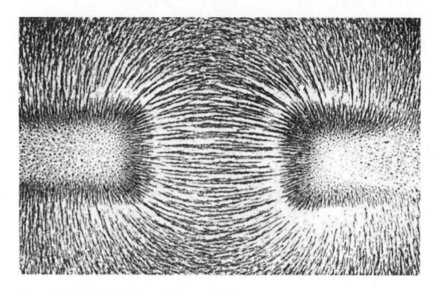

*Source:* Duff (1916, p. 315, Figure 234a)

You may remember a demonstration in your own high
school physics class that involved shaking some iron filings
onto a piece of paper, where they lay all higgledy-piggledy.
And then you put a magnet under the paper, and magic
happened! All the little scraps of iron lined up into neat
patterns (see Figure 10.1). The LPA tries to do that with
the culture and practices of a school. If we say we want
youngsters to be inquisitive and questioning, we need to
give them opportunities to develop those inclinations, and
make sure that those opportunities expand and deepen as
the students move through the school. If we want them to
become more resilient, we have to get them to strengthen
their learning stamina week by week. We have to get them
to think about resilience, to talk about its role in the lives
of people they admire (singers, sportsmen and women,
spiritual or community leaders, grandparents, whoever).
LPA teachers try to think through what these ambitions

actually mean for the way they teach. And school principals look for the wider implications for every aspect of school life: timetables, record keeping, relationships with parents—everything. It can be hard to see all the places where a tweak is possible—but if the school is to become an ever more effective incubator of those values, it has to be done.

Remember my story about banning the use of erasers for a while, to get students used to learning from their mistakes, not trying to pretend they never happened. If we want young people to grow up with a realistic view of what learning is like, and with the perseverance and willingness to make and learn from mistakes, then we might want to review the school policy on the use of erasers in classrooms. This could be the subject of a discussion in a staff meeting, and eventually of a whole-school decision. This would be one small example of how the day-to-day practice of a school can be knitted more tightly into its vision. If our vision were different, then the iron filings of pedagogy would line up differently. When a whole staff do try banning erasers, you will hear the tiny clicks of a lot of iron filings aligning themselves with the magnetic field of a coherent set of values. In contrast, approaches to school improvement sometimes seem to be more of a jumble—a few fun activities that are designed to exercise students' thinking skills, plus a new homework policy, plus an initiative on bullying, maybe—that fails to change the culture as a whole.

## Provisional and Growing, Not Set in Stone

The LPA is a work in progress, for several reasons. First, there are always going to be disagreements between professionals about how to express and prioritize the different elements of learning power, and fresh claims for introducing other elements that have been overlooked. Learning power does not claim to be a watertight scientific theory; its validity lies primarily in any practical value it has for real teachers in real schools, trying to do the best for their students. Is it a helpful framework that stimulates experiments in planning lessons and developing policy, or not?

And it is important that any description of learning power is not set in stone, because every school needs to make it their own. Some schools already have clear statements of their vision and values, and any new insights about the student attributes they are trying to cultivate ought to be integrated with those preexisting statements. Any framework needs to be thought about, discussed, and customized by the school community if there is going to be real understanding and buy-in. Without that engagement, there is the greater risk that it becomes just another damn initiative—the latest fad that flared up and died away like so many before it.

That's why we call the LPA an "approach," not a "program" or an "initiative." It offers suggestions, illustrations, and frameworks that can guide and support a school's development. It is like gardening. We give you some tools, some compost, some seeds, and some trelliswork, and hope you will go off and create your own learning garden in your school. Some other approaches to thinking and learning are more prescriptive. They seem to be offering the royal road to 21st century education, and they try to guard and quality-assure their intellectual property carefully. They may try to tell you that mind maps are the answer to everything, for instance, and that there is only One Right Way to do a mind map properly, which you have to be taught by a highly qualified instructor (usually for a sizeable fee).

Of course, people can always misinterpret ideas and mess them up. Give too much freedom and there is a risk that—with the best of intentions—they will introduce what Dylan Wiliam calls a "lethal mutation": an apparently innocuous change that kills the whole thing. But on balance, we think this is the lesser of two evils. If you hold the framework too tightly, you prevent people from discussing, critiquing, and customizing it to fit their own culture and traditions, and that keeps them from really owning it and understanding it. We want to give you enough information and guidance to help you get the feel and the spirit of the approach, and hope that this is enough to prevent the lethal mutations from creeping in.

## Wondering

This brings us nearly to the end of Book 1 of the Learning Power Approach series. I have tried to give you as clear a picture as possible of the What, the Why, and the How of the LPA: What is it all about? Why is it important? And how do you go about putting it into practice? So now let me invite you to reflect back over the ideas, frameworks, illustrations, and suggestions you have encountered on the way through the book.

What has stuck in your mind? Can you say why those ideas had the biggest impact on you?

Which bits did you disagree with the most, or were most suspicious of or irritated by? What seemed implausible or impractical to you? Why was that, do you think? What experiences, information, or beliefs do you have that might lead you to be skeptical? And what could you try out anyway? Compare notes with a colleague if you can.

If you were going to talk to a group of your students about the ideas in this book, how would you phrase them? And why not give it a try!

# Notes

1. John Holt, *How Children Fail,* p. 173.
2. See, for example, Ap Dijksterhuis, "Think Different"; and Timothy Wilson and Jonathan Schooler, "Thinking Too Much." See also my overview of this research in *Hare Brain, Tortoise Mind.*
3. See https://characterlab.org/research.
4. See Lisa Blackwell, Kali Trzensiewski, and Carol Dweck, "Implicit Theories on Intelligence Predict Achievement Across an Adolescent Transition."
5. E. D. Hirsch, "The 21st Century Skills Movement."
6. Interestingly, though she devotes two pages to describing my Building Learning Power as an example of a progressive approach, she then goes on to make no criticism of it at all, preferring to attack much easier stereotypes.
7. Angela Duckworth and David Yeager, "Measurement Matters: Assessing Personal Qualities Other Than Cognitive Ability for Educational Purposes."
8. See Note 3 and the reference section.
9. Margaret Carr, *Assessment in Early Childhood Settings.*
10. From http://www.elli.global/new-discoveries-often-happen-by-chance/. See also Ruth Deakin-Crick, Patricia Broadfoot, and Guy Claxton, "Developing an Effective Lifelong Learning Inventory: The ELLI Project."
11. Guy Claxton, Art Costa, and Bena Kallick, "Hard Thinking About Soft Skills." The views I express in this section are heavily influenced by this collaboration, but may have evolved in ways that Art and Bena might not entirely agree with, so please treat them as mine alone.
12. Raymond Nickerson, David Perkins, and Edward Smith, *Teaching Thinking.*
13. Po Bronson, "How Not to Talk to Your Kids: The Inverse Power of Praise."
14. Roy Baumeister, Jennifer Campbell, Joachim Kreuger, and Kathleen Vohs, "Does High Self-Esteem Cause Better Performance?"

15. Lauren Resnick, "Making America Smarter."
16. Jerome Bruner, *The Process of Education.*
17. See Ron Berger, *An Ethic of Excellence.*
18. For example, Michaela Community School in London is often criticized for it zero-tolerance discipline. But if you read the rationale on the school website, you will find that it is grounded in classical stoical philosophy, and in scientific evidence that the development of higher levels of self-discipline contributes significantly to a happy and successful life—especially in young people who may not have learned these habits at home. See http://mcsbrent.co.uk/pragmatic-education-staying-stoical-in-school.

# Joining the Culture Club

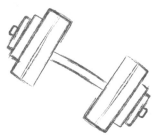

**11**

If we create a culture where every teacher believes they need to improve, not because they are not good enough but because they can be even better, there is no limit to what we can achieve.

Dylan Wiliam[1]

The Learning Power Approach (LPA) seems an obvious way ahead for education. Schools should be preparing kids to flourish in a complicated and demanding world. Just trying to squeeze better test scores out of them is not enough. We know that, in the long run, character counts for more than examination results. To prosper—to live good lives—today's students will need curiosity, determination, concentration, imagination, camaraderie, thoughtfulness, and self-discipline *as well as* literacy, numeracy, general knowledge, and the best possible grades. These attributes contribute hugely to people's success and fulfillment in life. And we also know that they are capable of being intentionally developed—or unintentionally stifled. The desire to cultivate them has to be at the heart of every school's endeavor.

Such dispositions cannot be "taught" directly. Sure, they can be made explicit and talked about, and that helps, but merely understanding the concept of "resilience," say, and even being able to write an A-grade essay about it, does not by itself make you any more resilient. Character is a constellation of habits, and habits are tendencies that are built up over time. If you regularly find yourself in a culture—a family, for example—where the people you look up to continually model, value, and expect politeness, honesty, or curiosity, you are likely to grow toward those qualities, as a plant grows toward the sun. Such habits begin to become part of your natural way of being. (Of course, nothing is for sure, in the complex world of human affairs, but such cultural messages exert a definite pull.)

As young people spend a good part of their waking hours in school, education becomes, for many of them, the second most powerful habit incubator in their lives, after their families. School stretches and shapes their developing dispositions, especially those that have to do with how they react to difficulties and uncertainties. In one classroom, learning mode becomes students' default response to challenge, and they grow in adventurousness, ingenuity, and determination. In another, perhaps next door, the culture steers students toward habitually being in performance mode, anxious for high marks and teacher approval, and their developing need to be "right" erodes that bold spirit. What teachers notice, what they approve of, the informal comments they make, the activities and tasks they devise, the way they lay out the desks or tables, the way they respond when things go wrong, how open they are about their own learning challenges past and present—all of these add to the currents that pull students in one direction or the other. We have to pay greater attention to the learning that is going on in the depths of the river, as well as the packages of knowledge floating by on the surface.

The LPA asks teachers to become more conscious of the cultures they create; to notice how their own classroom habits steer their learners toward or away from particular learning dispositions; to think about which outcomes they would prefer; and, if necessary, to adjust their habits accordingly. In order to strengthen the learning habits of our students, we teachers may need to gradually change our own habits. In order for learning power to develop in the classroom, we too will need to be powerful learners. And this means that the school as a whole needs to be a place where everyone—teachers and students alike—are, as much as possible, in learning (rather than performance) mode.

Changing habits requires effort and attention. Remember the old joke: How many therapists does it take to change a light bulb? Just one—but the light bulb has to really want to change. So we have to "get" why developing young people's learning power is important. We have to accept that our classroom is already an incubator of learning attitudes, and become interested in our role as a mind trainer (and not just a mind filler). We have to believe that slowly building students' learning power, providing it is done well, supports the achievement of grades and test scores rather than jeopardizing them. We have to have some ideas to try out that feel plausible and fruitful. We need the awareness to recognize opportunities to do it the new way rather than the way that feels more natural or familiar. We need courage to try things that are outside our current comfort zone, and resilience and resourcefulness to rethink and try again when they don't work the first time. We need determination to carry on when students, used to being instantly rescued and reassured, push back against the unfamiliar demand to take greater responsibility, think for themselves, and toughen up.

And we have to know that our willingness to be imaginative and experimental in our teaching is genuinely supported by our colleagues and by the leadership of the school. The school principal's role in culture change and habit change is crucial. We have found in our research that, for the LPA to become embedded in a school, there need to be frequent, heartfelt, and visible endorsements of the approach by senior leaders. Without that, it is all too easy for the pressures of normal life to crowd out the efforts that change requires.[2]

Dylan Wiliam's rallying cry, in the quotation at the beginning of this chapter, is a challenge. When he asks teachers to become "even better," he cannot just mean better at racking up test scores and college admissions. That is desirable, but it is not enough. We need a grander ambition: to get better at creating classrooms that systematically develop the broad, positive attitudes toward challenge and uncertainty that are the proven foundations of a fulfilled life. We need to be eagerly looking for an accumulation of little tweaks to our everyday habits that increase the likelihood that our students, whatever they end up doing, whether they go to Harvard or Hamburger University, will be living happy, satisfying, principled, and loving lives.

---

Throughout this book I have tried to make the LPA look easy. And in principle it is indeed quite straightforward—commonsense even. But in practice it can be a demanding, even daunting, journey. Even a minimal change to classroom procedure, like dropping the familiar hands-up routine, or banning the use of erasers for a while, can feel, to begin with, like a risk. Students used to being spoon-fed may kick back quite vigorously. Parents may react strongly when their fragile darlings complain that their teacher is no longer rushing to their aid when they are stuck, but requiring them to learn how to rescue themselves. In most schools, innovative principals will meet a spectrum of responses from teachers too, ranging from instant enthusiasm to entrenched cynicism, and they will need to think long term and sometimes "make haste slowly" in order not to polarize the staff room. Schools are complicated places, full of regular folk with diverse portfolios of beliefs, values, and vulnerabilities, and leadership, as Michael Fullan and others have pointed out, has to engage with these if it is to be effective.[3] The forthcoming books in this series, aimed at both teachers and principals, will address these challenges in much more detail.

The research that underpinned our earlier book *The Learning Powered School*, looking at schools where the LPA was thriving, seemed in the end to boil down to four words. First, the LPA is *vital*. There is widespread agreement that all youngsters need and deserve the strengths that the LPA aims to cultivate. Second, it is *difficult*. People say that it takes time, energy, and commitment if the LPA is to become embedded. It is very far from a quick fix. But third, it is *possible*. With patience and persistence, any classroom and any school, however difficult their circumstances, can, over two or three years, become deeply, ineradicably imbued with the learning power spirit.

And the last word is *rewarding*. When that learning spirit gets into the bone marrow of the institution, children from every conceivable background become amazing, and teaching becomes a luminous pleasure. Everyone wins. The children grow in confidence and pride, as they achieve things for themselves of which they never dreamed they were capable. Teachers—once they get used to sharing control with their classes—find that their students are much more gratifying to teach. College lecturers find their intakes from such schools significantly better prepared to grapple with the advanced learning challenges they will meet. And employers too are delighted to hire young workers who are imaginative, responsible, thoughtful, and convivial. In the immortal words of Hannah Montana, "What's not to like?"

There are hundreds, maybe thousands of schools around the world that have embraced different versions of the LPA, are well on the way to embedding the necessary changes, and are already seeing the difference it makes to students. But there are many more that talk the talk but have not yet made much change in practice. And there are teachers, principals, superintendents, and ministers of education who still think that education is all about literacy and numeracy, grades, and college entrance, and have not yet gotten the importance of the slower learning that goes on in the depths of the river. In short, good work is happening, but it is not scaling up fast enough.

We need to help more people to see the importance and the viability of the LPA; to understand the solid arguments and research findings that lie behind it; to discover the small, nonthreatening tweaks that make a difference; to become comfortable with talking, thinking, and writing about students as developing learners, and to have a rich vocabulary for unpacking what that means; and to appreciate the realities of culture and habit change, and have the mixture of patience and determination to see the journey through. That's what this book has tried to do—and what the ones to follow will spell out in greater detail. I hope you feel emboldened and inspired to try some new things out and see for yourself. Good luck!

## Notes

1. Dylan Wiliam, *How Do We Prepare Our Students for a World We Cannot Possibly Imagine?*
2. See Guy Claxton, Maryl Chambers, Graham Powell, and Bill Lucas, *The Learning Powered School.*
3. Michael Fullan, *Indelible Leadership: Always Leave Them Learning.*

# Bibliography
and References

Abbott, John (2010). *Over-Schooled but Under-Educated: How the Crisis in Education Is Jeopardising Our Adolescents.* London: Continuum Books.

Adey, Philip, and Shayer, Michael (2015). The effects of cognitive acceleration. In Lauren Resnick et al. (Eds.), *Socialising Intelligence Through Academic Talk and Dialogue,* pp. 127–142. Washington, DC: AERA.

Al-Ghazali, Abu Hamid (2016). *The Book of Knowledge* (Kenneth Honerkamp, Trans.). Louisville, KY: Fons Vitae.

Allison, Maria, and Duncan, Margaret (1988). Women, work, and flow. In M. Csikszentmihalyi and I. Csikszentmihalyi (Eds.), *Optimal Experience: Psychological Studies of Flow in Consciousness,* pp. 118–137. New York: Cambridge University Press.

Baird, John, and Northfield, Jeff (1992). *Learning From the PEEL Experience.* Melbourne, Australia: Monash University Press.

Barber, Nigel (2011). Conservatives big on fear, brain study finds. *Psychology Today.* Retrieved from https://www.psychologytoday.com/blog/the-human-beast/201104/conservatives-big-fear-brain-study-finds

Baumeister, Roy; Campbell, Jennifer; Kreuger, Joachim; and Vohs, Kathleen (2003). Does high self-esteem cause better performance, interpersonal success, happiness or healthier lifestyles? *Psychological Science in the Public Interest, 4*(1), 1–44.

Bedell, Geraldine (2016, February 27). Teenage mental health crisis: Rates of depression have soared in the past 25 years. *The Independent.* http://www.independent.co.uk/life-style/health-and-families/features/teenage-mental-health-crisis-rates-of-depression-have-soared-in-the-past-25-years-a6894676.html

Berger, Ron (2003). *An Ethic of Excellence: Building a Culture of Craftsmanship With Students.* Portsmouth, NH: Heinemann.

Berger, Ron; Woodfin, Libby; and Vilen, Anne (2016). *Learning That Lasts: Challenging, Engaging and Empowering Students with Deeper Instruction.* San Francisco: Jossey-Bass.

Bianco, Federica, and Lecce, Serena (2016). Translating child development research into practice: Can teachers foster children's theory of mind in primary school? *British Journal of Educational Psychology, 86,* 592–605.

Binet, Alfred (1909). *Modern Ideas About Children.* Paris: E. Flammarion.

Blackwell, Lisa; Trzesniewski, Kali; and Dweck, Carol (2007). Implicit theories on intelligence predict achievement across an adolescent transition: A longitudinal study and an intervention. *Child Development, 78*(1), 246–263.

Bloom, Benjamin, and Carroll, John (1971). *Mastery Learning: Theory and Practice.* New York: Holt, Rinehart and Winston.

Briceño, Eduardo (2016). How to get better at the things you care about. *TED Talk.* https://www.ted.com/talks/eduardo_briceno_how_to_get_better_at_the_things_you_care_about

Bronson, Po (2007, August 3). How not to talk to your kids: The inverse power of praise. *New York Magazine.* http://nymag.com/news/features/27840

Bruner, Jerome (1960). *The Process of Education.* Cambridge, MA: Harvard University Press.

Bucher, Anton (1998). The influence of models in forming moral identity. *International Journal of Educational Research, 27*(7), 619–627.

Burge, Bethan; Lenkeit, Jenny; and Sizmur, Juliet (2015). *PISA in Practice: Cognitive Activation in Maths.* Slough, UK: National Foundation for Educational Research.

Carr, Margaret (2001). *Assessment in Early Childhood Settings: Learning Stories.* Thousand Oaks, CA: Sage.

Carr, Margaret, and Claxton, Guy (2002). Tracking the development of learning dispositions. *Assessment in Education, 9*(1), 9–37.

Christodoulou, Daisy (2014). *Seven Myths About Education.* Abingdon, Oxfordshire, UK: Routledge.

Claro, Susana; Paunescu, David; and Dweck, Carol (2016). Growth mindset tempers the effect of poverty on academic achievement, *Proceedings of the National Academy of Sciences, 113*(31), 8664–8668.

Claxton, Guy (1984). *Live and Learn: The Psychology of Growth and Change in Everyday Life*. London: Harper & Row.

Claxton, Guy (1990). *Teaching to Learn: A Direction for Education*. London: Cassell.

Claxton, Guy (1997). *Hare Brain, Tortoise Mind: Why Intelligence Increases When You Think Less*. San Francisco: Harper Perennial.

Claxton, Guy (1999). *Wise Up: The Challenge of Lifelong Learning*. London and New York: Bloomsbury.

Claxton, Guy (2002). *Building Learning Power: Helping Young People Become Better Learners*. Bristol, UK: TLO.

Claxton, Guy (2008). *What's the Point of School?* London: Oneworld.

Claxton, Guy (2015). *Intelligence in the Flesh: Why Your Mind Needs Your Body Much More Than It Thinks*. New Haven: Yale University Press.

Claxton, Guy, and Carr, Margaret (2004). A framework for teaching learning: The dynamics of disposition. *Early Years, 24*(1), 87–97.

Claxton, Guy; Chambers, Maryl; Powell, Graham; and Lucas, Bill (2011). *The Learning Powered School: Pioneering 21st Century Education*. Bristol, UK: TLO.

Claxton, Guy; Costa, Art; and Kallick, Bena (2016). Hard thinking about soft skills, *Educational Leadership, 73*(6), 60–64.

Costa, Art (2014). *Dispositions: Reframing Teaching and Learning*. Thousand Oaks, CA: Corwin.

Costa, Art, and Kallick, Bena (2000a). *Discovering and Exploring Habits of Mind*. Alexandria, VA: ASCD.

Costa, Art, and Kallick, Bena (2000b). *Assessing and Reporting on Habits of Mind*. Alexandria, VA: ASCD.

Crooks, Terry (1988). The impact of classroom evaluation practices on students. *Review of Educational Research, 58*(4), 438–481.

Csikszentmihalyi, Mihaly (1992). *Flow: The Psychology of Happiness*. New York: Harper & Row.

Deakin-Crick, Ruth; Broadfoot, Patricia; and Claxton, Guy (2004). Developing an effective lifelong learning inventory: The ELLI project. *Assessment in Education, 11*(3), 247–272.

Dewey, John (1910). *How We Think*. Lexington, MA: D. C. Heath.

Dijksterhuis, Ap (2004). Think different: The merits of unconscious thought in preference development and decision making. *Journal of Personality and Social Psychology, 87*(4), 586–598.

Duckworth, Angela (2016). *Grit: The Power of Passion and Perseverance*. New York: Scribner.

Duckworth, Angela; Kirby, Teri; Gollwitzer, Anton; and Oettingen, Gabriele (2013). From fantasy to action: Mental contrasting with implementation intentions (MCII) improves academic performance in children. *Social Psychological and Personality Science, 4*, 745–753.

Duckworth, Angela, and Yeager, David (2015). Measurement matters: Assessing personal qualities other than cognitive ability for educational purposes. *Educational Researcher, 44*(4), 237–251.

Duff, Alexander Wilmer (Ed.) (1916). *A Textbook of Physics*. Philadelphia, PA: P. Blakiston's Son & Co.

Dweck, Carol (2006). *Mindset: The New Psychology of Success*. New York: Random House.

Edwards, Carolyn, and Gandini, Lella (2011). *The Hundred Languages of Children: The Reggio Emilia Experience in Transformation*. Santa Barbara, CA: Greenwood Press.

Ericsson, Anders, and Pool, Robert (2017). *Peak: How All of Us Can Achieve Extraordinary Things*. New York: Vintage.

Farrington, Camille; Roderick, Melissa; Allensworth, Elaine; Nagaoka, Jenny; Keyes, Tasha Seneca; Johnson, David; and Beechum, Nicole (2012). *Teaching adolescents to become learners. The role of non-cognitive factors in shaping school performance: A critical literature review*. Chicago, IL: The University of Chicago Consortium on Chicago School Research.

Flink, Cheryl; Boggiano, Ann; and Barrett, Marty (1990). Controlling teaching strategies: Undermining children's self-determination and performance. *Journal of Personality and Social Psychology, 59*(5), 916–924.

Fothergill, James (2012). *First Steps: A New Approach for Our Schools.* London: Confederation of British Industry.

Fullan, Michael (2017). *Indelible Leadership: Always Leave Them Learning.* Thousand Oaks, CA: Corwin.

Gambetta, Diego, and Hertog, Steffen (2016). *Engineers of Jihad.* Princeton, NJ: Princeton University Press.

Goleman, Daniel (2013). *Focus: The Hidden Driver of Excellence.* New York: Bloomsbury.

Harris, John (2016, December 29). A society too complex for the people risks everything. *The Guardian.* https://www.theguardian.com/commentisfree/2016/dec/29/trump-brexit-society-complex-people-populists

Hart, Susan; Dixon, Annabelle; Drummond, Mary Jane; and McIntyre, Donald (2004). *Learning Without Limits.* Maidenhead, UK: Open University Press.

Hattie, John (2012). *Visible Learning for Teachers.* London: Routledge.

Hetland, Lois; Winner, Ellen; Veenema, Shirley; and Sheridan, Kimberley (2007). *Studio Thinking: The Real Benefits of Visual Arts Education.* New York: Teachers College Press.

Higgins, Steve; Hall, Elaine; Baumfield, Viv; and Moseley, David (2005). *A Meta-Analysis of the Impact of the Implementation of Thinking Skills Approaches on Pupils.* London: Evidence for Policy and Practice Information and Co-ordinating Centre, Social Science Research Unit, Institute of Education, University of London.

Hirsch, E. D., Jr. (n.d.). *The 21st-Century Skills Movement.* Retrieved May 6, 2017, from http://greatminds.net/maps/documents/reports/hirsch.pdf

Holt, John (1964). *How Children Fail.* New York: Pitman.

Holt, John (1983). *How Children Learn.* New York: Merloyd Lawrence.

Hughes, Gwyneth (Ed.) (2014). *Ipsative Assessment: Motivation Through Marking Progress.* Basingstoke, UK: Palgrave Macmillan.

Johnson, David, and Johnson, Roger (1999). Making cooperative learning work. *Theory Into Practice, 38*(2), 67–73.

Kanai, Ryota; Feilden, Tom; Firth, Colin; and Rees, Geraint (2011). Political orientations are correlated with brain structure in young adults. *Current Biology, 21,* 677–680.

Kashdan, Todd (2010). *Curious?* New York: Harper.

Kautz, Tim; Heckman, James; Diris, Ron; ter Weel, Bas; and Borghans, Lex (2013). *Fostering and Measuring Skills: Improving Cognitive and Non-Cognitive Skills to Promote Lifetime Success.* Paris: OECD.

Lantieri, Linda; Nambiar, Madhavi; Harnett, Susanne; and Kyse, Eden (2016). Cultivating inner resilience in educators and students. In K. Schonert-Reichl and R. Roeser (Eds.), *Handbook of Mindfulness in Education,* pp. 119–132. New York: Springer-Verlag.

Lemov, Doug (2015). *Teach Like a Champion 2.0: 62 Techniques That Put Students on the Path to College.* San Francisco: Jossey-Bass.

Lipman, Matthew (1980). *Philosophy in the Classroom, 2e.* Philadelphia, PA: Temple University Press.

Lucas, Bill; Claxton, Guy; and Spencer, Ellen (2013). *Expansive Education: Teaching Learners for the Real World.* Melbourne, Australia: ACER Press; and Maidenhead, UK: Open University Press.

Lythcott-Haims, Julie (2015). *How to Raise an Adult.* London: Bluebird Main Market Edition.

Mannion, James, and Mercer, Neil (2016). Learning to learn: Improving attainment and closing the gap at Key Stage 3. *The Curriculum Journal.* http://dx.doi.org/10.1080/09585176.2015.1137778

Marzano, Robert (1992). *A Different Kind of Classroom: Teaching With Dimensions of Learning.* Alexandria, VA: ASCD.

Mercer, Neil (2000). *Words and Minds: How We Use Language to Think Together.* London: Routledge.

Mercer, Neil, and Littleton, Karen (2007). *Dialogue and the Development of Children's Thinking: A Socio-Cultural Approach.* London: Routledge.

Mitra, Sugata (2012). *Beyond the Hole in the Wall: Discover the Power of Self-Organized Learning* (e-book). TED Books. Kindle edition.

Mitra, Sugata (2016). *The Future of Learning* (e-book). Kindle edition.

Montessori, Maria (1992). *Maria Montessori's Own Handbook: A Short Guide to Her Ideas and Materials*. New York: Random House.

Mountstephen, Peter (2000). *Primary Tales: Learning by Heart*. Birmingham, UK: National Primary Trust.

Murdoch, Kath (2015). *The Power of Inquiry*. Available from www.kathmurdoch.com.au

Murray, Lynne (2014). *The Psychology of Babies*. London: Constable & Robinson.

Nickerson, Raymond; Perkins, David; and Smith, Edward (Eds.) (1985). *Teaching Thinking*. London: Routledge.

Nisbet, John, and Shucksmith, Janet (1973). *Learning Strategies*. London: Routledge and Kegan Paul.

Nottingham, James (2017). *The Learning Challenge*. Thousand Oaks, CA: Corwin.

Nuthall, Graham (2007). *The Hidden Lives of Learners*. Wellington, New Zealand: NZCER Press.

Ondaatje, Michael (1993). *The English Patient*. New York: Vintage Books.

Packham, Chris (2017). *Fingers in the Sparkle Jar: A Memoir*. London: Ebury Press.

Palincsar, Annemarie, and Brown, Ann (1984). Reciprocal teaching of comprehension-fostering and comprehension-monitoring strategies. *Cognition and Instruction 1*, 117–175.

Palincsar, Annemarie, and Schutz, Kristine (2011). Reconnecting strategy instruction with its theoretical roots. *Theory Into Practice, 50*, 85–92.

Palmer, Joy (Ed.) (2001). *Fifty Major Thinkers on Education: From Confucius to Dewey*. London and New York: Routledge.

Perkins, David (1993). Person-plus: A distributed view of thinking and learning. In Gavriel Salomon (Ed.), *Distributed Cognitions: Psychological and Educational Perspectives* (pp. 88–110). Cambridge, UK: Cambridge University Press.

Perkins, David (1995). *Outsmarting IQ: The Emerging Science of Learnable Intelligence*. New York: The Free Press.

Perkins, David (2009). *Making Learning Whole: How Seven Principles of Teaching Can Transform Education*. San Francisco: Jossey-Bass.

Perkins, David (2014). *Future Wise: Educating Our Children for a Changing World*. San Francisco: Jossey-Bass.

Petersen, Christopher, and Seligman, Martin (2004). *Character Strengths and Virtues*. New York: Oxford University Press.

Pham, Lien, and Taylor, Shelley (1999). From thought to action: Effect of process- vs. outcome-based mental simulations on performance. *Personality and Social Psychology Bulletin, 25,* 250–260.

Pirsig, Robert (1976). *Zen and the Art of Motorcycle Maintenance*. London: Bantam.

Postman, Andrew (2017, February 2). My dad predicted Trump in 1985. *The Guardian*. https://www.theguardian.com/media/2017/feb/02/amusing-ourselves-to-death-neil-postman-trump-orwell-huxley

Pressley, Michael (1976). Mental imagery helps eight-year-olds remember what they read. *Journal of Educational Psychology, 68*(3), 355–359.

Price, David (2013). *Open: How We'll Work, Live and Learn in the Future*. London: Crux.

Raine, Adrian; Reynolds, Chandra; Venables, Peter; and Mednick, Sarnoff (2002). Stimulation seeking and intelligence: A prospective longitudinal study. *Journal of Personality and Social Psychology, 82*(4), 663–674.

Resnick, Lauren (1999). Making America smarter. *Education Week, 18*(40), 38–40.

Richardson, Ken (2017). *Genes, Brains and Human Potential: The Science and Ideology of Intelligence*. New York: Columbia University Press.

Ritchhart, Ron (2002). *Intellectual Character: What It Is, Why It Matters, and How to Get It*. San Francisco: Jossey-Bass.

Ritchhart, Ron (2015). *Creating Cultures of Thinking: The Eight Forces We Must Master to Truly Transform Our Schools*. San Francisco: Jossey-Bass.

Ritchhart, Ron; Church, Mark; and Morrison, Karin (2011). *Making Thinking Visible: How to Promote Engagement, Understanding and Independence for All Learners*. San Francisco: Jossey-Bass.

Root-Bernstein, Robert, and Root-Bernstein, Michele (1999). *Sparks of Genius: The 13 Thinking Tools of the World's Most Creative People*. New York: Houghton Mifflin.

Rose, Martin (2015). *Immunising the Mind: How Can Education Contribute to Neutralising Violent Extremism?* London: British Council.

Scheffler, Israel (1991). *In Praise of Cognitive Emotions*. New York: Routledge.

Schön, Donald (1991). *The Reflective Practitioner: How Professional Think in Action*. New York: Routledge.

Shayer, Michael, and Adey, Philip (2002*). Learning Intelligence: Cognitive Acceleration Across the Curriculum from 5 to 15 Years*. Maidenhead, UK: Open University Press.

Simister, C. J. (2009). *The Bright Stuff*. London: Pearson Life.

Smallwood, Jonathan; Fishman, Daniel; and Schooler, Jonathan (2007). Counting the cost of an absent mind: Mind wandering as an under-recognised influence on educational performance. *Psychonomic Bulletin and Review, 14*(2), 230–236.

Sullivan, Anne McCrary (2000). Notes from a marine biologist's daughter: On the art and science of attention. *Harvard Educational Review, 70*(2), 211 227.

Toffler, Alvin (1970). *Future Shock*. New York: Pan.

Topping, Keith, and Trickey, Steve (2007). Collaborative philosophical enquiry for school children: Cognitive effects at 10–12 years. *British Journal of Educational Psychology, 77*, 271–288.

Tough, Paul (2012). *How Children Succeed: Grit, Curiosity and the Hidden Power of Character*. Boston: Houghton Mifflin Harcourt.

Tough, Paul (2016). *Helping Children Succeed: What Works and Why*. London: Random House.

Veevers, Nick, and Allison, Pete (2011). *Kurt Hahn: Inspirational, Visionary, Outdoor and Experiential Educator*. Boston: Sense Publishers.

Von Stumm, Sophie; Hell, Benedikt; and Chamorro-Premuzic, Tomas (2011). The hunger mind: Intellectual curiosity is the third pillar of academic performance. *Psychological Science, 6*(6), 574–588.

Watkins, Chris (2010). *Learning, Performance and Improvement.* London: International Network for School Improvement, University of London.

Watkins, Chris; Carnell, Eileen; and Lodge, Caroline (2007). *Effective Learning in Classrooms.* London and San Francisco: Sage.

Whimbey, Arthur (1975). *Intelligence Can Be Taught.* New York: Dutton.

Wiliam, Dylan (2012). *How Do We Prepare Our Students for a World We Cannot Possibly Imagine?* Keynote address, SSAT Conference, Liverpool, UK, December 5.

Wiliam, Dylan, and Leahy, Siobhan (2015). *Embedding Formative Assessment: Practical Techniques for K–12 Classrooms.* West Palm Beach, FL: Learning Sciences International.

Williams, Margery (1991). *The Velveteen Rabbit: Or How Toys Become Real.* New York: Doubleday.

Williams, Marion, and Burden, Robert (1998). *Thinking Through the Curriculum.* London: Routledge.

Wilson, Timothy, and Schooler, Jonathan (1991). Thinking too much: Introspection can reduce the quality of preferences and decisions. *Journal of Personality and Social Psychology, 60,* 181–192.

# Resources and Further Reading

Becky Carlzon blogs at www.learningpowerkids.com. Her blog is full of useful LPA ideas and reflections from her Year 1/2 classroom. Twitter: @beckycarlzon.

The Common Ground Collaborative can be found at www.thecgcproject.org.

Art Costa's Habits of Mind courses and materials can be found at www.artcostacentre.com.

EL Education (which used to be Expeditionary Learning) has many resources at www.eleducation.org.

The Expansive Education Network, at www.expansive education.net, contains lots of useful teacher research projects on LPA ideas.

The Partnership for 21st Century Learning can be found at www.p21.org.

The 21st Century Learning Initiative is at www.21learn.org.

Whole Education, led by David Crossley and Douglas Archibald, is at www.wholeeducation.org.

The Tools of the Mind approach developed by Elena Bodrova and Deborah Leong is at www.toolsofthemind.org.

The Effective Lifelong Learning Inventory (ELLI) can be found at www.elli.global.

Thinking Schools International is at www.thinkingschoolsinternational.com.

James Nottingham's Challenging Learning is at www.challenginglearning.com.

Jane Simister's Future Smart programs can be found at www.cjsimister.com.

David Price's Engaged Learning is at www.engagedlearning.co.uk.

Chris Watkins has a wide array of free resources at www.chriswatkins.net.

The UK Royal Society of Arts' Opening Minds project can be found at www.thersa.org.

Kath Murdoch's approach to Inquiry-Based Learning is described at www.kathmurdoch.com.au.

# Index

Abbott, John, 9
Accepting, 117
Achievement
  collaboration and, 199–200
  concentration and, 194–195
  curiosity and, 192–193
  empathy and, 201
  imagination and, 196–198
  versus improvement, 182–185
  reflection and, 201–202
  resilience and, 195–196
  thinking skills and, 198–199
Adey, Philip, 8, 203
Adventurous learners, 69
Aesthetic vision, 144
Aim of the learning power
  approach, 40–49
Al-Ghazali, Abu Hamid, 17, 18–19
American College Health
  Association, 98
American Educational Research
  Association, 106
Analyzing, 115
Anser Charter School, 130–136, 158
Archibald, Douglas, 9
*Assessment for Learning,* 10
Attenborough, David, 166
Attention, 109–110, 194–195
Attitudes of students, 4–5
*Austin's Butterfly,* 175, 177

Baird, John, 8
Ban Erasers, 66–67
Bartlett, Kevin, 9
Beckett, Samuel, 26
Berger, Ron, 8, 119, 130,
  175, 177, 229
Bialik College, 142–144, 170
Bianco, Federica, 201
Biles, Simone, 166
Binet, Alfred, 106
Black, Paul, 10

Blackwell, Lisa, 195
Blake, William, 233
Bloom, Benjamin, 11
Bodrova, Elena, 9
Bolt, Usain, 166
*Book of Knowledge, The,* 17
Brainstorming, 116
Brittle learners, 71
Broadfoot, Patricia, 223
Bruner, Jerome, 229
Building Learning Power (BLP), 6–7,
  12, 105, 139–141, 159, 169
Buoyancy, 112
Burden, Bob, 9

Capability, 42
Carlzon, Becky, 60, 127–129, 158,
  161–162, 164, 172, 184–185
Carpenter, Andy, 169
Carr, Margaret, 221, 222
Challenge, creating, 160–163
*Challenging Learning,* 10
*Character Education,* 11
Characteristics of learning power,
  103–106
*Character Strengths and
  Virtues,* 105
Chili Challenge, 60–61, 69, 164
Christ Church Infants School,
  127–129, 184–185
Christ Church Primary
  School, 153
Christodoulou, Daisy, 220
Circle-Ate, 66
Circle of Viewpoints, 170
Claro, Susana, 196
Classrooms, LPA
  allowing increasing amounts of
    independence, 177–180
  creating a feeling of safety,
    151–152
  creating challenge, 160–163

design principles, 147–150, 232
developing craftsmanship, 175–177
displays, 173–174
distinguishing between learning mode and performance mode in, 152–155
focus on improvement, not achievement, 182–185
giving students more responsibility, 180–182
habits, 243–244
leading by example in, 186–187
making ample time for collaboration and conversation, 157–159
making difficulty adjustable, 163–165
making use of protocols, templates, and routines in, 168–171
organizing compelling things to learn in, 156–157
showing the innards of learning, 166–167
using the environment in, 171–175
Coaches, learning, 150, 232
Cognitive Acceleration Through Science Education, 8, 203
Collaboration, 117, 157–159, 171, 172, 199–200
Collaborative learners, 70
Collapse of Complex Societies, The, 81
College, powerful learners doing better at, 90–92
Common Ground Collaborative, 9
Complexity of life, 79–81
Concentration, 106, 110, 194–195
Confederation of British Industry (CBI), 86–87
Confidence, 42, 84
Confusion and the learning challenge, 136–139
Connecting, 113
Contemplating, 110

Continuous learning, 20–21
Conversation, 157–159
Costa, Art, 8, 105, 223
Craftsmanship, 119, 175–177, 230, 232
Creativity and imagination, 196–198
Critiquing, 25, 115–116
Crooks, Terry, 183
Crossley, David, 9
Csikszentmihalyi, Mihaly, 95–96
Culture of the learning power approach, 241–246
Curiosity, 68–69, 107–109

Decline of deference, 155
Deducing, 115
Desserts, learning power approach, 64–67
Determination, 26, 69–70, 111–112
Dewey, John, 9, 193
Dimension of Learning, 105
Discussion, 28
Dispositions, learning, 67–71, 226, 242
Dixon, Phil, 150
Dorevitch, Nicky, 142
Drummond, Mary Jane, 10
Duckworth, Angela, 9, 198, 222
Dweck, Carol, 9, 69, 90, 111, 161, 195, 196

Edison, Thomas, 109
Educational Leadership, 223
Education Endowment Foundation (EEF), 201–202
Effective Lifelong Learning Inventory (ELLI), 9, 222–223
EL Education, 8
Elements of learning power, 107–124, 122–123 (figure)
attention, 109–110
curiosity, 107–109
determination, 69–70, 111–112
imagination, 26, 112–114
organization, 120–124
reflection, 28–29, 118–120

socializing, 116–118
thinking, 114–116
Empathy, 117–118, 201
*Engaged Learning,* 10
Ernst and Young, 80
Evaluation, 47, 119
Executive function, 110, 217
*Expansive Education Network,* 7, 9
Expeditionary Learning, 8, 119,
    130, 175–176, 229
    Workshop 2.0, 130–136, 168
Experimenting, 25–26
    and tinkering, 109
Exploring, 108

*Fingers in the Sparkle Jar:*
    *A Memoir,* 45
*First Steps: A New Approach for*
    *our Schools,* 86
Fixed mindset, 196
Flink, Cheryl, 154, 184
Ford, Henry, 42
*Formative Assessment,* 10, 160
Fothergill, James, 87
*Future Smart,* 10
*Future Wise,* 157

Gandhi, Mahatma, 1
Gardner, Howard, 8
Gerjuoy, Herbert, 39
Gervais, Ricky, 157
Ginnis, Paul, 10
Glen Waverley Secondary
    College, 177
Google, 80
    Future think tank, 80
Green, Julie, 171, 172
Growth mindset, 9, 106, 111, 196
"Gumption traps," 46

Habits, 225, 243–244
*Habits of Mind,* 8, 105, 229
Hahn, Kurt, 8
Happiness and learning, 95–97
Harkness table, 172
Harmony and security, 81–82
Harris Academies, 181–182

Hart, Susan, 176
*Harvard Educational Review,* 144
Hattie, John, 10–11, 160
Heckman, James, 85–86
Hemingway, Ernest, 25, 115, 217
Hetland, Lois, 7
*Hidden Lives of Learners, The,* 89
Hirsch, E. D., 227
Holt, John, 75
Howard, John, 178
*How Children Succeed,* 91
*How to Raise an Adult,* 98
*How We Think,* 193
Hughes, Gwyneth, 183
*Hundred Languages of Childhood,* 8
Hungry Mind Lab, 192

ICT (Independent-
    Collaborative-Teacher), 171, 172
Imagination, 26, 112–114,
    196–198
Imitating, 27–28, 117
Immersing, 110
Imposter syndrome, 41–49
Improvement versus
    achievement, 182–185
Inclination, 226
Incurious learners, 71, 193
Independent learners, 48,
    177–180
Independent Schools
    Victoria, 140
*Inquiry-Based Learning,* 10
*Intellectual Character/Visible*
    *Thinking,* 7, 105
*Intelligence Can Be Taught,* 106
Intelligence quotient, 106
    increased by curiosity, 193
Interested sensitivity, 30
*International Baccalaureate,* 8
Interthinking, 116
Intuition, 106, 114, 216
Ipsative assessment, 183
Isbell, Giselle, 130–136, 158, 162,
    168, 174, 186, 220

Jackson, Sarah, 153

Kallick, Bena, 8, 105, 223
Kinds of minds, 229–230
King, Martin Luther, 213
Kipling, Rudyard, 186

Lamina, Umu, 182
Landau Forte College, 180–181
Landry, Tom, 150
Lantieri, Linda, 194
Launchpad for learning, 22–23
Leading, 118
  by example, 186–187
Learnable intelligence, 9
Learners, 42–43
  adventurous, 69
  choosing to learn, 44–45
  collaborative, 70
  critiquing by, 25
  curious, 68–69
  designing their own
    learning, 45
  determined, 69–70
  discussion by, 28
  doing better at college,
    powerful, 90–92
  doing better at school,
    powerful, 88–90
  employers wanting to hire
    powerful, 86–88
  evaluation by, 47
  experimenting by, 25–26
  imagining by, 26
  imitating by, 27–28
  independent, 48, 177–180
  observing by, 24
  practicing by, 29–30
  pursuing their learning
    plans, 46
  reading by, 24–25
  reasoning by, 26–27
  reflecting by, 28–29
  research by, 45–46
  what is actually done by, 23–24
  willing, 44
Learning
  as continuous, 20–21
  curiosity effect on, 192–193

focusing on learning power,
    not just, 214–216
  getting better at, 32–33
  imagination and, 196–198
  launchpad for, 22–23
  making people happier, 95–97
  reasons for, 18–20
  versus thinking, 216–217
  types of classroom, 34–37
Learning agility, 80
Learning challenge, 136–139
Learning designers, teachers as, 150
Learning-designing, 120–121
Learning dispositions, 67–71,
    217–219, 226, 242
Learning muscles and the mind
    gym, 228–230
Learning power
  as acceleration, 18, 19 (figure)
  beginnings of, 30–32
  characteristics of, 103–106
  cognitive and social science
    research affirming, 106
  for complexity of life, 79–81
  definition of, 17–18
  developed in one context
    transferring to other
    contexts, 202–203
  elements of, 107–124,
    122–123 (figure)
  focusing on, 214–216
  lasting legacy of, 83–84
  life success with, 84–86
  making teaching easier and
    more rewarding, 93–95
  making the world a safer place,
    81–83
  quiz, 71–72
  young people's mental health
    dependent on, 97–99
Learning power approach (LPA),
    39–40
  in action, 49–53, 127–144
  aim of, 40–49
  as alternative to programs that
    focus overwhelmingly on
    academic attainment, 14

challenge of implementing, 244–245

classrooms (*See* Classrooms, LPA)

culture, 241–246

desserts, 64–67

different brands, 12–13

as ethos of the whole school, 233–235

evidence for success of, 221–223

friends and neighbors, 9–10

godparents, 9

implementation of, 55–59

learning muscles and the mind gym in, 228–230

mains, 62–64

as multifaceted concept, 191–192

near misses, 10–14

nuclear family, 7–8

origins of, 1–7

pedagogy rules, 230–233

precision about language of, 223–228

as provisional and growing, not set in stone, 235–237

reasons to implement, 78–99

socket set, 14–15, 213

starters, 59–61

student comments on, 204–206

teacher feedback on, 207–209

as "traditional" or "progressive," 219–221

willingness to implement, 78

*Learning Powered School, The,* 245

Learning stories, 222

Learning to Learn (L2L) intervention, 89, 90 (figure)

Learning versus performance mode, 152–155

*Learning Without Limits,* 10, 176

Lecce, Serena, 201

Legacy of learning power, 83–84

Lemov, Doug, 11

Leo, Jane, 154–155

Leong, Deborah, 9

Limiting assumptions, 6

Lipman, Matthew, 9, 136

*Live and Learn,* 6

LPA. *See* Learning power approach (LPA)

Lucas, Bill, 7, 9

Lythcott-Haims, Julie, 98

Mains, learning power approach, 62–64

Maker Movement, 166

"Making America Smarter," 106

*Making Learning Whole,* 112

Marzano, Robert, 105

*Mastery Learning,* 11

"Mayonnaise model" of learning, 58

McLuhan, Marshall, 147

Mental health and learning power, 97–99

Mercer, Neil, 116

Metacognition, 29, 118, 202

Mindfulness, 99, 118

*Mindset,* 90

Mitchell, Ian, 8

Mitra, Sugata, 179

Montessori, Maria, 8

Motivation, 226–227

Murdoch, Kath, 10, 180

Muscles, learning, 228–230

Nisbet, John, 9

No Hands Up, 62

Non-cognitive skills, 85

No-Put-Down Zone, 64

Northfield, Jeff, 8

"Notes From a Marine Biologist's Daughter: On the Art and Science of Attention," 144

Noticing, 109–110

Nottingham, James, 10, 136–139, 162–163, 168, 172

Nuthall, Graham, 89

Observation, 24

O'Donnell, Annie, 97

*Office, The,* 157

Ondaatje, Michael, 119
*Opening Minds* project, 10
Optimism, 111
Organisation for Economic
    Co-operation and Development
    (OECD), 84–85, 162
Organization, 120–124
*Outsmarting IQ: The Emerging
    Science of Learnable
    Intelligence,* 106

*P21, the Partnership for
    21st Century Learning,* 9
Packham, Chris, 45
Paunescu, David, 196
Pearson, 80
Pedagogy rules, 230–233
Peer marking, 128–129
Performance versus learning
    mode, 152–155
Perkins, David, 7, 9, 43, 106, 112,
    142, 157
Persevering, 111
Pestalozzi, Johann, 8
Petersen, Christopher, 105
Philosophy for Children, 9, 136, 199
Piaget, Jean, 42
Pirsig, Robert, 46
*Planet Earth II,* 166
Planning, 121
Playing with ideas, 113
Postman, Andrew, 103
Powell, Graham, 6
*Power of Inquiry, The,* 180
Practicing, 29–30, 112
Price, David, 10
PricewaterhouseCoopers, 80
Problem-solving skills, 227
Professional learning
    communities, 57–58
*Project for the Enhancement of
    Effective Learning (PEEL),* 8
Project Zero, 7–8
Protocols, 168–171
Purpose of education, 76–78

Questioning, 108

Reading, 24–25
Reasoning, 26–27
Reasons for learning, 18–20
Reciprocal Teaching, 200
Recovering, 112
Reflection, 28–29, 118–120,
    201–202, 217
*Reflective Practitioner, The,* 118
Research by learners, 45–46
Resilience and grit, 106, 111,
    195–196
Resnick, Lauren, 106, 229
Resourcing, 121
Respectful skepticism, 30
Responsibility, student, 180–182
Richardson, Louise, 82
Riskometer, 64–66, 69, 164–165
Ritchhart, Ron, 7, 105, 142, 170
Root-Bernstein, Michèle, 105
Root-Bernstein, Robert, 105
*Round Square* schools, 8
Routines, 168–171

Safety
    creating a feeling of, 151–152
    enhanced through learning
        power, 81–83
Scheffler, Israel, 9
Schön, Donald, 188
Schools for the Future, 172
Self-awareness, 217
Self-efficacy, 111
Self-esteem, 227–228
Self-evaluation, 119
Self-regulation, 110, 195
Seligman, Martin, 105
*Service Education,* 11
*Seven Myths About Education,* 220
Shayer, Michael, 8, 203
Simister, Jane, 10
Simon, Paul, 166
Skills (terminology), 223–225
Smallwood, Jonathan, 194
Socializing, 116–118
Social referencing, 151
Solitary learners, 71
*Sparks of Genius,* 105

Split-Screen Teaching, 169–170
Starters, learning power
    approach, 59–61
St. Mary's Primary School, 154
*Stranger to Stranger,* 166
Stress, 98–99
Stuck Posters, 62–63, 174
*Studio Thinking,* 7
Sullivan, Anne McCrary, 144
Systems thinking, 116

Tainter, Joseph, 81
*Teachers' Toolkit,* 10
Teaching, LPA and easier and more
    rewarding, 93–95, 245–246
*Teaching to Learn,* 6
*Teach Like a Champion,* 11
Templates, 168–171
Tendency, 226
Terrorism, 82–83
Thinkering, 119–120
Thinking, 114–116, 198–199
    versus learning, 216–217
Thinking Routines, 170
*Thinking Schools International,* 10
*Thinking Skills,* 11
Tinkering, 109
TLO Limited (The Learning
    Organisation), 6
*Tools of the Mind,* 9
Topping, Keith, 199
Tough, Paul, 91, 106
"Tracking the Development of
    Learning Dispositions," 221
Transferability of learning power,
    202–203
Trickey, Steve, 199

Troubleshooting, 46–47
Try Three Before Me, 61, 70
Trzesniewski, Kali, 195
*21st Century Learning Initiative,* 9

Unadventurous learners, 71
Upwork.com, 80

*Visible Learning,* 10–11, 160
Visible Thinking, 142–144, 170
Vision, aesthetic, 144
Visualizing, 113–114, 196–198
Von Stumm, Sophie, 192
VUCA world, 80

Watkins, Chris, 8, 88
*Where's Waldo?,* 24
Whimbey, Arthur, 106
White, Dick, 8
*Whole Education,* 9
Wiliam, Dylan, 10, 160, 202,
    241, 244
Willing learners, 44
*Wise Up: The Challenge of Lifelong
    Learning,* 6
Witnessing, 120
Wondering, 107–108
Wonder Wall, 59,
    60 (figure), 69
World Bank, 86–87

Yeager, David, 222
Young Minds, 98

*Zen and the Art of Motorcycle
    Maintenance,* 46

A SAGE Publishing Company

Helping educators make the greatest impact

**CORWIN HAS ONE MISSION:** to enhance education through intentional professional learning.

We build long-term relationships with our authors, educators, clients, and associations who partner with us to develop and continuously improve the best evidence-based practices that establish and support lifelong learning.

# Solutions you want. Experts you trust. Results you need.

## Author Consulting

On-site professional learning with sustainable results! Let us help you design a professional learning plan to meet the unique needs of your school or district. www.corwin.com/pd

## Institutes

Corwin Institutes provide collaborative learning experiences that equip your team with tools and action plans ready for immediate implementation. www.corwin.com/institutes

## eCourses

Practical, flexible online professional learning designed to let you go at your own pace. www.corwin.com/ecourses

## Read2Earn

Did you know you can earn graduate credit for reading this book? Find out how: www.corwin.com/read2earn

Contact an account manager at (800) 831-6640 or visit **www.corwin.com** for more information.

CORWIN